The Bark River
Chronicles

Stories from a Wisconsin Watershed

Milton J. Bates

Wisconsin Historical Society Press

Published by the Wisconsin Historical Society Press
Publishers since 1855

© 2012 by the State Historical Society of Wisconsin

wisconsinhistory.org

Photographs identified with WHi or WHS are from the Society's collections; address requests to reproduce these photos to the Visual Materials Archivist at the Wisconsin Historical Society, 816 State Street, Madison, WI 53706.

Printed in the United States of America

Designed by Diana Boger, dianaboger.com
Front cover photo by Emily Dyreson, Aerialscapes.com
All maps created by Michael Custode Illustration, www.custode.com
Cattail drawing by Jeremy Bates

16 15 14 13 12   1 2 3 4 5

Library of Congress Cataloging-in-Publication Data
Bates, Milton J.
　　The Bark River chronicles : stories from a Wisconsin watershed / Milton J. Bates.
　　　p. cm.
　　Includes bibliographical references and index.
　　ISBN 978-0-87020-502-6 (pbk. : alk. paper) 1. Bark River (Washington County-Jefferson County, Wis.)—Description and travel. 2. Bark River Valley (Washington County-Jefferson County, Wis.)—Description and travel. 3. Bark River Valley (Washington County-Jefferson County, Wis.)—History. 4. Natural history—Wisconsin—Bark River Valley (Washington County-Jefferson County) 5. Bates, Milton—Travel—Wisconsin—Bark River (Washington County-Jefferson County) I. Title.
　　F587.B24B38 2012
　　977.5'91--dc23
　　　　　　　2012002694

∞ The paper used in this publication meets the minimum requirements of the American National Standard for Information Sciences—Permanence of Paper for Printed Library Materials, ANSI Z39.48-1992.

For Puck

and in memory of
Milton F. and Helen H. Bates

CONTENTS

Preface and Acknowledgments

The stories in this book are true. I tell them as factually as possible, basing my account on research, personal observation, and the testimony of people who are or were in a position to know what happened. The characters, living and dead, are all real and go by their actual names.

The canoe journey that serves as the narrative frame for these chronicles is a composite of numerous outings that my wife and I have enjoyed on the Bark River since 1982, sometimes in the company of family or friends. In 1994 I began to keep a journal of our excursions. Drawing extensively on the journal, I have compressed the experiences of many seasons into an adventure extending from April through October of a single year. It is a year that can be found on every calendar and on none.

To vary the treatment of historical and other material, I sometimes present it in the form of a dialogue, freely incorporating research into conversations between my wife (and occasionally friends) and me. I have not taken the same liberty with conversations involving other people, chiefly residents of the Bark

River valley. These are either transcribed verbatim from taped interviews or recalled as accurately as memory permits.

A caveat for readers who may be inspired to explore the Bark River on their own: this is not a guidebook. The beaver dams, fallen trees, and other blockages mentioned in the narrative have in many cases been removed, but they have a way of reappearing elsewhere. Especially on a river as small as the Bark, the time of year and the amount of recent rainfall also affect navigation. No two voyages of discovery are the same. No true explorer would want them to be.

Much of the Bark River adventure unfolded in libraries, research collections, and museums while our vessel was in dry dock. I am particularly indebted to the following institutions for opening up their resources to me: the Wisconsin Historical Society Library and Archives, Madison; the Office of the State Archaeologist, Madison; the Robert L. Parkinson Library and Research Center, Circus World Museum, Baraboo; the Waukesha County Museum Research Center, Waukesha (thanks especially to Terry Biwer Becker and Eric Vanden Heuvel); the Frank P. Zeidler Humanities Reading Room, Milwaukee Public Library; the Harry H. Anderson Research Library, Milwaukee County Historical Society; the University of Wisconsin–Milwaukee Area Research Center; the Washington County Historical Society, West Bend; the Special Collections and Interlibrary Loan Departments, Raynor Memorial Libraries, Marquette University; the Hoard Historical Museum (thanks to Sue Hartwick and Karen O'Connor) and the Dwight Foster Public Library (thanks to Amy Lutzke), both in Fort Atkinson; the Bark River Woods Historical Society (thanks to Olive and Don Gross); and the Department of Natural Resources offices in Madison (thanks to Bill Sturtevant, Meg Galloway, and Eleanor Lawry), Fitchburg (thanks to Rob Davis), Waukesha (thanks to Michelle Schneider), and Milwaukee (thanks to Stephen Galarneau).

Among the people who responded to my queries or directed me to useful sources of information are Margaret Zerwekh, Michael Gauger, Yance Marti, Marlin Johnson, David Overstreet, and Patrick J. Jung. Thomas L. Jeffers and Tim Machan read and responded to early drafts of a couple of chapters. Three chapters (4, 6, and 12) benefited from the scrutiny of editors at the *Wisconsin Magazine of History*, where they appeared in somewhat different form. To Marquette University I am grateful for stipends that supported two summers of research and writing.

Considering how perilous the passage from book manuscript to printed book can be, I feel fortunate to have had the support and guidance of the dedicated people at the Wisconsin Historical Society Press. Kate Thompson recognized the potential in the manuscript and drew it out with marvelous tact and intelligence. Mike Nemer managed the production of the book, enlisting the freelance skills of Diana Boger (cover and interior design), Michael Custode (maps), Emily Dyreson of Aerialscapes (cover photograph), and Melissa York (copyediting).

I cannot imagine a journey on the Bark, much less on the river of life, without my stalwart companion, Puck. To her I dedicate these chronicles, with an appreciative nod to our children, Jeremy and Elizabeth. Finding a canoe paddle in their hands at an early age, they adapted more or less cheerfully to their parents' notion of fun.

The Bark River Route

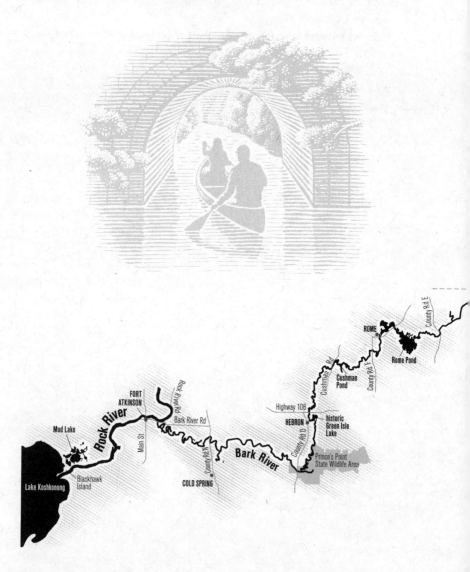

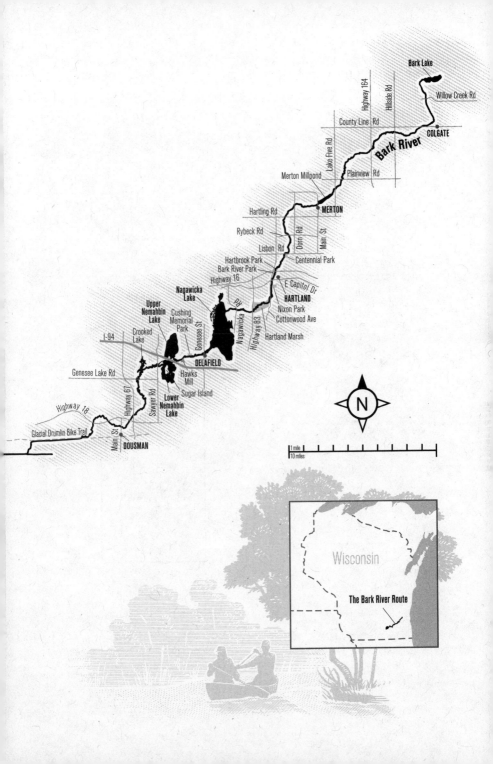

Bark Lake

Highway 164

Hillside Rd

Willow Creek Rd

County Line Rd

Lake Five Rd

Bark River

COLGATE

Plainview Rd

Merton Millpond

Hartling Rd

MERTON

Rybeck Rd

Dorn Rd

Main St

Lisbon Rd

Centennial Park

Hartbrook Park
Bark River Park
Highway 16

E Capitol Dr

Nagawicka
Lake

HARTLAND

Upper
Nemahbin
Lake

Cushing
Memorial
Park

Nixon Park

Cottonwood Ave

I-94

Crooked
Lake

Genesee St

Nagawicka

Highway 83

Hartland Marsh

Genesee Lake Rd

DELAFIELD

Hawks
Mill

Highway 67

Sawyer Rd

Sugar Island

Highway 18

Lower
Nemahbin
Lake

Glacial Drumlin Bike Trail

Main St

DOUSMAN

N

1 mile
10 miles

Wisconsin

The Bark River Route

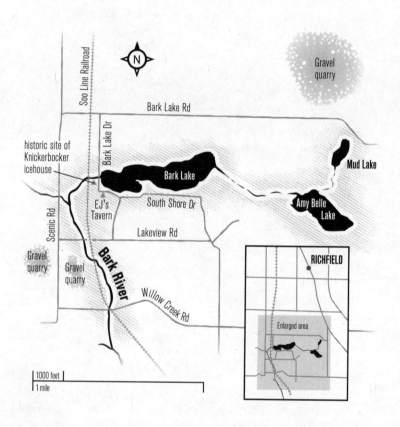

CHAPTER 1

Bark Lake to
Willow Creek Road

A green canoe floats, leaflike, on Bark Lake in the town of Richfield, Washington County, Wisconsin. Two figures occupy the boat. Except for the difference in height, they look much the same in their floppy hats and shapeless fleece jackets. An artist would notice how the straw-yellow sunlight of early April picks out a wisp of the woman's blonde hair and glances off the man's gray beard. The canoe's inverted image wavers slightly on the surface of the water. Overhead, the saturated blue of the sky stretches cloudless to the horizon.

My wife and I have chosen this morning, which happens to be Easter Sunday, as an auspicious moment to begin our voyage of rediscovery on the Bark River. Arriving at the lakeshore, we had gone first to a tavern on its southwest corner. Noticing a man outside, near the entrance, we asked if we could launch our boat at the access across the road, which a hand-lettered sign identified as tavern property. "You're welcome to use it," he offered, adding that this was the only place on the lake where we could put in. He doesn't mind as long as people ask his permission. "We'll drop in later for a beer," I said. Then we parked at the access and unloaded our gear.

Now we paddle the lake counterclockwise, hugging the shore. A few people are out, working in their yards or simply enjoying the sunshine. A woman sits on her dock with a young girl, possibly her granddaughter. "The fish are back," the girl says, sowing the surface of the water with breadcrumbs. Indeed they are, though the fishermen aren't, not yet. The only other boat on the lake is a yellow canoe doing the same thing that we're doing, but in the opposite direction.

The cottages are mostly small one-story structures on narrow, clutter-friendly lots. There are exceptions, large two- and three-story modern houses set on double lots with manicured lawns and elaborate docks. Here and there are access lots, but they are privately owned and not for use by outsiders. Posted like stern sentinels along South Shore Drive are signs that say NO PARKING, STOPPING, OR STANDING. In 2007 the township established ownership of two of these "boat lots," each twenty feet deep with ten feet of shoreline, and offered them for sale on eBay. The bidding pushed the purchase price up to eight thousand dollars, more than four times the opening figure.

Unruffled by wind, the lake allows us a clear view of its bottom. We glide over silt and marl on the west end, gravel and rock in the midsection, and a spongy accumulation of organic matter on the east shore, bordering a cattail marsh. Numerous painted turtles sun themselves along the marsh, and carp boil away at our approach. A great blue heron flushes from the cattails and flies deeper into the wetland. We discover a narrow creek flowing out of the marsh and follow it upstream, heading east at first, then north. Where the creek exits a grove of trees we notice a low mound of dirt along the bank.

"It looks as though someone was trying to dredge or widen the creek," Puck observes. On formal occasions she goes by the name Elizabeth. On canoe outings she favors a nickname borrowed from Shakespeare's mischievous sprite in *A Midsummer Night's Dream*, particularly as the Canadian actress Geneviève Bujold interpreted the role in the 1960s.

I consult two maps in a clear plastic holder attached to the rear thwart. "The creek appears as a squiggly line on the federal survey map of 1836," I respond. "It's still there on our Geological Survey map, but straightened to follow the section line. It extends about a mile due north."

"But why the dredging?"

"Your guess is as good as mine. There are a couple of other man-made channels in the marsh, including one that almost connects Bark Lake with

Amy Belle Lake to the east. Both were popular tourist destinations in the late nineteenth century. People could travel by rail from Milwaukee or Waukesha to a platform on the west shore of Bark Lake. Perhaps resort owners dredged the canals for access by steam launch."

The area's lakes and rivers owe their existence to a far more ambitious dredging operation dating to the Ice Age. Though the Laurentide Ice Sheet advanced from the north and retreated many times during the last two million years, today's topography is largely the product of its last campaign, called the Wisconsin Glaciation. One geologist has compared the current landscape to a chalkboard that has been written on and mostly erased many times. Only the most recent markings are clearly legible.

Bark Lake is located just east of the region known as Kettle Moraine, where the markings are especially easy to read. It was here that two lobes of the glacier converged about twenty-four thousand years ago, creating fantastical landforms with equally improbable names: eskers, moulin kames, drumlins, moraines, and kettles. The Green Bay and Lake Michigan Lobes, named for the valleys they followed in their southwesterly advance, covered the land for about ten thousand years, then "wasted back" (in geologist-speak) to the north. Sediment that had hitchhiked for many miles on the advancing ice took one last giddy ride on its meltwater, washing onto the surface of stranded ice blocks. When the ice melted, the gravel, sand, and silt sank to the bottom of the resulting lake or wetland.

Bark Lake occupies sixty-four acres of a large kettle or basin that was formed in this way. Spreading over several square miles, the basin consists mostly of wetland. Besides Bark Lake, it includes a couple of other depressions where the ice penetrated far enough below the water table to assure a year-round supply of water. These are Amy Belle and Mud Lakes, which cover thirty-three and fourteen acres, respectively. Though the basin has no official geological name, we might call it Glacial Bark Lake, by analogy with more extensive Pleistocene bodies of water such as Glacial Lake Wisconsin in the central part of the state and Glacial Lake Scuppernong in Jefferson and western Waukesha Counties.

Glacial Bark Lake is geologically interesting due to its location at the western edge of the Lake Michigan Lobe and its position with respect to the subcontinental divide that separates the Great Lakes and Mississippi River watersheds. As the Lake Michigan Lobe retreated to the east, following the downward slope of the land, it prevented meltwater from draining in that direction. An ice dam about two miles southwest of today's Bark Lake likewise blocked drainage to the west until the swollen lake breached the dam, discharging a torrent of water, ice, and sediment toward the southwest. This cataclysmic event committed the lake and the Bark River to the Mississippi watershed, with consequences for today's human residents.

After scouring a channel, the great flood subsided into braided meltwater rivers like those in Alaska, flowing southwest toward Glacial Lake Scuppernong. As the Lake Michigan Lobe continued its retreat to the east, the land rebounded from its heavy freight of ice. West of the uplift, deprived of meltwater from both lobes of the diminishing ice sheet, the braided rivers narrowed to the dimensions of today's Bark and Oconomowoc Rivers.

~~~~~~~~~

Our nameless creek is one of many small arteries and even smaller veins that supply Bark Lake and Bark River with their lifeblood. The wetland that was once part of Glacial Bark Lake acts as a giant sponge, absorbing runoff from the surrounding area and releasing it gradually into the three remaining lakes. It also serves as a filter, removing sediment and contaminants from the water. That is why property owners on Bark and Amy Belle Lakes united in 1975 to oppose the expansion of a nearby quarry.

The same geological forces that gouged out the lakes also deposited pockets of glacial drift that have attracted quarry operations to the area, seeking gravel and sand for highway construction. One of these operated for years on the north side of Bark Lake Road, just west of Highway 175. When a new owner acquired the quarry and adjoining farmland in the early 1970s, he planned to expand the gravel pit. This entailed rezoning sixty-nine acres from agricultural to general industrial use. Though the Richfield Town Board approved his request, they did so in a session that appeared to violate the state's open meeting law.

The Bark and Amy Belle Lakes owners associations took advantage of a procedural challenge to mobilize resistance to the gravel pit expansion. They feared that quarry operations would release sediment into the wetland, reducing its capacity to filter water entering the lakes. The pit might also lower the water table to the point where the wetland would dry up. If the gravel pit were later turned into a landfill, as often happens, the lakes might be contaminated by seepage from refuse dumped in the pit.

Nearly four years elapsed between submission of the rezoning application and final approval in March 1979. Though the lakeshore owners were unable to prevent expansion of the gravel pit, they won several victories. The expansion was scaled back to twenty-four acres. The pit could not be excavated below the normal ground water level, and no water could be used in the operation. Looking to the future, the township passed a stricter mineral extraction and processing ordinance. It requires a detailed operations plan, a restoration plan with a performance bond to assure satisfactory completion, public hearings, minimum setbacks, fencing and landscaping, and consultation with the state Department of Natural Resources (DNR) and other agencies when appropriate.

~~~~~~~

Fallen trees block further progress up the creek, so we return to the lake and resume our circuit. The north shore contrasts sharply with the south. On the south shore a steep escarpment rises 110 feet above the lake. On the north the land eventually rises to about the same height to form the opposing rim of the glacial basin. Close to shore, however, it appears nearly level, as though scraped by an enormous bulldozer.

The soil, composed of silty sand, reminds us of a kayak trip that we took years ago to the Muir Glacier in Alaska. For several days we had paddled from Glacier Bay National Park near Gustavus to the ice sheet that John Muir first encountered in 1879. What we found at the head of Glacier Bay bore little resemblance to historical photos, which show a dazzling Taj Mahal of ice, its walls rising vertically from the water. All that remained was a dirty, ruined slum, stranded on its own till. To view it up close, we had to disembark from our boats and walk about fifty yards. This proved more difficult than we anticipated, as walking on wet glacial silt is like walking on wet grease. We mostly crawled the first ten yards, alternately dragging our kayaks and clinging to them for balance.

For the farmers who settled Bark Lake's north shore in the 1840s, the silty soil and level topography were an attraction rather than a deterrent. When exposed to air and water, glacial silt breaks down chemically and fosters plant growth. In contrast to the neighboring Town of Erin, settled by immigrants from Ireland, this part of Richfield Township drew families from Prussia, Upper Darmstadt, and Bavaria. On an 1892 plat map, farms belonging to families named Frank, Neuberg, Becker, Kurzhais, Schneider, Zeinbach, and Braun encircle the lake.

The farmers' boon became the cottagers' bane in the twentieth century. Most of their homes are set well back from the lake to provide a margin for the occasional high-water year. Unfortunately, not all of their septic systems have such a margin. The combination of a high water table and glacial silt, which retards percolation, causes many to fail, posing a more immediate threat to the lake than quarrying operations. In 1988 an inspector for the DNR testified that he had seen human waste oozing to the surface near the lake.

His testimony followed several years of frustrating and ultimately fruitless attempts to solve the problem. In 1984 Richfield had formed the Bark Lake Sanitary District. Consultants hired by the district recommended that a treatment plant be built near the Bark River outflow to process the wastewater generated by the lake's 135 residents. However, the DNR opposed the release of wastewater—about thirty-five thousand gallons per day—into the river. The DNR had recently embarked on a program to improve the river's water quality, and it maintained that phosphorus in the plant's discharge would foster weed growth and threaten two endangered species of fish that had appeared downriver in 1970s surveys—the starhead topminnow and a small catfish called the slender madtom.

Joining in the DNR's opposition to the treatment plant was the agency responsible for oversight of water and sanitation in the region, the Southeastern Wisconsin Regional Planning Commission. SEWRPC proposed that household waste be collected in a community holding tank and periodically trucked away. Alternatively, SEWRPC and the DNR suggested, the Bark Lake Sanitary District might link up with the Milwaukee Metropolitan Sewerage District (MMSD). That sounded like a good idea to the Bark Lake Sanitary District, and it formally requested such a connection in 1986. The District was prepared to build a three-and-a-half-mile pipeline to Germantown, which was already linked to MMSD, at an estimated cost of $1.5 million, later increased to $1.8 million. Sixty percent of the cost would be paid by the state, with the balance to be shared among lake residents.

Unfortunately, the area's glacial history thwarted this solution. The rebounding land that blocked Glacial Bark Lake's easterly drainage now blocked access to the watershed served by MMSD. Because Bark Lake lies just west of the subcontinental divide, in the Mississippi watershed, MMSD declined to process its residents' sewage. In 1989, stymied in its efforts to fix the problem, the Bark Lake Sanitary District asked Richfield to vote the district out of existence. The town board delayed a decision while it looked into building a regional interceptor system that would serve Bark Lake and other isolated communities. Today the district has a posthumous life as a name on

SEWRPC maps and plans but remains otherwise inactive. Lakeshore households continue to discharge waste into septic systems and holding tanks.

~~~~~~

We reach the end of our circumnavigation at the culvert where the river exits Bark Lake. There is no dam of any kind here, which makes it unique among the lakes and millponds through which the river passes. The culvert is a needle's eye too small to thread with our canoe, so we carry the boat across Bark Lake Drive and slide it into the downstream current. A gauge just downstream from the culvert shows 7.38—presumably feet. At higher lake levels the water must simply run over the road. We pass a woman sitting beside a backyard campfire on the right, then a young man fishing. Ahead looms a railroad bed, perforated by two large culverts.

The Wisconsin Central Railroad (now the Soo Line) accounted for Bark Lake's popularity as a sporting destination, resort, and commercial resource in the days before auto and truck transportation. Passengers could disembark at a flag station just south of Bark Lake Road. From there anglers could walk a half mile to the lake for a day of fishing. Families arriving for a longer stay could take a horse-drawn jitney to cottages on the north shore of Bark Lake or on Amy Belle Lake. The people who vacationed on these lakes may have lacked the social standing of those who frequented the larger Waukesha County lakes, but they often followed the pattern of seasonal migration described by Thorstein Veblen in his 1901 study *The Theory of the Leisure Class*. Summer weekdays found the husband and father laboring in the city while his wife and children enjoyed life at a resort, bearing witness to their financial security. The paterfamilias joined his family, and often the fishermen, on weekends.

Fishing underwent a brief hiatus in the late fall as ice thickened on the lake, then resumed in its winter form. Both fishermen and skaters had to keep their distance from a commercial operation that shifted into high gear when the ice reached a depth of at least twelve inches. Each January and February—sometimes earlier, sometimes later—Bark Lake reverted to the Pleistocene ice slab it had once been. During the nineteenth century, though, there were entrepreneurs on the scene who had figured out a way to turn some of that ice into money.

It was Frederic Tudor, the Ice King of Boston, who showed them how. In 1807 he sent a shipload of ice to the West Indies for use in treating yellow fever. Though his initial ventures were not especially profitable—indeed, they were often an object of derision—he eventually amassed a fortune shipping his product to the West and East Indies, Calcutta, Cuba, the Caribbean, and domestic ports such as Charleston, Savannah, and New Orleans. Tudor's ice was used not only to reduce fever but also to make ice cream in the American South and cool the drinks of British civil servants in India.

Tudor developed techniques for harvesting, storing, and transporting ice that were imitated throughout the United States. His ingenious partner Nathaniel Wyeth invented the ice plow, an essential harvesting tool that was widely copied by blacksmiths. Tudor designed the first aboveground storage houses and constantly experimented with ways to insulate the ice so as to minimize melting during storage and transport in the hold of a ship or a railroad boxcar.

The Ice King preferred to harvest his ice from bodies of water such as Fresh Pond, close enough to Boston for efficient transport but far enough away to be spared the effects of urban pollution. He unwittingly entered American literary history in 1846 when he dispatched a crew to harvest the ice on Walden Pond. Henry David Thoreau was then engaged in his own business venture on the pond, trading, as he put it, with the Celestial Empire. A delightful passage in Thoreau's *Walden* immortalizes the labor of Tudor's crew. Its humor stems chiefly from the similarity between harvesting ice with Wyeth's horse-drawn plow and more conventional forms of agriculture.

Walden Pond had the merits of pristine clarity (Thoreau drank directly from its waters), proximity to Boston, and a railroad that often figures in Thoreau's reflections on Yankee industriousness and ingenuity. It lacked a proper icehouse, however, and the harvesters' makeshift structure of hay and planks allowed the crop to seep back into the pond. Tudor never felt the loss, for the Walden harvest was merely a hedge against competition, to be sold or not as the market dictated.

As the demand for ice grew and East Coast entrepreneurs sought purer waters in colder climates, the Kennebec River in Maine came to be the Bordeaux of ice production. "Kennebec ice" was the *appellation d'origine contrôlée* that bespoke clarity, hardness, and purity. Its Midwestern equivalent came from the lake country of Wisconsin's Waukesha and Washington Counties. At first the Milwaukee River was the area's principal source of ice. Then concern over pollution of the river below the North Avenue dam, where the city's factories were located, prompted the ice companies to move upstream and to the inland lakes.

It was on the Milwaukee River, rather late in the ice-harvesting era, that one of naval history's more bizarre battles took place. During the winter of 1901–1902 the newly formed Pike and North Lake Ice Company built ice houses on its namesake lakes and filled them with ice, hoping to capitalize on Milwaukeeans' doubts regarding ice taken from the river. They neglected, however, to buy or obtain easements to the land that separated the icehouses from a nearby railroad. By the time they discovered their oversight, the property was no longer available. Agents of their main competitor, so they alleged, had secured the land and were unwilling to sell or grant them access. Without the real estate on which to construct railroad spurs, they could not get their product to market.

The company took revenge on its competitor, the Wisconsin Lakes Ice and Cartage Company, by purchasing a steam launch and outfitting it as an ice cutter. Under the pretext of conducting Milwaukee River excursions, complete with musical entertainment provided by a German band, the *Julius Goll* plowed through the ice fields of the Wisconsin Lakes Company, sending its floes over the North Avenue dam. The excursions continued for nearly six weeks, preventing river ice from being harvested for the rest of the season. The Wisconsin Lakes Company tried stringing barbed wire across the river, launching spike-studded timbers at the *Julius Goll*, and even attacking the vessel in smaller boats, to no avail. Young men aboard the ice-breaker deflected the attacks with pike poles and repaired the occasional puncture.

These skirmishes had an *opera buffa* quality, especially as reported in the local newspapers. But they had their serious side, too, inasmuch as the combatants depended on the ice harvest to support their families that winter. They also exacerbated ethnic tensions, for the Wisconsin Lakes Company employed about two hundred Polish immigrants, and the Pike and North Lake Company employed an unknown number of mostly German workers.

It was the German immigrants who brought to the city a taste for the beer that would make Milwaukee famous. Unlike the heavier malt liquors that prevailed before their arrival, the lighter, more effervescent lager beer required ice for warm-weather brewing and storage. By the early 1880s Milwaukee brewers were using 335,000 tons of ice per year. As people began to prefer their beer chilled, they increased the demand for ice in taverns, hotels, and homes.

After brewing, meatpacking was the enterprise that depended most heavily on a reliable source of ice. Locally, this included the Cudahy Packing Company. The industry giants were Swift and Armour of Chicago. Gustavus

Swift developed refrigerated railroad cars ("reefers") that allowed meat to be processed in Chicago and shipped to markets around the country. Especially after the Chicago River became too foul to supply their needs, Chicago packers turned to Wisconsin lakes and rivers as far north as Sturgeon Bay. The Madison lakes and Pewaukee Lake were favorites, being far enough north for a reliable freeze yet within a few hours' transport by rail. It was on Pewaukee that Armour built its largest icehouse, a structure that could hold over 175,000 tons of ice.

Natural ice played a key role not only in brewing and meatpacking but also in the dairy business, where it served to chill milk, butter, and cheese. Mortuaries, too, used it to retard spoilage. Ice consumption spread gradually from the commercial sphere to the domestic, as efficient and affordable iceboxes became available. By the late nineteenth century half of the ice harvest found its way into American households, delivered by icemen in colorful horse-drawn wagons.

Tudor and Wyeth developed the harvesting technique that so amused Thoreau at Walden Pond. It was still the method used during the nineteenth and early twentieth centuries on Wisconsin lakes, millponds, and rivers. Each fall the ice companies marked their fields by submerging long poles in the lake bottom. The extent of a company's field was based on the amount of lake frontage it owned, following a formula developed for Fresh Pond in Massachusetts. If weeds grew too close to the surface, as they often did on Pewaukee Lake, the companies removed them with weed-cutting scows.

When the ice was thick enough to bear the weight of horses, the animals dragged scrapers over the surface to remove the snow. Without snow for insulation, the ice froze to a greater depth. The harvester scored the ice with two base lines, forming a right angle. Then he hitched his horse to the marker, a plowlike instrument that cut a line three inches deep and parallel to one of the base lines. A guide attached to the marker maintained a distance of twenty-two inches from the base line and all subsequent lines to the other end of the ice field. Then, working from the second base line, the harvester marked lines that were likewise twenty-two inches apart and perpendicular to the first set. The dimensions of the blocks varied according to the intended market.

Next, the harvester hitched his horse to an ice plow, which resembled the marker in having progressively longer teeth from front to back. With each pass over the marked lines, this instrument sawed a couple of inches deeper until the cut was two-thirds of the way through the ice. Workers with saws or

Photograph courtesy of the Milwaukee Public Museum

Photograph courtesy of the Milwaukee Public Museum

Marking and cutting ice on the Milwaukee River (top) and then guiding it to the elevator (above), about 1910

long chisel-pointed bars then broke off sections consisting of perhaps a dozen ice squares. Using horses or long-handled hooks, they towed or prodded the sections along an open channel of water to the icehouse.

There the floes were divided into smaller sections or individual blocks and guided onto a steam-driven elevator that carried them to storage chambers. As the cakes of ice slid into a chamber, men with hooks arranged them in tiers until the room was full, then moved up to the next chamber. The icehouse was double walled on the outside, with sawdust, marsh hay, or peat providing insulation between the walls. The same material was packed between the tiers of ice and between the top tier and the ceiling of each chamber.

Ice harvesting on this scale required hundreds of workers and dozens of horses. Farmers looking for off-season employment provided some of the muscle and livestock. Other workers were recruited from neighboring villages and cities, including almshouses in Milwaukee. The larger icehouses on Pewaukee Lake became virtual villages, with barracks, barns, equipment storage sheds, and repair shops. Boisterous young strangers suddenly overran the tranquil lakeside communities, lacking any diversion besides what they could find in local taverns. Perhaps it was just as well that they worked ten-hour days in physically demanding and sometimes dangerous circumstances.

Though it was usually workers and their horses who fell into the frigid water and had to be rescued, nonworkers were also at risk. Early on, Wisconsin enacted legislation that required ice companies to erect a perimeter of brush and blocks of ice. When this failed to warn people off, the state required secure fencing around the operation. The result could be fatal when harvesters ignored the law. In January 1891 the *Waukesha Daily Freeman* reported the drowning of a young woman in Fowler Lake. During a nighttime skating party she and her escort had slipped into water left open and unsecured by the ice cutters.

The season's ice crop usually remained in icehouses until the following summer, when it was removed for shipment in reefers or conventional boxcars lined with marsh hay or sawdust. Reversing the order of storage, workers emptied the upper chambers first, using pike poles to guide the blocks onto a slide or conveyor inclined toward the railroad cars. When full, the cars were towed to an "Alaska" (weighing station) to determine how much the railroad would charge for transporting the ice to Milwaukee or Chicago.

For a brief interval at the turn of the century the weight also determined the tax to be paid on Wisconsin ice bound for Chicago. In 1898 the Knickerbocker Ice Company consolidated most of the Chicago-area natural ice companies except for those belonging to the meat packers. The consolidated company behaved suspiciously like a trust, prompting the state of Wisconsin, under Governor Robert M. La Follette, to pass the Overbeck Ice Bill in 1901. The bill levied a tax of ten cents per ton on ice shipped out of state, with the proceeds going to the state school fund. To ensure compliance, the bill required nonresident ice-harvesting companies and individuals to post a bond of ten thousand dollars. A Knickerbocker agent promptly tested the bill's constitutionality by posting no bond and shipping ice from Racine-area lakes to Chicago. Found guilty in a circuit court, he appealed to the state supreme court, which overturned the lower court's decision. The Overbeck Ice Bill was repealed in 1903.

Knickerbocker won the battle against the Wisconsin tax but lost the war against more convenient and less costly methods of cooling. Though there was still a market for natural ice as late as the 1920s, it had mostly given way to artificial (man-made) ice and refrigeration. Knickerbocker abandoned its icehouses and was eventually absorbed by an artificial ice company. A Knickerbocker icehouse was located on the south bank of the Bark River just downstream from Bark Lake. A spur off the Wisconsin Central Railroad line facilitated easy shipment of Bark Lake ice to Chicago. Today the icehouse can be found only on old maps and in the records of the Office of the State Archaeologist.

~~~~~~~~~~

Of the two culverts passing under the railroad bed, the one on the right appears to have the deeper channel, so we take that route and continue our voyage downriver. A train rumbles past, northbound. We hear five more over the next three hours, suggesting that this stretch of track is well used. Where the river is too shallow to paddle we step out and wade until it deepens. Noticing a sunny, somewhat elevated bank on the right, we pull over for lunch. The skunk cabbage has unfurled, and a couple of animal bones lie bleaching in the sun, perhaps from a deer leg.

Back in the boat after lunch, we hear an animal, probably a deer, crashing through the underbrush. Where a tributary enters the river on the right, a Canada goose eyes us warily from her nest. We have to thread our way through overhanging branches here and there, but otherwise make good progress until just upstream from Lakeview Road, where a fallen tree blocks the channel. We pull over to the right and drag our boat around the downfall, steering clear of a pothole hidden in the thick brush. At Lakeview Road we manage to squeeze through the culvert, then paddle through property heavily posted with no trespassing signs. Here the grass is mowed almost to the water's edge. Shortly afterward, for the second time in a couple of hours, we negotiate a culvert under the Soo Line tracks.

West of the river, hidden from sight by a high ridge, is a huge quarry. A climb up to Scenic Road provides a good overview of the operation, which is currently in recovery. Mature trees and other vegetation have reclaimed the part of the quarry west of the road, while the part to the east is still fairly raw. Each view is like a snapshot of the plant succession that followed the glacier's retreat some thirteen thousand years ago.

From Lakeview Road to Willow Creek Road the river teems with marsh marigolds and turtles, including a snapping turtle as big as a dinner plate. At our approach the snapper tunnels under the mat of river vegetation and vanishes. Despite the early season an algae bloom testifies to ample sunlight and, very likely, septic runoff into Bark Lake.

At Willow Creek Road we encounter the Soo Line for the third and last time. Here the river passes under two culverts in quick succession. The first, under the railroad tracks, is wide enough for a canoe to pass through, but today the water is too shallow. The second, which passes under the road, is too narrow. So we take out upstream from the railroad culvert, along the shoulder of Willow Creek Road.

"Good news—our shuttle vehicle is still here," Puck says, pointing to the railroad gate where I cabled my bicycle early this morning. "You won't have to walk." A few minutes later I am pedaling back to our minivan, parked near the lake access.

When I return to the take-out, we load our canoe onto the rooftop carrier and drive back to the tavern on Bark Lake. Initials on the outside of the building identify it as EJ's. The owner, the man whom we'd met that morning, explains that he wanted a short name for answering the telephone, after running a place with a longer name in Menomonee Falls. So he named the bar after his wife, Erika, and himself, Jim.

Our eyes adjust to the dim light as we sip the draft beer. EJ's could be any rural Wisconsin bar on a Sunday afternoon. Three television sets are on, two of them tuned to a NASCAR race. Three men watch from their stools, occasionally commenting on the commentary. The door opens and two more patrons enter, taking the stools next to ours. Ignoring the TV screens, one of them strikes up a conversation.

"Is that your van with the canoe?"

"Yes." It's hard to miss among the pickup trucks, and we're no doubt just as conspicuous among EJ's regulars.

"Out fishing on the lake?"

"Not today. Just paddling and sightseeing. We also got down the Bark River a ways, to Willow Creek Road."

"I didn't know you could get that far in a boat. You know, there's some nice canoeing on the river where it leaves Lower Nemahbin Lake."

"I know the stretch you mean. But my wife and I plan to paddle the entire river this year, from the lake down to the Rock River."

"So that's where it goes. Is this a contest or something?"

"No contest. We just want to see the whole river, see what kind of country it passes through. The Bark valley has an interesting history. I like to read about the events, then see where they happened. Maybe collect the stories in a book."

"Sounds like something I'd enjoy reading. I like historical stuff—Civil War mainly, but just about anything on the History Channel. Does it have a title, this book you're writing?"

"Possibly *The Bark River Chronicles*, if I ever finish it. My wife and I are teachers, which keeps us pretty busy during the school year. During the summer I usually do research related to my work. I'm an English professor."

"Well, I wish you luck. What part of the river are you going to do next?"

"From Willow Creek Road down to Colgate, on County Line Road."

"You'll need all the luck you can get. I don't think you can get through there in a boat. It's nothing but swamp."

"We'll find out. If you hear about two people disappearing in the marsh, you'll know who it was."

Bark Lake

Willow Creek Rd

COLGATE

County Line Rd

LaFarge
North America
quarry

Hillside Rd

North Rd

Bark River

Highway 164

Song Bird Hills
Golf Course

Lake Five Rd

Genesee Aggregate
Corporation quarry

Plainview Rd

Geniese Aggregate
Corporation quarry

Merton
Millpond

Chicago and Northwestern RR right-of-way

Bugline Recreation Trail

Mill St

Merton Feed
Company

MERTON

Main St

historic site
of "cross" effigy mound

County Highway VV

Golden Swan
antique furniture store

N

1 mile

CHAPTER 2

Willow Creek Road
to Merton

The following Sunday finds us back on Willow Creek Road, gazing dubiously downstream. The Bark River is visible for only a short distance before it disappears into a heavily wooded swamp. It is not a place where we would want to be after the mosquitoes have hatched. Later in the spring there probably won't be enough water to float a canoe. Fortunately, County Line Road is just a mile and a half downstream. How long could that take? We plan to paddle an additional mile or so to Hillside Road, where we have left the bike.

As we start to unload our canoe a passing car slows down, then stops. The driver, a man in his early twenties, offers to help. During the next quarter of an hour, we learn that he lives on a farm west of the river. He and his brother had once paddled the section we're about to do, and it had lodged in his memory as an epic adventure from the golden age before southern Washington County became a suburb of Milwaukee. The area was then, in his words, "a little slice of heaven." Wishing us luck, he waits for a Ford

Explorer—its very name a bit of suburban wishful thinking—to pass. Then he crosses the road and drives off.

After an auspicious launch, we enjoy thirty yards of clear sailing before we plunge into a jungle of tag alder, willow, and red osier dogwood. Here our Sunday morning service begins in earnest. Canoeing is a religion for some people, but no one, as far as I know, has taken the trouble to compose its catechism or New England Primer. For the benefit of anyone who is curious about the mysteries of our faith, especially as they apply to this section of the Bark River, I offer the following as a first draft.

Q: How do you propel a seventeen-foot canoe through impenetrable swamp?
A: You don't. If God had wanted a canoe to pass through the swamp He wouldn't have made it impenetrable. Go home and enjoy your day of rest.

Q: Seriously, how?
A: Okay, if you really want to know. Kneel in the bow, well forward of the front seat. Then, as the person in the stern propels the boat forward with a paddle planted in the riverbed, you do the Moses Stroke. This resembles the breaststroke, except that it's used for parting waters and water-loving vegetation. The alders separate to either side of the bow, which drives forward like an entering wedge. Then they smack the stern paddler in the face because— you forgot, didn't you?—the canoe gets narrower back there.

Q: Suppose I don't want to antagonize the only person who would venture into a swamp with me?
A: The secret to tandem bushwhacking is to glide over, not between. Maybe it would help to think butterfly rather than breaststroke. Reach forward and above the branches, palms down. Bring your arms straight down close to the bow, pressing the alders under the water. Follow through, lifting the bow over the submerged branches and launching it forward. Your partner, no longer distracted by alder facials, pushes you deeper into the heart of darkness.

Q: Hey, I think we're getting the hang of it. But what about that tree trunk lying across the river? We can't butterfly over that, can we?
A: Here's how, amphibian. Step ashore and have your partner do the same. Each of you lifts an end of the boat and you carry it around the downfall.

Q: *What shore? We left* terra firma *behind us half an hour ago. Now we're surrounded by primal ooze and wrecked trees. Even if we could walk on this goo, we'd have to detour a mile out of our way.*

A: Right. The carry-around is a lubberly maneuver, anyway. For sheer elegance it's hard to beat the lift-over. Angle the bow up to the section of tree trunk with the fewest branches. The bow paddler steps onto the trunk and holds the boat steady as the stern paddler walks forward and steps onto the trunk facing him. Each paddler grabs a gunwale near the bow. Then one, two, three—*lift!* With the bow on the trunk between you, you can slide the boat up and over, passing your hands along the gunwales. Reverse the procedure on the downstream side to re-embark. The bow paddler steps into the stern, walks forward, and so forth. You get the idea.

Q: *What's that I smell?*

A: Mink scat. What did you expect to find on a mink highway? You may take some home with you guilt free. It's a renewable resource.

Two hours downstream from Willow Creek Road, with a dozen carries-around or lifts-over to our credit, we emerge from the swamp into a sunny meadow upstream from the County Line bridge. Cars whoosh by, Explorers and nonexplorers. The interior of our canoe is a sight to behold, so littered with sticks that it resembles an enormous heron nest. My forearms look as though I've spent the morning wrestling mountain lions. Stepping ashore, we unpack our bagel sandwiches and Kool-Aid, spread our PFDs (personal fanny devices) on the grass, and sit with our backs to the highway. A little slice of heaven.

Q: *What could be finer?*

A: Amen.

~~~~~~

After dining and de-littering our canoe, we continue downstream, passing under County Line Road into Waukesha County. Two hundred yards farther on we pass through a culvert under North Road, where spiders have set an ambush for unsuspecting paddlers. Breaking through the gossamer curtain into a farmer's pasture, we encounter a sturdier web of barbed wire, presumably set for cows. Puck is currently in the bow. She lifts the lowest strand and ducks under. I do the same when it reaches me, and the boat glides under. These maneuvers attract the attention of a couple of farm kids, about twelve and eight years old, who run down to see what we're doing. They mention that another canoe had come through the previous year, adding wistfully that they've never gone down the river themselves.

Our hearts sink as we leave the pasture, for it looks initially as though we have more alder bashing ahead of us. Almost immediately, however, the river opens into a spacious wetland, a mixture of cattail marsh, sedge meadow, and hardwood swamp. It is a noisy, teeming place, an aviary without walls or roof. Dozens of Canada geese announce our arrival. Some frantically steer their goslings toward the safety of the cattails as others honk an alarm from hummocks of marsh hay and old tree stumps. Most of the trees are dead, though still in demand as woodpecker and tree swallow dwellings. The air is alive with twittering swallows, weaving intricate flight patterns. Others perch on dead snags, showing off the stylish contrast of blue-black and white that gives them their scientific name, *Tachycineta bicolor*. Black-and-white warblers, blue-winged teal, wood ducks, a kingfisher, and a great blue heron add their colors to the palette.

Contributing to the sense of aviarylike enclosure is a high ridge to the southwest, rising abruptly from cattail marsh to a height of about a hundred feet. The glacier was clearly at work here, depositing an irregular kame or a terminal moraine. Beneath the swallows' airy falsetto we can hear the guttural grunts of machinery. Someone is at work in the LaFarge North America quarry, extracting sand and gravel for use in construction. A conveyor belt juts above the horizon like the head and neck of some prehistoric monster.

Unable to discern any channel in the flooded woods, we pick our way through the maze of standing and fallen trees in what seems to be the right direction. Finding ourselves near solid ground on the south end of the swamp, we pause for a snack. The most promising spot is an earthen dike that separates the wooded swamp from an elevated cattail marsh. The top of the dike seems to have been cleared and leveled, perhaps for access by quarry vehicles. Now it is mostly overgrown, though we find open ground on which to munch our trail mix and admire nature's attempt at a Georgia O'Keeffe painting—violets pushing through the bleached bones of a deer skeleton.

Back in the canoe, we proceed from open hardwood swamp to a wetland dominated by large willows, some cradling old ducks' nests. Houses and yards begin to appear on the higher ground to the right. In one of the backyards, on a trailer parked near the water, is a metal-flake red runabout that looks fast even when standing still. From its stern dangles an enormous Mercury outboard. Its bow points toward a distant horizon.

The higher banks funnel the water toward an exit stream. It is blocked by a nearly submerged beaver dam, which accounts for some of the flooding upstream. As we ponder which section of the dam to run, one of the little engineers swims out and climbs onto a willow stump to check us out. Satisfied that we aren't dam saboteurs from the DNR or Edward Abbey's Monkey Wrench Gang, he slips back into the water and disappears. We slide over his handiwork into a quicker current, relieved to be back in water that behaves like a river.

Barely twenty yards downstream another beaver dam blocks the channel, requiring us to perform a precarious lift-over while balanced on freshly peeled branches. We are a good two feet lower when we resume our journey, as though we had come through a set of locks. We pass a beaver lodge on the left bank, then negotiate the ruins of yet another beaver dam before arriving at our take-out on Hillside Road.

Checking my wristwatch, I find that we've traveled two miles in the two hours since lunch. Is that too slow, too fast, or just about right? It depends on where you're going and what you hope to encounter along the way. We have arguably traveled farther in two hours, really traveled, than the red runabout has in two years. Next time we'll slow down and see even more of the world.

~~~~~~~

A couple of fellow travelers join us when we resume our journey at the end of April. Kent and Gail have paddled many northern Wisconsin rivers with us, stunning wilderness rivers with serious whitewater. It was near one of these, the Wolf River, that we proposed an outing on the Bark. Sitting around our campfire after supper, we traded war stories about the day's run through the magnificent Dells section of the Wolf, on the Menominee Reservation.

"Is there any better stretch of river in the state?" I asked. It was a rhetorical question, but Gail answered.

"There are parts of the Peshtigo and Oconto that come pretty close."

"Give me the Montreal below Saxon Falls," Kent ventured.

"Don't forget the Pine and the Popple," Puck chimed in.

"Those are all righteous rivers," I had to concede. "We're lucky to have so many to choose from. But suppose we factor distance from home into our ranking. Which rivers have the highest QPQ—quality-proximity quotient?"

We are all from the Milwaukee area, so the usual suspects came to mind: the upper sections of the Milwaukee, the Oconomowoc near Monches, the Rock where it enters Horicon Marsh.

"My favorite backyard river is the Bark," Puck said.

"We've done the section from Lower Nemahbin Lake to Dousman several times," Gail offered. "It scores fairly high on the QPQ scale."

"Puck and I are going to run the whole thing this season," I said. "Want to come along?"

"I don't know about the whole thing," Kent responded. "Probably not. But keep us posted on your progress, and we'll join you when we're available."

Today they're available. We selfishly appreciate having a second car to replace the bike as shuttle vehicle. We plan to paddle from Hillside Road to the village of Merton. Considering that the river sets its own pace, however, we leave a car at the bridge on Highway 164, less than halfway to Merton. It's our hedge against unforeseen delays.

We are scarcely launched when we have to carry around the first obstacle, a rickety wooden footbridge fifteen yards downstream from Hillside Road. Except for this bridge, a small dock, and birdhouses, there is little human encroachment on the river here, despite the subdivisions visible on both banks. Most of these suburban pioneers had the good sense to build on higher ground, though one home on the left appears to be in the flood plain. Kent draws our attention to black hoses coming from the basement.

"I'll bet they're getting more of the Bark River than they bargained for."

Passing through a willow thicket, we come out into an open sedge meadow. I see what appears to be a cat close at hand in the brush. It turns out to be a young raccoon, more curious than alarmed at our approach. Though wood duck nesting boxes line the river, Canada geese have claimed the neighborhood. One pair has built their nest on a gravel bar in the middle of the river. We count five ivory-colored eggs. This is the first of two dozen nests that we will encounter, all with eggs.

The river bottom is gravelly here, with an occasional boulder in the channel. Some of these are quite large, probably erratics deposited by the glacier. Where the meadow narrows to forested, brushy banks we notice a large deposit of small boulders, some of which have been arranged to form a low dam or footbridge across the channel just above a drop in river level. Carrying around a downed tree, we notice a county sign prohibiting the cutting of trees and shrubs along the banks.

This noble effort at creating a riparian buffer soon gives way to manicured lawns that extend to the river's edge. Where the valley opens out we can see, directly ahead, an enormous new house crowning an eroded hilltop. The castle in Orson Welles's *Citizen Kane* comes to mind. Gail points to tree stumps at the base of the hill.

"A couple of weeks ago," she says, "we were looking at real estate in North Carolina. Our agent had a phrase for that kind of tree removal. He called it 'view enhancement.'"

This particular view will be enhanced at some cost to a lovely wetland at the base of the hill. Clouds of minnows scatter as we paddle into it. Minute particles of vegetation signal a slight current. Sure enough, a bit farther on we find natural springs boiling up through the sand.

Leaving the wetland, we return to the river, which soon passes through a culvert under a driveway. We carry over the driveway, resume paddling, and enter a large cattail marsh alive with geese, some of them on nests. We are puzzled, at first, by an old wooden bridge in the middle of the marsh, surrounded entirely by water. The mystery of the Bridge to Nowhere is resolved when we notice signs leading away from it, marking a snowmobile trail.

Due to downed trees and flooding from recent rains, we must cast about until we locate the river channel. At last we discover where it pours over a beaver dam and threads its way westward among willows and dogwoods. Hearing voices on the higher ground to our left, we look up and are startled to see golfers loitering at a tee on the Song Bird Hills golf course. They studiously ignore us, though it can't be every day that they see boats on their water hazard.

We arrive at Highway 164 at 12:30, about two hours from our put-in. The weather is still clear and warm. No one is ready to call it a day, so we reshuttle the cars and are back in our boats by 1:30. I have misgivings about the next section, which skirts the Genesee Aggregate Corporation. The company has posted the land forbiddingly, and quarries generally treat adjacent waterways as a nuisance. So I'm pleasantly surprised when this proves to be one of the more attractive and less spoiled sections of the river.

We begin by shooting a small drop on the upstream side of the Highway 164 bridge, then enter a wooded area downstream. The river is exceptionally clear, with occasional boulders and fish, probably smallmouth bass, in the ten- to twelve-inch range. I am struck by the contrast with the Menomonee River in Milwaukee County, where we'd helped to pick up litter the day before. Two inches of rain had fallen in the previous forty-eight hours, and the Menomonee was running fast, high, and turbid, to the point where we were concerned about the safety of the volunteers. Though the Bark had received the same rainfall, its wetlands had absorbed the extra water and were releasing it more slowly.

After a couple of lifts-over and carries-around we pass a building, possibly a quarry company office, on the left. Then we pull over for lunch on the right.

"Look at all the skunk cabbage," Puck remarks.

"Lots of spring beauties, too," Gail adds. We are unable to identify most of the other wildflowers.

After lunch we come to a wooden bridge constructed of recycled telephone poles, apparently for snowmobiles. At a lift-over just downstream from the bridge Gail nearly loses her balance but avoids a swim by grabbing the gunwales of the canoe. We hear the hoarse chuckling and fluting of sandhill cranes in the distance and see evidence of beavers, including an artfully sculpted tree and a dam we are able to skid over. In a thicket of willows and dogwood we spot a doe that remains motionless as we glide by, watching us over her shoulder.

Where the river meets a high landform and veers sharply to the left we get out of our boats and climb the hill.

"How did *this* get here?" Kent asks, marveling at the clearly delineated ridge that separates the river from a farmer's field.

"Oh."

He recognizes it as an esker, the raised bed of sediment from a meltwater stream that tunneled through the ice sheet during the Pleistocene. This ancient upside-down river still shapes the course of today's Bark River. We follow a game trail along the esker's sinuous crest, noting the abundant bird life, then scramble down its slope through hickory trees to a sedge meadow. Where the meadow meets the base of the esker a small tributary stream joins the Bark.

Returning to our boats, we hear splashing upstream and look in time to see a doe and her fawn crossing the river toward the quarry. The doe clears the river in two effortless leaps as the fawn struggles to lift its hooves high enough to clear the water. From the esker to the Merton millpond the river meanders through a cattail marsh where we see muskrats and nesting geese.

A few minutes' paddle above Plainview Road we're reminded that this is quarry land. Bulldozed dirt and gravel encroach on the river as close as twenty yards, though berms generally hide the excavations from view. In 2002 Genesee Aggregate received the county's blessing to expand its operations by more than a hundred acres in the direction of the Bark. In years to come, the upstream section may look more like this one.

Kent and Gail are in the lead when we reach Plainview Road. They discover that they can squeeze through a culvert, avoiding a portage, and we do the same. Soon we pass under the right-of-way for the Chicago and Northwestern Railroad, which once shipped ice from North Lake to meat packers in Chicago. Downstream from the railroad bridge, where the river bends right, the owners of a large beam-and-stucco house have put out feeders for both the wild waterfowl and their own ducks and geese.

A damaged culvert blocks our passage under Lake Five Road, requiring a short portage over the asphalt. Almost immediately we pass under another railroad bridge. Once used by the Chicago, Milwaukee, St. Paul, and Pacific Railroad, and before that by the Milwaukee and Superior Railroad, it is now part of the popular Bugline Recreation Trail between Menomonee Falls and Merton. From here to our take-out at the Merton dam, a distance of about a mile, we are on the millpond. It is heavily silted in and might not be passable later in the season when vegetation claims the surface. The only other craft on the pond is a bass fishing boat, jury-rigged with a raised platform. On each side of the platform a bow hunter scans the murky water for carp. They acknowledge us with a nod but pay no attention to the cyclists who pass on either side. Skinny tires hum along the Bugline on the north shore while fat tires grind up the rougher mountain bike trail on the south.

Two hours after leaving Highway 164, we take out to the left of the dam and carry our boats across the parking lot to the shuttle car.

"Well, what do you think?" I ask our fellow voyageurs after we've retrieved the other car and loaded up our gear. "Is it as good as the Wolf?"

"No way," Kent says. "But in terms of QPQ—not bad."

"What do you say to next Sunday, nine o'clock at this parking lot?"

Gail looks at Kent, hesitating. Then she smiles broadly. "Okay. You're on."

"We'll see you then. We're going to stroll up the street before driving home."

~~~~~~~

We wave to our friends as they leave the parking lot, then walk south along Main Street. The buildings in the immediate neighborhood reflect the village's origins as a rural farm community. In 1871, when the Old Settlers Club of Waukesha County asked members of the newly formed Merton chapter for an account of their past, they began their chronology in 1837, when Ralph B. Allen built a cabin west of the village. The following year a young man named Stephen Warren arrived and stayed with Allen and other early settlers while looking for land for himself and his father, Sylvanus Warren.

The Warren family, as prolific as it was nomadic, came to the town of Merton from Canada by way of New York State and Michigan. Once the clan descended on the town, they shaped its history by their sheer numbers and the extent of their land holdings. Though the family's impact was greater on the village of Hartland, located six miles downstream from Merton on the border between Merton and Delafield Townships, the town of Merton was originally called Warren. The name had to be changed in 1848 when a post office was opened and the town learned that there was already a Warren post office in the state. A resident suggested that they adopt the name of her hometown in England, and so it came to pass.

Like Hartland, Merton grew up around mills on the Bark River. "Bark River put us on the map," an early memoirist contended, and went on to cite the sawmills, gristmills—three of each, according to the Old Settlers group— and cider mill that once formed the village's commercial nucleus.

Turning right on Mill Street, which is more a driveway than a street, we visit the last surviving mill, built in 1856. The Merton Feed Company used the river as a source of power until the early 1960s, when it transferred ownership of the dam to the village. Entering the tiny store where mill business is conducted, we find Don Serres behind the counter and chat for a while about the history of the mill and his decades of experience in local politics. When it is time to move on we buy a couple of smoked beef bones for my brother's dogs, pause to check out the baby chicks and ducklings in metal cages near the entryway, and descend the wooden steps.

Returning to Main Street, we admire the facade of the Golden Swan antique furniture store across the way. It was called H. E. Beckman's General Store when Serres worked there as a teenager. A small adjoining building served within the memory of older residents as the village post office. A short walk south on Main Street is the current post office, where locals often pause to grind the daily grist of news, gossip, and rumor.

Main Street follows the old Immigrant Trail where it descended to the Bark River. After fording its waters, pioneers resumed their westerly journey along the north bank. A half mile below the ford, near a campsite beside a large natural spring, some of them buried their dead.

A far older burying ground preceded the pioneer cemetery. In 1851 Increase Lapham surveyed the Indian mounds near Merton for his book *The Antiquities of Wisconsin*. His map shows several clusters of round and oval mounds located west and south of the village. On the elevation known as Fort Hill he found two oblong embankments, apparently man-made. Northwest of the intersection of County Highway VV and Lake Five Road lay the most striking earthwork, an effigy mound that Lapham called "the cross." "This last is certainly entitled to the name," he wrote, "from its striking resemblance to the cross as emblematically used and represented by the Roman Church in every part of the world; and yet there can be no doubt that this mound was erected long before the first Jesuits visited this country, and spread the doctrines, and presented the emblem of the Christian faith."

Measuring the unusual mound, Lapham found that one beam of the cross extended 226 feet, the other 320 feet. He learned that someone had dug into the mound and unearthed large bones, apparently those of an American Indian, at the intersection of the two members. Today the site is a farmer's field, and no trace of the mound remains.

The Merton cross was not the first effigy mound to arouse Lapham's curiosity. When he arrived in Milwaukee in 1836 he was already, at the age of twenty-five, an experienced surveyor and civil engineer whom Byron Kilbourn had hired to lay out the new city and supervise construction of a canal from Milwaukee to the Rock River. Though Lapham had little formal schooling, his quick mind and curiosity soon made him an expert in the territory's geology, plant and animal life, archeology, and meteorology. Visiting an effigy mound in Prairieville (later Waukesha) shortly after his arrival, he was both intrigued and appalled by what he saw. The mound resembled a turtle, with a body measuring fifty-six feet long and a tail extending another 250 feet. To Lapham's dismay, local Indians had worn a path through the tail and excavated a new grave on its back. The farmer who owned the land had dug out a potato cellar in a large round burial mound near the tip of the tail, discarding the human remains turned up by his shovel.

Several days later Lapham fired off a letter regarding the turtle mound to the editor of Milwaukee's sole newspaper, the *Advertiser*. "Such sacrilege should be made a punishable offence by the law," he wrote, and urged residents of the new territory to show greater respect than settlers of other

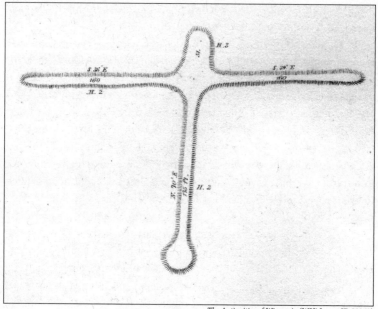

The Antiquities of Wisconsin (WHi Image ID 90269)
Increase Lapham's plat of the "cross" effigy mound near the village of Merton

states for Indian antiquities. Unfortunately, Wisconsin acquitted itself no
better than New York, Kentucky, or Ohio, where Lapham had watched the
ancient mounds disappear under the plow before anyone could unlock
their secrets. Of the fifteen to twenty thousand mounds thought to be in
the Wisconsin Territory when Europeans arrived, only about four thousand
remain, and many of these were plundered before trained archeologists
could study them.

Lapham drew attention to the mounds, especially the effigy mounds, in
his 1844 volume *Geographical and Topographical Description of Wisconsin*,
written for new arrivals and prospective settlers in the territory. In 1850,
after several years of seeking financial support for a comprehensive survey
of the Wisconsin mounds, he received $500 for expenses (about $14,400
today) from the American Antiquarian Society, but no personal remunera-
tion. He set off on his first excursion in June of that year and completed his
fieldwork two years later. *The Antiquities of Wisconsin*, published jointly by
the American Antiquarian Society and the Smithsonian Institution, finally
appeared in 1855.

The *Antiquities* was a groundbreaking study. Previous accounts of the earthen works in Ohio and other parts of the Midwest had resorted to variations on the "lost race" theory. According to the theory representatives of an advanced, nonnative civilization—perhaps from Greece, Rome, or Egypt—had built the marvelous earthen structures. Or the builders had belonged to one of the lost tribes of Israel. One man claimed that he had found a pair of golden candlesticks from Solomon's temple in a Waukesha mound.

Whoever these people were, they had vanished or were driven out by the savages who inhabited the country at the time of European contact. Aaron Rankin expressed a typical pioneer belief in his account of the effigy mounds and intaglios he had seen in Waukesha and Jefferson Counties. "I never saw an Indian who knew anything about these mounds," he wrote, "or had any tradition in relation to them. I am satisfied that these mounds were built by a race of people of much more intelligence than our native Indian." Especially during the time of Indian removals, it was convenient to draw a clear line between contemporary tribes and a highly developed pre-Columbian civilization.

Lapham believed, to the contrary, that ancestors of the territory's historic Indians had built the mounds. Then their culture had evolved away from mound building, though they continued to bury their dead in the ancient structures. He speculated that the effigies and earthworks at Aztalan, named for their resemblance to Aztec ruins in Mexico, were the oldest mounds. Conical (round and oval) burial mounds came later, followed by geometrical garden beds and finally the irregular garden beds planted by contemporary Indians.

Lapham thus hypothesized a cultural evolution—or devolution—from more sophisticated earthen structures to less sophisticated. Modern archeologists share his belief that ancestors of historic-era native people built the mounds. However, radiocarbon dating, combined with the study of grave artifacts, has enabled them to determine the age of the mounds more precisely. Reversing Lapham's progression, they believe that native people of the late Archaic period began building conical burial mounds in Wisconsin around 800 BC. The practice persisted through the Woodland period (500 BC–1200 AD). It was during the late Woodland period, between 700 and 1200 AD, that the spectacular effigy mounds were built, often at sites already occupied by burial mounds.

Sometime after 900 AD Indians belonging to the Middle Mississippian culture centered in southern Illinois established a northern outpost in Aztalan, on the west bank of the Crawfish River. Among other earthworks they built flat-topped pyramids like those in the ancient city of Cahokia, near the present-day site of East St. Louis. Broken, cut, and charred human bones unearthed at Aztalan may be a byproduct of funerary practices. Or they may indicate that this warlike people inflicted a violent death on prisoners, perhaps even consuming parts of their bodies in ritual cannibalism.

Not far from Aztalan, along the Rock River and Lake Koshkonong, a late Woodland group developed the distinctive Upper Mississippian culture known as the Oneota. From these the Ho-Chunk (Winnebago) and related Indians of the historic period—including the Dakota, Ioway, and possibly the Menominee—are thought to have descended. So far the evidence is largely cultural, deriving from oral tradition and similarity of practices and beliefs. DNA testing may eventually establish genetic connections, but it can proceed only with the cooperation of contemporary Ho-Chunk people. Considering the history of grave robbing by white settlers, they are understandably wary of procedures that would further violate the remains of people whom they regard as ancestors.

Though the Ho-Chunk are also reluctant to reveal details of their spiritual beliefs to outsiders, ethnographic study of their beliefs and those of other Midwestern native people has helped to unlock the mystery of the effigy mounds. Lapham was onto something when he compared the Merton effigy to the Christian cross, for it is a religious symbol. Like the great cathedrals, mosques, and temples of the world, the effigy mounds embody a coherent cosmology.

The Woodland Indians of Wisconsin represented the upper world of the sky with bird-shaped mounds, of which the Merton "cross" is one example. They represented the lower world of earth with mounds shaped like bears, deer, elk, bison, and other terrestrial animals. Beneath the earth was the still lower world of water, represented by the long-tailed water spirits that settlers called turtles, lizards, or panthers. The Waukesha turtle mound was one of these. Another is the mound that Lapham surveyed near Hartland, just north of a pioneer cemetery on present-day Lisbon Road. Dorn Road, which connects Hartland and Merton, had obliterated part of the water spirit mound. Between Dorn Road and the Bark River Lapham found an animal (earth) effigy and several linear mounds, the latter possibly also a kind of effigy. Farther downstream and west of the river, in the town of Summit, he mapped a large group of mounds representing the complete cosmology, with air, earth, and water effigies distributed among conical and linear mounds.

Noticing that the mound builders often located their structures along rivers or beside lakes, Lapham organized *The Antiquities of Wisconsin* around major watersheds. Archeological evidence confirms that the native people who used these sites for seasonal hunting, fishing, and food gathering also used them for religious rituals and burials. Mound sites located at a distance from surface water are often close to springs, regarded as portals to the watery underworld of the water spirits. As represented on Late Woodland clay pipes, these have horns and clawed feet, reflecting their occasionally mischievous behavior.

Mischief, indeed. Puck and I recall inching our way onto a wave-lapped ledge on the Ontario shore of Lake Superior. There, on Agawa Rock, we studied the red-ochre images of several Ojibwe water spirits, including Misshepezhieu, the "great horned lynx." Like the water spirit—sometimes called "water panther"—of the effigy mound builders, Misshepezhieu has horns on its head, clawed feet, and a long tail. Archeologists believe that an Ojibwe war party painted the image in gratitude for a successful crossing of the big lake. Having paddled on Lake Superior in heavy weather, we understand why they would placate a spirit that could upset their canoes with a flick of its tail.

Like the Potawatomi, Sac, and Fox tribes, the Ojibwe came to Wisconsin after 1200 AD, during the unsettled period following European contact in eastern North America. The resemblance between Misshepezhieu and the mound builders' water spirit suggests that native people of the Great Lakes region shared a mythology. It provided a model not only for the universe but also for social organization. Kinship systems were apparently based on the division between the upper (air)

Wisconsin Historical Society, drawing by Richard Dolan

Late Woodland pipe bowl featuring an image of a horned water spirit, found near Mauston and lower (earth and water) worlds. These moieties were divided into clans named after the creatures inhabiting each realm. The scheme might dictate, for example, that a man belonging to the upper-world thunderbird clan would seek his mate from a lower-world bear or water spirit clan.

Native people of the historic period often buried their dead in the ancient mounds, so Lapham had no way of knowing whether the bones removed from the Merton "cross" had been placed there by the mound builders. Effigy mounds typically covered the remains of one person, usually located in a significant position—in this case, where the bird's wings joined the body. The conical mounds often contain more remains, buried in various ways according to the customs of the group. The bodies were sometimes placed intact in an extended or flexed (for example, seated or fetal) position. Or they were exposed on platforms or in trees, after which the bones were cleaned and gathered into bundles for interment. Or they were cremated on the mound. Some groups apparently gathered at specified intervals to bury their dead in mass graves covered by a single large mound. Other mounds grew by increments, each burial adding to their height and diameter.

During his survey of the Merton mounds Lapham may occasionally have glimpsed, seven miles to the north, a glacial kame that bore his name. Atop Lapham Peak were three conical mounds. According to one improbable legend, the Jesuit missionary and explorer Père Jacques Marquette visited the hilltop in the seventeenth century. During the 1850s it became the property of the Catholic Church, which eventually built a Carmelite monastery on the site. By the early twentieth century it was a popular destination for pilgrims seeking spiritual renewal or a cure for physical infirmity. Lapham Peak became Holy Hill, effacing both the mounds and the connection to their surveyor. In 1916 Government Hill, a kame located south of Delafield in the Kettle Moraine State Forest, was renamed Lapham Peak in his honor.

Holy Hill thus embodies the kind of religious succession seen so often in Europe, where a cathedral may occupy the site of a mosque, constructed in turn over a place that was sacred to the Romans or the Celts.

"So what do you think will replace the cathedrals?" I ask Puck, with whom I've shared these reflections on Lapham and the Merton cross.

"I wonder," she says, as we turn into the millpond parking lot. "So many of the churches in these little villages have lost their congregations and become temples of commerce. Boutiques."

"True. Even on Holy Hill, except for Sundays, the gift shop seems busier than the church."

"Still, it's comforting to know that this place was once inhabited by people who regarded the Bark River as the dwelling place of spirits. Its water wasn't just for driving turbines and disposing of waste. They knew something that we've forgotten."

"That's why the mounds were built—to help people remember. But let's not mess with that water panther, okay?"

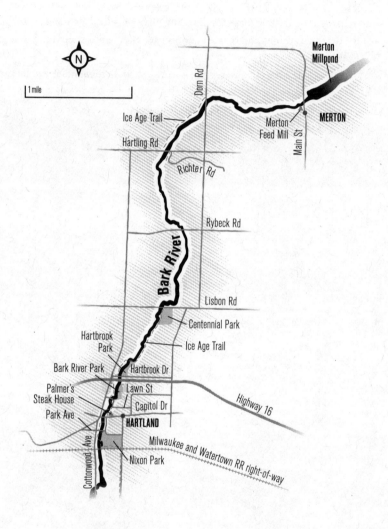

N

1 mile

Merton
Millpond

Dorn Rd

Ice Age Trail

Merton
Feed Mill

MERTON

MERTON

Main St

Hartling Rd

Richter Rd

Rybeck Rd

Bark River

Lisbon Rd

Centennial Park

Ice Age Trail

Hartbrook
Park

Bark River Park

Hartbrook Dr

Palmer's
Steak House

Lawn St

Park Ave

Capitol Dr

Highway 16

HARTLAND

Cottonwood Ave

Milwaukee and Watertown RR right-of-way

Nixon Park

CHAPTER 3

Merton to Hartland

The following weekend finds the four of us—Kent, Gail, Puck, and me—back in the parking lot beside the Merton dam. We've spotted one car about five miles downstream, near Highway 16, and parked the other well away from the millpond. Though the pond no longer drives mill turbines, it still supplies water for the local fire department's pumping trucks. With Merton's suburban growth has come suburban mischief. In July 2003 someone cut the lock that secured a chain on the dam's crank and wheel, causing the gate—and consequently the pond—to drop a foot. For the twenty-four hours it took to refill the pond, insurers of Merton's homes had cause to be nervous.

The weather is perfect for the beginning of May—sunny and clear in the high sixties. Puck and I slide our canoe into the water downstream from the dam, paddle under the Main Street bridge, and pull over to wait for Kent and Gail. A large dark green frog seems not to mind sharing his slackwater with our large dark green boat. When our fellow paddlers catch up, we follow the river as it swings left and drops sharply, requiring some maneuvering around downfalls. Through the trees on our port side we can see the maroon steel siding of the Merton Feed Mill. Beyond a narrow portal framed by box elders the channel straightens and opens out. A great horned owl flushes from cover, disappears briefly into a grove of trees, then emerges with a flock of noisy crows in pursuit.

"Sorry, Old Timer," Gail says. "We didn't mean to disturb your nap."

The river has a wild appearance here, if you ignore the occasional house on a ridge to the left and trash washed down from the millpond. Kent spots a deer in the flooded woods on our right, where a flock of ducks—wood ducks, to judge by their frantic piping—take flight as we pass. Because the trees haven't leafed out fully we can see warblers, including yellow-throats and palm warblers, that will be nearly invisible in a couple of weeks.

Considering the flooded woods, we aren't surprised to come upon a large beaver dam, the first of many in this section of the river. Upstream from the dam, the water gives off the funky smell of organic rot. Downstream, it quickens into a Class I rapids through a rock garden. We spot a pair of green herons and small shore birds just before the wooded banks give way to open meadow. Numerous carp patrol the silty bottom. They are grateful to the beavers for building a dam upstream from the Dorn Road bridge.

We lift over the dam. Below Dorn Road the river widens to about fifty feet as it passes through a mixture of cattail marsh and sedge meadow. The meadow is bounded on the right by a steep wooded ridge, probably a terminal moraine where the glacier paused long enough to discharge some of its cargo.

Just then, I notice movement in the marsh hay and point in its direction.

"Over there—what is that?" The animal is running from the river toward the ridge.

"Must be a fox—kind of reddish brown."

"But the tail—long and skinny, not bushy."

"Doesn't seem to be a dog or a coyote."

"Maybe a cougar?" Puck suggests. She adds sheepishly, "I know they aren't supposed to be around here, but . . . ."

Whatever it was has disappeared. Hoping to find tracks, we paddle up to the shore where I had first glimpsed the creature. No tracks, just some ancient scat with animal hair in it, deposited mostly likely by a fox. So a fox it would have to be, in the annals of our expedition.

An expedition paddles on its stomach, and we are ready for lunch. Ahead, the river narrows to a twenty-foot slot overshadowed by large trees. Bridging the channel are the remnants of a footbridge. High water has apparently washed its planking downstream, leaving the steel frame and support posts. We pull over to the right, where a grassy opening serves as both a portage trail and a wayside for hungry voyageurs. We lay out our life jackets as cushions and liberate our sandwiches from waterproof bags. We are comfortably settled when Puck notices a triangular blue trail marker on a nearby willow.

"The Ice Age Trail! I thought that you could only hike it in one of the Kettle Moraine units, north of Kewaskum or south of Eagle."

"We're on the part of the trail known as the Mid-Kettle Gap," I respond. "The Merton Segment, to be specific."

"So the trail actually links the two units?"

"Yes and no. The people who envisioned the Kettle Moraine State Forest in the 1930s assumed that it would encompass the entire ninety-mile stretch of wooded ridges between Glenbeulah in Sheboygan County and the Whitewater Lakes in Walworth County. That's where the lobes of the Wisconsin Glacier came together to create the most dramatic landforms."

"Those visionaries must not have gotten everything they wanted," Gail observes. "What would it take to close the gap?"

"Land was relatively cheap in the 1930s," I continue. "Creating another state forest in the forty-mile gap would be well-nigh impossible today. Washington County is the fastest-growing county in the state, and Waukesha County isn't far behind. Subdivisions already occupy the glacial ridges, and quarries are turning kames and eskers into building material. It may still be possible, though, to preserve noncontiguous parcels in the gap, plus a two-hundred-foot-wide corridor for the Ice Age Trail."

Kent gestures at the shady swath of trail before us, tending in a northerly direction toward the wooded ridge. "Obviously this part escaped development. How far does it go?"

"Only up to Dorn Road," I answer. "Or you can take it south to Hartling Road, where it crosses the river and follows the east bank for two hundred yards to Richter Road. That's about it for off-road hiking between Merton and Lisbon Road. The rest is on pavement. There's another section of off-road trail between the river and the Four Winds subdivision, south of Rybeck Road. But it's stranded until conservation easements can be acquired to link it to the main trail."

"Easements?" Puck wants to know. "Who's 'acquiring,' and how?"

"I read something about it in the newspaper," Gail says. "Isn't there a group that's using state money to buy parcels of land and easements for the trail?"

"You're thinking of the Kettle Moraine Task Force," I say, "organized by the Wisconsin Academy of Sciences, Arts and Letters. In 1996 it recommended that the DNR create a partnership of state agencies and environmental groups to consolidate holdings in the two Kettle Moraine units and acquire at least enough land in the gap for the Ice Age Trail. They targeted five areas in particular, one being this section of the Bark River. Since then task force partners have been gradually piecing the trail together, often with matching grants from the state's Warren Knowles–Gaylord Nelson Stewardship Project."

"If I owned valuable real estate in the gap," Kent says, "I'd think twice about opening it up to you tree-hugger types. What's in it for me?"

Puck and Gail roll their eyes. Always the devil's advocate.

"Money, for one thing," I respond. "If you allow an easement, you can keep the property but take a deduction on your state and federal taxes based on its market value. You'll also have the satisfaction of knowing that you're doing the right thing. Mid-Kettle partners put a good deal of effort into educating property owners about the significance of this landscape and the advantages of preserving it. Not only individual owners, but also developers and municipalities that want to do the right thing but don't know how. Developers learn how to design conservation subdivisions. Municipalities learn how to use zoning restrictions to preserve the ridges."

"What Henry Reuss hath wrought!" Kent exclaims, shaking his head in mock dismay. He is alluding to the long-term US representative who deserves much of the credit for establishing the 1,200-mile Ice Age National Scenic Trail, scrawled like a lazy backwards S across the state.

"Reuss was a co-chair of that Kettle Moraine Task Force I read about," Gail says, "together with Ody Fish of the Wisconsin Academy."

"You've heard that Reuss died recently, haven't you?" Puck asks. "He'd retired to California, but his body was returned to Wisconsin. The family scattered some of his ashes at his home on North Lake, a couple of miles west of here."

"To Chairman Reuss, then," Kent proposes, and we raise our water bottles in a toast. "May he live as long as there are drumlins to climb."

"And rivers to paddle," Gail adds, as the bottles come together.

～～～～～

Back on the Bark after lunch, we approach Hartling Road. Peacocks cry out as we pass under the bridge and negotiate a quick little rapids through a wooded section. The exotic birds presumably belong to the farmer on the right, whose outbuildings are nestled against the base of a drumlin. Where the trees open out, a great blue heron lifts from the shallows and flies downstream. He is perched high atop an oak tree when we catch up with him, posing like a crane on a Chinese scroll.

Upscale homes crop up on the right as we approach Rybeck Road, then tennis courts and a horse corral. Horses run up to the fence to watch us pass. A couple of twists and turns later, just upstream from Rybeck Road, we encounter the largest beaver dam of the day, a veritable TVA project. It inspires divergent strategies within our fleet. Kent and Gail use the lift-over method to good effect. Lacking their patience, Puck and I build up a head of steam and try to power over, but stop short of the downstream slope. As we teeter on the brink we notice that we have an audience. The picture window of a home on the left bank frames a pair of amused faces. Today, though, they won't have the satisfaction of watching us swim. After considerable rocking and shifting of places, we manage the descent and resume our journey with a wave to the gallery.

Just before gliding under the bridge we glimpse a small pond on the left, apparently the feature identified as a spring on old plat maps of the area. Its outflow refreshes the water that carries us under Rybeck Road. Below the bridge we detour to the right around a small island. From here to Lisbon Road the Bark meanders over a bottom of sand, gravel, and occasional rocks. Box elder and willows shade the banks. A two-foot northern pike cruises for minnows. A great horned owl, our second of the day, incites an uproar among the crows as he vacates his roost in one of the trees.

Downstream from Lisbon Road we skirt the western border of Centennial Park, with its open green space and recreational path. From here to Hartbrook Park on the north side of Highway 16 is our slowest going of the day. Though volunteer groups periodically clear the channel of fallen limbs, this section remains a jungle of downfalls to be lifted over or carried around. We change places frequently in the boat, stepping into whichever end, bow or stern, happens to be closer. Garlic mustard flourishes in the damp floodplain on the right, safe from park department mowers, and buckthorn is rapidly filling the intervals between the larger trees. Noticing our struggles with the untamed vegetation, passers-by stop to chat. All ask the same question: "How far have you come?" Finally we paddle by a small farm on the right, notable for its goat, and under the arched pedestrian bridge that marks the beginning of the Hartbrook Park picnic area, where we've left our shuttle vehicle.

While Puck and Gail drive back to Merton to get the other car, Kent and I paddle down to the two concrete culverts under Hartbrook Drive and Highway 16 to find out whether they can be run. Due to a bend midway through the culverts, we can't see their exit from the bank. From the river, though, we can see the other end and forge tentatively ahead. Besides that distant rectangle of light, nothing else is visible. We seem to be suspended in space. The hull of the canoe becomes a second skin, and I feel with my knees for any vibration that might signal an obstacle in the channel. Water drips from the ceiling.

Reaching the downstream side, we come about and paddle upstream through the other culvert, this time trying to calculate the distance. We count about twenty canoe lengths. A canoe length is roughly a rod (16½ feet), which may be why canoe portages are measured in rods. So we figure that the culverts cover about 110 yards of the Bark River.

When Gail and Puck return, we load up the boats and check our calendars.

"Are you up for the next stretch," I ask our friends, "from here to Delafield?"

"Can't make it next weekend," Kent responds. "But aren't you leading a cleanup trip the following Saturday in Delafield?"

"We are, and we could use your help—9:30 at the old fish hatchery. It sure beats mowing your lawn."

"What lawn?"

"Right. See you in a couple of weeks."

~~~~~~

When Puck and I resume our downriver journey a week later, we do so *à deux* but not exactly by ourselves. We launch at Bark River Park, downstream from Highway 16, where the river marks the outfield boundary of a baseball diamond. A noisy little league game is in progress. At least two dozen baseballs and softballs are strewn along the banks, looking like windfalls from some synthetic tree. Are they trash or treasure? No one seems interested in harvesting the fruit, least of all a man and two boys, probably his sons, who are catching crayfish.

A century ago, in another season, this space would likewise have teemed with human activity. Then it was part of a fourteen-acre millpond that extended half a mile upstream from Capitol Drive. On winter nights, a resident from that era recalled, the pond was "black with skaters." One of the more daring skaters inspired Orson Warren, a descendant of the village's founding family, to compose a poem. It opens on a nostalgic note:

> I was only a boy and Hartland was young
> But I remember the day
> On the ground where Hartland now nestles
> A mill pond held full sway.

The poem tells the story of a man who bets he can skate across the pond on a morning when the ice is still perilously thin. Warren's language rises from American Primitive to epic grandeur as he recalls the feat:

> When the skater struck the glittering ice
> It seemed he fairly flew
> You could see the water spatter
> Where his skates had chizzled through.

> [The] higher the water spattered
> The faster he seemed to glide
> But it wasn't only a minute
> Till he reached the other side.

Downstream from Bark River Park we pass under Lawn Street and several pedestrian walkways before arriving at the rapids under Capitol Drive. We've taken the precaution of scouting this stretch during our shuttle, so we know there isn't a logjam waiting in ambush under the bridge. It is nonetheless a challenge to maneuver in the dark, canyonlike narrows, with box elders overhanging the chute that we want to hit on the right. Overlooking the rapids on the left is a pleasant outdoor deck behind Palmer's Steak House, formerly the Cobblestone Inn, which looks like a good place for an après-paddle drink.

Today the river gods decree a clean if somewhat bumpy run under Capitol Drive. The river continues to drop perceptibly for another thirty yards below the bridge, then levels out and meanders through parklike green space. A strolling elderly couple glance in our direction but don't seem surprised to see a canoe in the village. There are two more bridges before Nixon Park, one consisting of three large culverts. Peering into the darkness from my position in the bow, I reject two on account of snags in the channel. The third has its own deterrent, which I don't notice until we are already committed. Dozens of large spiders dangle from the top of the culvert, each from a single thread. In silhouette they look like ornaments hung at regular intervals but irregular heights. Using my paddle as a swatter, I clear a course through the middle.

Just upstream from a low rock dam in Nixon Park a channel branches to the left and passes under a footbridge to supply the water for a small pond. We pull over to that side and stop for lunch in the shade of majestic cottonwood trees. Considering the spaciousness of the grounds and the sharp drop in the riverbed upstream, we're not surprised that Christian Hershey chose this site for a gristmill. In 1847 he purchased from Samuel Bartlett thirty acres of a tract that had once belonged to Stephen Warren and built an imposing four-story structure on the west bank of the river, just upstream from what became the right-of-way for the Milwaukee and Watertown Railroad.

From a dam at Capitol Drive, the millrace ran between the river and Cottonwood Avenue until it reached the mill, then veered east to return its water to the Bark. A waste weir at the dam allowed the miller to release excess water into the river when it was running dangerously high. A tree stump in the millpond served as a gauge. When water covered the top of the stump, it was time to remove a flashboard on the weir.

As the miller of grist for the village and outlying farms, Hershey became almost important enough to impose his name on the community. For a while the village was known as Hersheyville. But the mill passed to other owners, including Alvin and Edward Ordway, James Pawling, William Manegold, and finally Henry Van Buren, who purchased it in 1891. Van Buren's daughter, SaraBelle, wrote a memoir that provides an engaging account of a small-town gristmill in operation. I've read the memoir and Puck hasn't, so as we sit in SaraBelle's backyard eating our sandwiches, I propose a game.

"Poor SaraBelle, denied by an accident of birth the chance to appear as a celebrity author on *The Oprah Winfrey Show*."

"An accident?"

"I mean her timing, or maybe I should say her parents' timing. She was born too soon. Suppose we give her the opportunity that she missed in life. You can be Oprah. Ask the standard Oprah questions, and I'll do my best to channel SaraBelle."

"You're kidding, right?"

"Just humor me. It passes the time."

Okay, SaraBelle. What inspired you to write your memoir?

"Partly, I suppose, it is a tribute to my parents. My father was related to our eighth president and Stephen A. Douglas—you know, the man who ran against Lincoln. Father was born in Vernon, on the Wisconsin frontier, and went into the milling business there. He and my mother, Isabella Carmichael Van Buren, lost their first child to scarlet fever. My older brother, Peter, and I grew up around the Vernon mill. We moved to Hartland when I was sixteen. A couple of years later we built the home where I still live, over a half century later. That house is so full of memories for me!"

Did you ever consider becoming a miller yourself? Was that an option for women then?

"Milling was a man's work in those days. I became a schoolteacher and stayed with it for forty-seven years. I never married, or I might have followed in my mother's footsteps as a miller's wife. It was the wife's job to test the flour in her kitchen before it was shipped out. Today we'd call it quality control. Our best brand was Golden Eagle Flour. We also made Hartland's Pride, Cook's Delight, and Sunrise.

"I have to tell you about another advantage of being a flour mill princess, besides sampling all that homemade bread. After the wheat was ground it was passed through a bolter for sifting. The bolter was made of expensive silk, which had to be replaced if it developed the tiniest hole. I was the best-dressed young lady in Hartland, and there was still plenty of material left over for my friends."

Many of our viewers have never heard of a bolter and have no idea how flour was made in those days. Could you describe it for us?

"Let me take you on a tour of the mill, starting in the basement. There you could see the two big turbines that drove the whole operation. Water turned metal wheels in the turbines, and each wheel turned a pair of millstones on the main floor. When my father bought the mill, those stones ground all of the grain for human and livestock consumption. Later he introduced the newer type of roller machines to mill wheat flour. These could turn out fifty barrels a day and required far less maintenance than the old burrstones. He still used one set of stones for cornmeal, rye, buckwheat, and graham flour, and the other for livestock feed. All of that machinery was on the milling floor, plus a couple of platform scales to measure the flour into fifty-pound sacks.

"The second and third floors of the mill held large bins of grain waiting to be milled. The bolter was on the fourth floor, and there was yet another half story at the top, for miscellaneous machinery. It was an impressive building, the closest thing to a skyscraper in Hartland."

A cross-section of a typical flour mill, showing a turbine next to the foundation, a pair of millstones to the left of the figure on the main floor, and storage on the upper floor

You mentioned that your brother followed your father in the business. Does he run the mill today?

"I wish that were possible. One summer night in 1898, when I was twenty-three and just a year into my teaching career, the mill burned to the ground. We're sure it was arson. The hardest part was watching the mill go up in flames and hearing people say, 'Isn't it a beautiful sight?' Their entertainment was our tragedy. Insurance didn't cover the cost of rebuilding. We had to sell much of the mill property. Most of the buildings along the east side of Cottonwood Avenue are built over the old millrace. The dam was removed and the millpond drained.

"Fortunately, Peter's skills as a miller and millwright were much in demand. He built mills all over the country and even in Mexico before moving back to Hartland to retire. Today I'm surrounded by family again, though Mother and Father are buried in Vernon, near their firstborn."

Leaving SaraBelle to her bittersweet memories, we gaze across the river, where the village is undergoing yet another metamorphosis. Several of the buildings constructed over the millrace have been razed to make way for new commercial outlets. Among these is a restaurant with a patio overlooking the river and park. Several patrons are seated at the tables, enjoying the sunlight. The patio reflects a shift in the village's relationship with the Bark. Following the pattern of many communities that owe their start to waterpower, Hartland turned its back on the river when it no longer needed the power. The drained pond became a wasteland of weeds and stumps, the channel an open sewer.

In 1939 a local newspaper columnist, W. J. C. Ralph, deplored this state of affairs. "It is not a river of any importance," he said of the Bark. "But it is important to Hartland and that is the reason for this article." After the mill burned down, Ralph recalled, the village treated its river as merely a place to dispose of waste. Recently, though, he thought he had detected a change in attitude. Volunteers had cleared the waterway of rubbish, and the Lions Club had planted willows above and below the Park Avenue bridge. Ralph hoped that Hartland, then crossing the threshold into its second century, would come to regard the Bark as a natural resource whose possibilities "have yet to be discovered and worked out."

Rediscovery and working out had to wait until 1982, when a citizens group developed a plan to beautify the river. Then the Chamber of Commerce undertook construction of a river walkway in tandem with revitalization of the village center. To publicize their efforts a Hartland real estate developer organized a Bark River Splash, a onetime event modeled on Milwaukee's annual New Year's Day "polar bear" plunge in Lake Michigan. "Why should people have to fly all the way to Florida to enjoy a little sun and water?" the chief Splasher asked on the appointed day. He didn't wait for an answer before getting into warmer clothes. Onlookers outnumbered participants 150 to 13.

Once Hartland embraced the river as a recreational and commercial resource, it generally linked improved river access to business development in the village center. The results are pleasantly apparent to us as we gather our gear and return to the canoe. We are placing it in the water when two boys stop to ask where we'd paddled from and where we're going. Then they run ahead to a pedestrian bridge upstream from the railroad right-of-way to guide us through the shallow rapids. One train had come through during lunch; another passes shortly after we paddle under the old stone bridge. As it approaches the Cottonwood Avenue crossing, its air horn issues a blast that sounds like the trump of doom.

Railroads certainly signaled the doom or at least the decline of previous forms of transportation. When it reached Hartland in 1854, the Milwaukee and Watertown Railroad provided an efficient link to ports on the Great Lakes. The Van Buren mill, for example, used the railroad to bring in grain from Chicago and ship its milled products throughout the region. Preceding the railroad by six years was the Milwaukee-Watertown Plank Road, which had first made the village a commercial center.

The third member of the nineteenth century's transportation trinity, a canal, would in turn have preceded the road if a few things had fallen out differently. Then people standing near the flour mill might have looked upstream at the plank road, downstream at the railway, and across the river at a feeder channel carrying water in a southeasterly direction from the millpond to the Milwaukee and Rock River Canal, located about a quarter-mile away. The tragicomic story of that canal, whose fortunes were bound intimately to the Bark River valley, requires a chapter in itself.

CHAPTER 4

The Milwaukee and Rock River Canal

On the morning of July 4, 1839, a group of dignitaries gathered on the corner of Third and Chestnut Streets in the part of Milwaukee known as Kilbourntown. Forming a procession behind a brass band, they marched north to a triangular plot of ground located east of Third between Cherry and Vliet Streets. There Byron Kilbourn, the president of the Milwaukee and Rock River Canal Company, was to turn the first spade full of earth for a major shipping artery between Lake Michigan and the Mississippi River.

Anticipating the volume of wheat that would soon be streaming down the canal and through the port of Milwaukee, someone—perhaps Kilbourn himself—had chosen a grain scoop as the ceremonial implement. What happened at the climactic moment did not augur well for the project. Here is how an eyewitness described it, in mock-heroic prose:

> When at last the auspicious moment arrived, Kilbourn, in anticipation of the severity of the labor to be performed, divested himself of his

coat, standing before the assembled multitude, the very personification of a sinewy son of toil, seized the treacherous scoop, placed its point upon the virgin soil, so soon to become historic, placed his foot upon its heel, and like the Indian upon the lake bluff so graphically described by the poet, Egbert Herring Smith, in his epic,

> "He took a good look at the village and town,
>   With its thousands of houses and people,
> And cast his bold eye up and down,
>   O'er many a mansion and steeple,"

gave the fatal thrust and all was over, *i.e.*, with that scoop, it doubling up like a piece of tin. The look of mingled disappointment, mortification, rage and disgust which came over the face of Mr. Kilbourn, at this *faux pas*, I shall never forget while life remains. He threw the treacherous and disabled scoop upon the ground with an exclamation that sounded like profanity. His assistant, however, quickly placed in his trembling hands a tool suitable for the work, with which the ground was at once broken, the barrow filled with earth, wheeled off, and deposited at the spot selected. . . .

When Kilbourn recovered his dignity the procession re-formed and marched to the American House hotel on Third and West Water Streets for dinner, champagne toasts, and an oration by John Hustis. The rhetoric was splendid. Unfortunately, the crumpled grain scoop proved more prophetic of the canal's future than the speechmaking. Just over two years later, the territorial governor would effectively terminate the project after only a mile and a quarter of the canal had been dug.

If the stars did not quite line up, it was not for lack of trying. In choosing the Fourth of July as the day to break ground, promoters obviously hoped to partake in the magic of the Erie Canal, the nation's most ambitious and successful internal improvement before the Civil War. Eight years after Judge John Richardson broke ground for the Erie on Independence Day in 1817, that waterway opened amid spectacular pageantry. The income from tolls exceeded the most optimistic projections, and the canal opened public land on the Great Lakes to settlement.

Were it not for the Erie Canal, Kilbourn and his little band of notables would probably not have been delving into the soil of southeastern Wisconsin in 1839. Prior to the 1830s, trade and settlement concentrated in two other regions of the territory. The early fur trade, dominated by the French, opened a diagonal corridor between Green Bay and Prairie du Chien along the Fox and Wisconsin Rivers, linking the Great Lakes with the Mississippi River. In the 1820s it was lead mining that drew young adventurers to southwestern Wisconsin and northwestern Illinois. Coming from Kentucky, Tennessee, Ohio, Missouri, and southern Illinois, they lent a distinctly southern flavor to the communities of Mineral Point and Galena. The population of the mining region boomed, increasing from twenty people in 1822 to ten thousand in 1828. Wisconsin's first public land sale was held in Mineral Point in 1834. Two years later the Legislative Assembly convened for the first time, in nearby Belmont.

The Erie Canal inaugurated another shift in trade and population, this time from the big river on the territory's western border to the big lake on the east. In 1833 about 60,000 people made the eight-day journey by canal from Albany to Buffalo, many in search of cheap public land on the Great Lakes. By the 1840s 100,000 people, enough to populate ten fair-sized cities, were passing through Buffalo each year. In 1834 Milwaukee was little more than a fur-trading post run by Solomon Juneau, an agent of John Jacob Astor who considered himself a resident of Green Bay. Between 1835 and 1837 Milwaukee's population rose from 500 to 6,000, swelled by the flood of land-hungry settlers and speculators. In contrast to the people who settled in Green Bay and Mineral Point, these were mostly Yankees from New England and New York State, followed after 1839 by immigrants from Europe. By 1850 Germans accounted for about a third of Milwaukee's 45,000 residents. The Erie Canal contributed to Wisconsin's ethnic diversity and linked it firmly to the Union side in the Civil War.

The Ohio canal system likewise channeled settlers and speculators to Lake Erie and thence to Milwaukee. Among them was Kilbourn, who arrived in late 1834, in time to purchase town sites at the second public land sale, held the following August in Green Bay. Though Kilbourn came on official business as a federal deputy surveyor, few people considered it a conflict of interest for a surveyor to speculate in the lands he was mapping for the United States. With financial backing from Micajah T. Williams, an Ohio canal commissioner who had served as surveyor general of the Northwest Territory, Kilbourn bought land west of the Milwaukee River and north of the Menomonee. Kilbourntown would eventually unite with Juneau's holdings, located between the Milwaukee

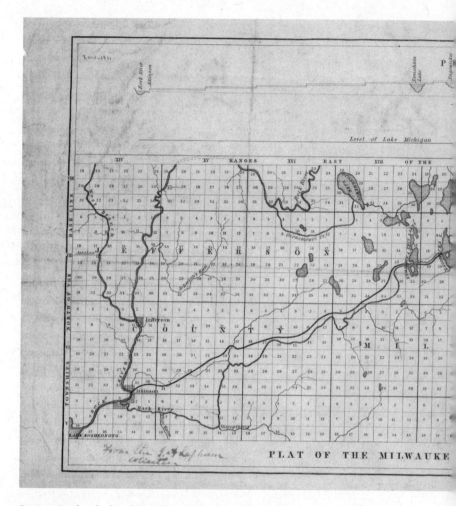

Increase Lapham's plat of the Milwaukee and Rock River Canal

River and Lake Michigan (Juneautown), and those of George H. Walker, located west of the Milwaukee and south of the Menomonee (Walker's Point), to form the city of Milwaukee.

Kilbourn understood that the value of his investment depended on the city's attractiveness as a Great Lakes port, which depended in turn on a steady flow of commodities such as lead and wheat from the west. Reliable, efficient, and inexpensive transportation was the key. Kilbourn consequently

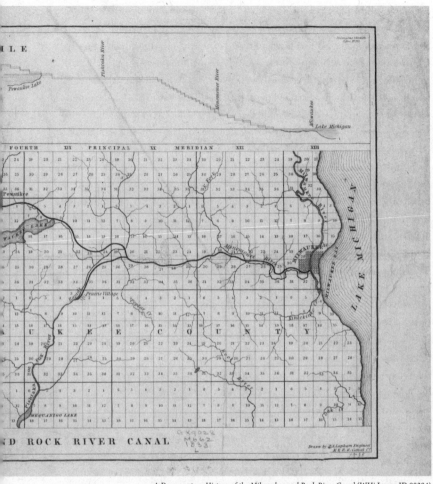

A Documentary History of the Milwaukee and Rock River Canal (WHi Image ID 90384)

devoted himself to projects such as improved access to the Milwaukee harbor, a railroad line to the Mississippi, and a canal to the Rock River. Though he served as secretary of a public meeting held in September 1836 to consider building a railroad from Milwaukee to Mineral Point, he decided that rail transport was not yet feasible financially. Though railways cost less than canals to build, mile for mile, and do not freeze over in the winter, efficient rail service requires tracks in both directions, nearly doubling the cost. Canal construction materials were available locally, whereas locomotives and rails had to be shipped from the east at considerable expense. Kilbourn, who had worked as surveyor and engineer on two canals in Ohio, turned naturally to water transport as the more practical option.

The canal's long-term success was likely to depend, as the ceremonial grain scoop suggests, on a steady flow of agricultural products through Milwaukee. There was clearly a demand for Midwestern grain in eastern cities, but it could not compete with European imports until the cost of shipping was reduced. In Wisconsin, moreover, the wheat fields had yet to be cleared and planted. Consequently, much as the Erie Canal depended initially on revenue from salt mines near Rochester, Milwaukee entrepreneurs looked to the lead mines of southwestern Wisconsin to repay their investment. Lead was much in demand for pipe, lead sheeting, bullets, and printer's type. It was also a key ingredient in house paint. By the early nineteenth century Americans had taken to painting frame buildings (with unsuspected consequences for the health of their children). Fourteen million pounds of the mineral traveled annually to New York by way of Galena and New Orleans. A canal to divert this trade through Milwaukee and on to Buffalo would not only enrich those ports but also save an estimated $110,000 (about $2.7 million today) per year in shipping costs.

Competition with Chicago as the chief port on Lake Michigan was another inducement. As far back as 1673 the French explorer Joliet had proposed a canal from the lake to the Illinois River, thereby opening a waterway to the Mississippi. After debating the project for a decade, the state of Illinois broke ground for a canal on (of course) July 4, 1836.

Henry Dodge was sworn in as the first territorial governor of Wisconsin that same day. Could Milwaukee, despite its late start, overtake Chicago as the gateway to the West? The groundbreaking for the Illinois and Michigan Canal lent urgency to building a rival waterway in Wisconsin. During the summer of 1836, anticipating the inaugural meeting of the Legislative Assembly that fall, Kilbourn scouted possible routes with Increase Lapham, his talented and trusted assistant on the Ohio canals. Kilbourn then asked the legislature to pass a general act incorporating a company to construct a canal from navigable water on the Milwaukee River to navigable water on the Rock River. But the legislature, preoccupied with more pressing issues, did not take up the canal bill.

In preparation for the assembly's second session, to be convened in Burlington in 1837, Kilbourn used the pages of his newspaper, the *Milwaukee Advertiser*, to make his case for a canal and lay out possible routes. In five articles published in May and June 1837, he sketched in the particulars, especially with regard to the lead trade. Mines located closer to the Mississippi and Galena would, he granted, continue to ship their mineral by the customary route. But he believed that those located east of Mineral Point, about half the number in operation, would send their lead down the Pecatonica and Sugar Rivers to the Rock River, then upstream to the western terminus of the projected canal. From Milwaukee, Kilbourn claimed, the lead could be shipped for a nominal charge as ballast or return freight to Buffalo and thence to New York. With cheap transportation as an incentive, miners would prospect for lead deposits closer to the Rock River, further reducing the cost of shipment. Geological evidence and the remains of Indian smelting pits suggested that lead and copper might be found as close to Milwaukee as Prairieville (now Waukesha) and Mukwonago.

Why, indeed, should Wisconsin send its mineral wealth to the Atlantic seaboard for others to process? Metal-bearing ore could be smelted in Milwaukee, Kilbourn suggested, and shipped in manufactured forms to markets on the Great Lakes and in the East. At the western terminus of the proposed canal, iron ore had been found in Dodge County and in the vicinity of Johnson's Rapids (now Watertown) on the Rock River. This combination of raw material and waterpower would make Watertown, in Kilbourn's phrase, the "Birmingham of Wisconsin." No one could accuse him of lacking entrepreneurial vision. In contrast to the Midlands industrial center, England's second-largest city, Wisconsin's Birmingham counted fewer than two dozen residents in 1838.

The *Advertiser* articles drew attention to other nonagricultural resources, such as limestone from quarries near Menomonee Falls and timber from the forested tracts west of Milwaukee. These might be shipped by canal to the Rock River and down the Rock to communities in Illinois that needed building materials.

How, specifically, would the canal connect these widely spaced dots on the map? The canal route was not finalized until May 1839, shortly before groundbreaking. Kilbourn nevertheless described a likely route in the *Advertiser*. Originating at the Milwaukee River, the canal would proceed up the Menomonee River valley nearly to the mouth of Honey Creek. Where the Menomonee veers north, the canal would maintain a westerly course to the Pishtaka (Fox) River. Crossing the Fox, it would continue up the Pewaukee River valley, then pass around the north shore of Pewaukee Lake to Hartland, where it would meet a feeder canal from the Bark River. For the rest of its journey to the Rock River the canal could follow the Bark River valley to Fort Atkinson. Or for the last seven miles it could shortcut a bend in the Bark River and join the Rock above Fort Atkinson, near the mouth of Deer Creek.

From Hartland to Fort Atkinson the Bark descends only about eighty feet in thirty miles, with no significant rapids to be negotiated. Why didn't Kilbourn and Lapham propose simply to use the natural channels of the Menomonee, Pewaukee, and Bark Rivers, dredging and widening where necessary? Centuries of canal-building experience had taught engineers to avoid flood-prone rivers in favor of man-made channels, where they could regulate the depth and rate of flow with waste gates and feeder canals. The canal would therefore parallel these rivers, occasionally tapping into their waters behind strategically placed dams. It would have the same dimensions as the Erie Canal, forty feet wide at the surface and four feet deep, to accommodate barges with the standard two-foot draft. Kilbourn and Lapham originally planned to skirt several lakes with towpaths, then decided that small steamboats could tow barges across these expanses, saving on construction costs. Steamboats were not feasible on most of the route, for their wake would erode the canal banks. Mules, traveling at the less damaging rate of two to four miles per hour, provided just the right amount of locomotion.

Crucial to the success of the enterprise was the feeder canal at Hartland. Barges proceeding west from Milwaukee would have to pass through a series of locks to gain sufficient elevation to cross the subcontinental divide separating the Menomonee and Fox River watersheds and then the still higher Hartland summit. These would presumably have been modeled on the locks used in New York and Ohio, which were based in turn on a design first used by Leonardo da Vinci in the fifteenth century. On the New York and Ohio canals double gates at each end of the lock formed a shallow V pointing upstream, so that the current pressed them tightly together. When a barge approached the downstream end, the lock keeper opened the downstream gates inward by pushing against huge wooden counterbalance beams. After the mules were unhitched the barge entered the narrow stone or wooden walls of the lock. The lock keeper closed the downstream gates and opened valves to raise the water—and consequently the barge—to the level of the next section of canal. Finally, the upstream gates opened outward, the mules were rehitched, and the barge continued on its way. By repeating this procedure twenty-nine times between Milwaukee and Hartland, a barge would gain 314 vertical feet over 22 miles.

It is the perverse nature of a watershed to shed water. Consequently, canal engineers have always wrestled with the challenge of supplying water to peak elevations. To provide adequate water for the famed seventeenth-century Canal du Midi in France, linking the Atlantic Ocean and the Mediterranean Sea, engineers had to create an artificial lake at the canal's 620-foot summit. Kilbourn and Lapham's task was relatively easy in comparison, for the Hartland summit is, as Kilbourn put it, a "mere bar" between the Fox and Rock River watersheds. A deep cut about a mile long and no more than ten feet deep would traverse it. Fortuitously for the proposed canal, the Bark River lies just west of the summit and renews itself downstream in such natural reservoirs as Nagawicka and Nemahbin Lakes. To Kilbourn the Bark's location seemed "almost a providential arrangement."

Besides the main artery between Milwaukee and Fort Atkinson, Kilbourn envisioned a system of smaller veins and capillaries linking all of the commercially significant parts of the territory. Where the canal crossed the Fox River a lateral line would follow the Fox downstream to the rapids at Waukesha. Below the rapids light steamboats could travel all the way down to Ottawa, Illinois, where the Fox joins the Illinois River. From Upper Nemahbin Lake a northern branch would pass through Twin Lakes (that is, Lower and Upper Nashotah Lakes), Oconomowoc Lake, and Lac La Belle to join the Rock River either at the mouth of the Oconomowoc River, about eight miles upstream from Watertown, or at the Rock's easternmost bend, about fifteen miles upstream from Watertown. On the Rock River steamboats could travel upstream to within eighteen miles of Lake Winnebago, thereby connecting Milwaukee with the old fur trade route between Green Bay and Prairie du Chien. Or they could go down the Rock to the Mississippi, with links along the way to the future seat of government in Madison by way of Catfish Creek (the Yahara River) and to the lead mining region via the Pecatonica and Sugar Rivers.

Increase Lapham's *A Documentary History of the Milwaukee and Rock River Canal*, published in 1840 at the behest of the canal company directors, included a plat of the route set forth in the *Advertiser*. By the time the report appeared, however, the directors had approved a more northerly link between the Milwaukee and Rock Rivers. A dam and lock on the Milwaukee just downstream from North Avenue would supply water for a canal along the west bank of the river. A barge heading west would enter the canal near present-day McKinley Avenue. It would be towed north a mile and a quarter to the lock, where it would be raised ten feet. The slack water above the dam would afford an easy four-mile tow to the mouth of Lincoln Creek. Leaving the Milwaukee at that point, the barge would veer northwest through Granville and the upper Menomonee and Fox River watersheds. Then it would tend in a southwesterly direction to Lac La Belle and ultimately the Rock River, entering the Rock above Jefferson.

The Milwaukee and Rock River Canal was conceived in the spirit of an age that built more than 4,400 miles of canals prior to the Civil War, chiefly in Virginia, Maryland, South Carolina, Pennsylvania, New York, Massachusetts, Ohio, Indiana, Connecticut, Delaware, Illinois, and New Jersey. Though most of the canal construction took place in the two decades following the 1825 opening of the Erie, canals were promoted from the earliest days of the republic as a way to unify the country. Joel Barlow traced that impulse even further back in his 1787 poem "The Vision of Columbus." Barlow's Columbus imagines the day when canals will extend his voyage into the American heartland:

> He saw, as widely spreads the unchannell'd plain
> Where inland realms for ages bloom'd in vain,
> Canals, long winding, ope a watery flight,
> And distant streams, and seas and lakes unite.

> From fair Albania [Albany], tow'rd the falling sun,
> Back through the midland lengthening channels run;
> Meet the far lakes, the beauteous towns that lave,
> And Hudson joined to broad Ohio's wave.

George Washington, who considered canals "fundamental to nationhood," sought a canal route from the Potomac to the Ohio River and ultimately Lake Erie in the years following the Revolutionary War. The vulnerable new nation was then bordered on three sides by vast territories to which European powers lay claim. Washington feared that western settlers, lacking canal links to the colonies, would go over to Britain on the north or Spain on the south. After the War of 1812 and the Louisiana Purchase, when foreign powers were no longer an internal threat, canal construction was driven partly by Manifest Destiny.

Some promoters of the Wisconsin canal regarded it as a link in the watery chain that would eventually connect the Atlantic with the Pacific. Byron Kilbourn was not above appealing to nationalistic fervor and territorial pride in promoting the canal. So grand an internal improvement would, he said, confound those who "fancy Wisconsin a wilderness, and only a fit resort for Badgers." Always the businessman, however, Kilbourn stressed the commercial benefits of the canal over the ideological. "The more such lines of intercourse can be extended," he told readers of the *Advertiser* after laying out possible routes, "—the more minutely they are made to penetrate the lesser as well as the greater sections of the country, the nearer together will the whole country be brought, practically in its business transactions; and the more compact and concentrated the business of the country can be rendered, the greater will be the development of its native resources."

The *Milwaukee Sentinel*, founded by Kilbourn's rival, Solomon Juneau, and published by Harrison Reed, was no less enthusiastic at first. It predicted that the canal would facilitate the export of agricultural products from farmland "as fertile as the delta of the Nile" and minerals from a region "of more real value than the mines of Peru."

Riding a wave of popular support, the canal won the Legislative Assembly's approval in the fall of 1837. The following January, Territorial Governor Henry Dodge signed the bill authorizing incorporation of the Milwaukee and Rock River Canal Company and the sale of capital stock. At a meeting on February 3 the stockholders elected Kilbourn president of the company and Lapham the chief engineer. Solomon Juneau was on the original board of directors, though he soon withdrew his support of the project.

Once the euphoria subsided, the company had to face a sobering challenge. Lapham estimated that the canal would cost almost $800,000 to build; shortly after groundbreaking he adjusted the figure to nearly $1 million. Alexander Mitchell, the territorial engineer, thought it closer to $1.2 million (about $28.2 million today). How was the company to raise that kind of money? Theirs was a challenge endemic to the federalist form of government. The great canal projects of the world—China's Grand Canal (completed in the early seventh century), for example, and France's Canal du Midi—had been constructed under highly centralized governments with large treasuries. In a nation organized along federalist principles, local entities, particularly those in sparsely populated areas, lacked the resources for large-scale internal improve-ments. For this reason Thomas Jefferson was famously skeptical of canal projects, though it was his secretary of the treasury, Albert Gallatin, who laid out a model of cost sharing between the public and private sectors in his 1808 *Report on Roads and Canals*.

Gallatin's blueprint notwithstanding, the state of New York failed to obtain federal funding for the Erie Canal and had to finance the project itself. The state assumed the construction cost of eight million dollars, and it was able to pay off its debt by 1835. If New York could build a canal and make it pay, why not Wisconsin? The territory's endeavor was far less ambitious than New York's, as these numbers suggest:

	Erie Canal	Milwaukee & Rock River Canal
Length	363 miles	51 miles (estimate)
Difference in elevation between terminals	568 feet	237 feet
Maximum continuous climb/descent	420 feet	314 feet
Number of locks	83	36 (estimate)
Cost	$8,000,000	$800,000–$1,200,000 (estimate)

Wisconsin lacked some of New York's advantages, to be sure. Whereas New York State's white population passed the one million mark soon after the 1810 census, Wisconsin counted fewer than twenty-three thousand white inhabitants in 1836. It therefore lacked a large revenue base. Furthermore, the Legislative Assembly, anxious to avoid the debts incurred by neighboring states, forbade territorial financing of internal improvements.

Partly offsetting these handicaps was the fact that most of the land along the proposed route did not have to be purchased from individual owners. It still belonged to the United States, and the federal government might be persuaded to grant the land to the territory, which could then sell off the surplus—any not occupied by the canal itself—to finance construction. Kilbourn petitioned Congress for such a grant, citing as precedent its gift to the state of Ohio for construction of the Miami Canal.

After weeks of intense lobbying in Washington, Kilbourn got his way. In June 1838 Congress granted the territory all of the odd-numbered sections in a ten-mile-wide swath of public land along the entire length of the canal. The size of the grant varied according to the route chosen, amounting to nearly 140,000 acres along the waterway that was eventually approved. Congress was persuaded not only by the commercial reasons dear to Kilbourn's heart but also, apparently, by the canal's potential military value. The Senate Committee on Public Lands noted that six years earlier, during the Black Hawk War, the United States had been unable to move troops and supplies expeditiously to the Rock River region. General George W. Jones, Wisconsin's territorial delegate to the House, underscored the military argument when the bill came before that body. President Martin Van Buren signed the measure into law on June 18, 1838.

Unfortunately, this remarkable windfall included a provision that would ultimately scuttle the project. The land grant included parcels that had already been taken up and improved by settlers who assumed that when it was offered for sale they would be able to purchase it at the standard minimum price of $1.25 an acre (about $30 today). Known as the right of preemption, this privilege had been confirmed by a series of bills passed between 1830 and 1834. Squatters assumed that the right of preemption would be renewed in 1836. But the Jackson and Van Buren administrations delayed renewal until 1838, due partly to abuses of preemption in southeastern Wisconsin, where much of the preempted land was going to speculators rather than settlers.

The territorial canal bill included a clause that gave settlers the right to preempt up to 160 acres. The federal land grant bill included a similar provision until it was amended in a Senate committee. As amended, the bill specified that the even-numbered sections belonging to the United States were to be sold at not less than $2.50 an acre, thereby assuring that the United States would realize the same profit as if it had sold all sections at the $1.25 minimum. The House committee further amended the bill to require that the odd-numbered sections, too, be sold for at least $2.50 an acre. Kilbourn did not protest these amendments, for he believed that land in the canal strip was still a bargain at the higher price.

Settlers saw the matter differently, of course, and Kilbourn's opponents rallied to their cause. Among these was Alanson Sweet, one of Milwaukee's two representatives in the Territorial Council, which together with the House of Representatives made up the Legislative Assembly. When Sweet opposed the canal project on the grounds that it provided no right of preemption, Kilbourn wrote him an angry and impolitic letter. "I have the screw upon you," Kilbourn threatened, "and can turn it at any time at my own pleasure." Sweet passed the letter on to the *Milwaukee Sentinel*, which by this time, reflecting the opinion of Solomon Juneau and Harrison Reed, had also turned against the canal as a venture that placed Kilbourn's interests above those of the settlers. The newspaper published Kilbourn's letter on July 31, 1838, along with Sweet's response.

Sweet's letter reflects widespread suspicion of Kilbourn as an outside speculator motivated chiefly by greed. "Your course at the land sale at Green Bay in '35," Sweet wrote, "was such as to convince me that you was [sic] the friend of the settler only so long as you could further your own views. You commenced your career in Wisconsin at that sale, by linking yourself with eastern capitalists to cheat the settler out of his improvements on the public land, as many an honest man at the present day can testify. I was satisfied that your object was to amass wealth by your operations, and if possible reign triumphant over the County of Milwaukee, and have its citizens subservient to your nod."

The Legislative Assembly sent memorials to Congress in 1838 and 1839, urging it to extend preemption rights to canal strip settlers, but Congress chose not to reconsider the matter. Powerless to alter the price of the granted sections, the assembly passed a bill allowing for easier terms of sale: 10 percent down, with the balance to be paid in four installments beginning in 1844. Territorial Governor Henry Dodge, a Black Hawk War hero appointed by President Andrew Jackson, also took up the cause of the settlers. In his annual address of 1839, he placed them, and by implication the canal, in the grand Jacksonian tradition of the American frontier: "The settlers upon the Canal reservations, are a part of that same band of pioneers in the march of improvement, who are rapidly extending the empire of this Union, and whose spirit of adventure and enterprize will ere long cross the Rocky Mountains and plant the American standard on the shores of the Pacific."

Much as the Erie Canal was called Clinton's Big Ditch by its detractors, the Milwaukee and Rock River Canal came to be known as Kilbourn's Canal, so strongly were the man and his pet project identified in the public mind. The preemption issue provided those who disliked either Kilbourn or his canal with a popular cause. Besides Sweet, Juneau, and Reed, the opposition included James Duane Doty, who was contemplating a rival canal along the Fox-Wisconsin route from Green Bay to Prairie du Chien. In 1839 Doty ran against Kilbourn as the territorial delegate to Congress and won. When President John Tyler took office in 1841, he appointed Doty territorial governor in place of Dodge.

The canal was by then in financial trouble. Due partly to the liberal terms of purchase, the public land auction of 1839 yielded less than $12,400 for construction. Looking for ways to reduce construction costs, the canal company proposed the substitution of wooden locks for stone wherever possible. That measure would save an estimated $120,000 (about $2.9 million today), though the wooden locks would eventually rot and have to be replaced with stone. The Legislative Assembly amended the original canal bill to permit the strictly regulated sale of territorial bonds worth $50,000 and later $100,000 to private investors.

It was Governor Dodge who authorized Kilbourn to sell the bonds. Under Dodge's successor, Doty, a select committee of the assembly declared in 1842 that most of the second bond issue had been "illegally and fraudulently disposed of" and vented its displeasure in a series of "repudiating resolutions." Kilbourn had doubtless bent the rules in a desperate effort to raise money, supplying Doty with a pretext to revoke his authority to sell canal bonds. That was the *coup de grace* for the Milwaukee and Rock River Canal, though its legal and financial afterlife extended through Wisconsin's admission to statehood in 1848. Under the state constitution, the canal land grant became part of the half-million acres accorded newly admitted states. Purchasers who had paid more than $1.25 an acre for canal land received a refund of the overcharge.

Kilbourn didn't miss a beat before turning to his railroad ventures. For years it had been obvious that railways, powered first by horses and then by steam locomotives, would replace canals as the faster and cheaper way to move goods and people across the country. He must have been disappointed, nonetheless, at the demise of a project in which he had invested so much of his time and personal resources. He was partly to blame for its failure, inasmuch as his high-handed style created political enemies where he needed allies. Not all of the mayhem can be laid at his door, however. Opposing him were influential men who supported rival projects or had the backing of cash-poor farmers.

Yet the canal's chief adversary was not a person but a freak of bad economic timing. The panic of 1837, triggered by President Jackson's banking policies and rampant speculation in public land, ruined many potential investors. Though the panic enriched the few—including Kilbourn and Doty—who could profit from others' losses, it also jeopardized some of their pet projects. Money was in such short supply during the late 1830s that only 8 percent of canal stock was paid for by 1840, depriving the company of the means to extend the canal much beyond the refractory soil in which Kilbourn inserted his spade that hopeful morning in 1839.

Milwaukee County Historical Society

An early photograph of the completed section of the
Milwaukee and Rock River Canal along the west bank of
the Milwaukee River

Historic Photo Collection / Milwaukee Public Library

North Commerce Street in 1959

Milton J. Bates

North Commerce Street in 2007

Kilbourn had not taken up that implement in vain, however. The canal company managed to build a dam on the Milwaukee River just downstream from North Avenue, creating a ten-foot head of water. From there a lock diverted water to a section of canal that hugged the river's west bank for a mile and a quarter before rejoining it near today's McKinley Avenue. For westbound pioneers the canal led nowhere. But for German immigrants and others who made their home in Milwaukee it led to jobs and middle-class affluence. Kilbourn's Canal became a millrace, and by 1849 it was driving the turbines of twenty-five industries, including flour mills, wood turners, foundries, and a tannery.

The original dam was constructed of whole trees covered with 100,000 cubic feet of gravel. When it washed out in 1866, the trees took out five bridges on their way to Lake Michigan. Though the dam was rebuilt and power restored, the factory owners had learned a lesson. They switched from water power to steam. In 1884 the city filled in the old canal, paved it over, and gave it a name that would have pleased Kilbourn: Commerce Street. Over a century later, during the 1990s, developers turned the derelict, weed-infested property into a neighborhood with upscale condominiums, a microbrewery, and a stylish new restaurant.

West of Milwaukee, communities such as Hartland and Delafield owe their existence partly to the canal that never was. Settlers purchased land in the canal strip believing that its value could only increase. Farmers, millers, and other entrepreneurs anticipated ready access to markets on the Great Lakes and in the East. Fortunately for them, the canal's demise was only a temporary setback, for railroads soon moved into the breach.

Over a century and a half later, railroads like the one that crosses the Bark River in Hartland remain visibly and audibly present. The Milwaukee and Rock River Canal is there too, as a spectral presence. South of the village, where the feeder canal would have joined the main artery, you can almost hear the sounds of might-have-been: the clip-clopping cadence of mules on a towpath and the voices of bargemen singing:

> Low bridge, everybody down!
> Low bridge, 'cause we're coming to a town!
> And you'll always know your neighbor,
> You'll always know your pal,
> If you ever navigated on the Kilbourn Canal.

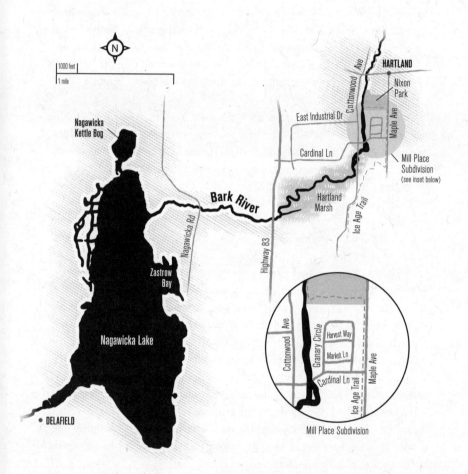

N

1000 feet
1 mile

Nagawicka
Kettle Bog

HARTLAND

Nixon
Park

Cottonwood Ave

East Industrial Dr

Maple Ave

Cardinal Ln

Mill Place
Subdivision
(see inset below)

Bark River

Nagawicka Rd

Hartland
Marsh

Ice Age Trail

Highway 83

Zastrow
Bay

Nagawicka Lake

DELAFIELD

Cottonwood Ave

Granary Circle

Harvest Way

Market Ln

Cardinal Ln

Maple Ave

Ice Age Trail

Mill Place Subdivision

CHAPTER 5

Hartland to Nagawicka Lake

Downstream from Nixon Park in Hartland the Bark River straightens out and stretches its legs. The sunlight is full in our faces as we ride the brisk current directly south, gliding past the backyards of homes facing Cottonwood Avenue. The river's cheery mood is deceptive, however, for it would be hard to find another place on the Bark where misery has pressed so close on both banks.

The misery on the left was human and chiefly financial. Here in the 1990s the Dynacon Development Corporation planned to build a subdivision called Mill Place. Its street names recall Hartland's milling history: Granary Circle, Harvest Way, Market Lane. Fewer than half of the projected forty-five homes had been built by April 1997, when the owners of five completed homes began to receive foreclosure notices. That was their first clue that Dynacon had not fully paid for the lots on which their homes were situated. In fact, it still owed the mortgage company $1.23 million. When police seized Dynacon's business records in June of that year, they discovered evidence of fraud and theft. After

Dynacon filed for bankruptcy late that summer, the mortgage company worked out a settlement with the homeowners that allowed them to keep their property. Construction eventually resumed under another developer, and today Mill Place is fully built up.

The misery on the right, though also human and financial, posed a serious threat to the health of the ecosystem as well. In 1970 the Chrysler Corporation hired Keller Transit of Hartland to remove barrels of toxic waste from a subsidiary plant that manufactured outboard marine engines in Hartford. The waste included cadmium, chromium, lead, and trichloroethylene (TCE), a cleaning solvent believed to be a carcinogen. Lee Hasslinger, the president of Keller Transit, had no license or permit to haul hazardous waste and later testified he was unaware that the barrels contained toxic material. He dumped about five hundred of the fifty-five-gallon drums in a marshy area on his farm and covered them with gravel and other fill. He subsequently sold the farm to Bark River Properties, a real estate partnership that was planning to develop a shopping plaza on the west side of Cottonwood Avenue between East Industrial Drive and Cardinal Lane. In 1992 a contractor unearthed more than four hundred of the rusting barrels while excavating the plaza site.

Bark River Properties notified the DNR, which ordered Chrysler to remove the barrels and contaminated soil. This did not solve the larger environmental problem, however. The DNR determined that leaking barrels had generated a plume of ground water contamination extending at least a half mile, with the Bark River only two hundred feet away. Wonderful word, *plume*. The DNR's term conjures up the rakish ornament on a cavalier's hat. But this plume was deadly, for the ground water contained chlorinated solvents in concentrations up to ten times the safe drinking-water standard.

Because a municipal well had registered high levels of TCE eleven years previously, when its source was unknown, the State Division of Public Health (Department of Health Services) undertook an epidemiological study to determine whether cancer cases in Hartland might be linked to well water. The well used by an elementary school located about two hundred yards north of the Bark on Highway 83 had to be disconnected due to unsafe levels of TCE, and a private well near the school registered much higher concentrations. In 1995 the state filed suit in a Waukesha County circuit court against the Chrysler Corporation, seeking full remediation of the Cottonwood Avenue site.

The suit was controversial for a couple of reasons. First, the state asked the court to hold the generator of waste (Chrysler) liable for damage rather than, as was usually the case, the current owner of the disposal site (Bark River Properties). Second, it argued that, even though Chrysler had dumped the waste prior to Wisconsin's 1978 hazardous substance discharge law, the company was not protected by the statute of limitations because its waste was still contaminating the site.

The county circuit court dismissed the state's case, declaring that the statute of limitations had expired and Chrysler was no longer liable. However, the State Court of Appeals called for closer scrutiny of the case and forwarded it to the State Supreme Court. In 1998 the Supreme Court determined in a 4–3 split decision that Chrysler continued to "own" the waste until it was destroyed. Each day's discharge constituted a new release, hence a new violation of the 1978 law. Chrysler would therefore have to pay for cleaning up the site. Environmentalists applauded the decision as a victory for Wisconsin taxpayers, who would otherwise have had to foot the bill. They also saw it as an important precedent, providing the state with a way to handle any toxic treasures that had yet to be unearthed.

To its credit, Chrysler did the job right. The corporation employed a remediation company that used an innovative on-site steam injection process to remove 6,700 pounds of chlorinated solvents from the soil and ground water on a one-acre plot southeast of the Piggly Wiggly grocery store. The cleanup took three years and cost $3.2 million. As is usually the case with environmental damage, an ounce of prevention would have saved many pounds of cure. Chrysler put the best face on its legal setback by presenting one of its 1999 CHEER (Continuously Honors Environmental Excellence with Recognition) awards to the supply partner that researched and implemented the cleanup technology.

Passing the site in our canoe, we add our own silent cheer to Chrysler's, though we cannot help but wonder how much TCE leached into the river between 1970 and 1998. Today it lies undetected in the sediment of downstream lakes and millponds where people swim and fish. An inexact procedure at best, remediation never restores a natural community to its original state. There are merely degrees of paradise lost.

We float under the Cardinal Lane bridge, which links the Mill Place subdivision to Cottonwood Avenue, then turn sharply right through cattail marsh. Approaching the Cottonwood Avenue bridge, we realize that we won't be able to squeeze under at the current water level. So we pull over to the left and carry around. Downstream from the bridge we enter another world, a realm of sedge meadow, cattail marsh, and glacial landforms. This was once the least inviting section of the Bark River, with wind-toppled willows and human refuse blocking the channel. On a trip in the 1990s it took us nearly three hours to cover the one and a quarter miles between Cottonwood Avenue and Highway 83, lifting over tree trunks and dragging around river bends clogged with debris.

Today a cruise down the 3.3-mile canoe trail between Nixon Park and Nagawicka Lake is an ideal way to see what volunteers have accomplished in the area known as Hartland Marsh. It was Henry Reuss who proposed turning the marsh into a nature conservancy. He was on the board of the Ice Age Park and Trail Foundation, which owned one hundred acres along the Bark River between Maple Avenue and Highway 83. The village of Hartland owned eighty acres; a private owner held another twenty-eight acres. The strategy that was working so well in the Mid-Kettle Gap—buying private land and consolidating parcels held by conservation-minded groups—was applied to Hartland Marsh. In 1999 Reuss asked Marlin Johnson, the manager of the University of Wisconsin–Waukesha Field Station in Waterville, to coordinate the effort. He also contributed twenty-five thousand dollars of his own money.

The Hartland Marsh project was as remarkable for the way it happened as it was for the outcome. The local chapter of the Ice Age Park and Trail Foundation partnered with the Waukesha Land Conservancy and municipal agencies such as Hartland and the Pewaukee Sanitary District, which owned 225 acres of marsh east of Hartland. They enlisted the help of volunteers from Arrowhead and Kettle Moraine High Schools, the Boy Scouts, the Kiwanis and Rotary Clubs, and a group called Friends of Hartland Marsh to remove trash, build waysides and overlooks, plant native wildflowers, install birdhouses, and remove invasive plants. Two volunteers in particular, Paul Mozina and Pati Holman, devoted so many hours to buckthorn removal that Hartland declared a day in their honor on June 16, 2010.

Two of the overlooks are named after prominent state environmentalists, Aldo Leopold and John Muir. A third, added later for disabled visitors, memorializes John Wesley Powell, who spent part of his boyhood on a farm in Walworth County. Though Powell lost an arm in the Civil War, the handicap didn't prevent him from leading two exploratory expeditions down the Colorado River. One day, perhaps, an overlook will be named after Henry Reuss, as the preservation of Hartland Marsh proved to be his last gift to his native state.

Five minutes below the Cottonwood Avenue bridge we come to a high ridge on the right, linked by a wooden footbridge to a home site on the left bank. Remnants of its foundation remain. The Waukesha Land Conservancy purchased this private parcel with the help of a grant from the state's Stewardship Program. Puck and I stop for lunch on the ridge, where piles of brush testify to the labor of volunteers who have cleared the woods of buckthorn, honeysuckle, and other invasive species. What remains is not exactly oak woodland or savanna—there are too many shagbark hickories, maples, black cherries, red pines, junipers, and spruces to qualify—but something closer to the landscape encountered by early settlers. Controlled burns would maintain the landscape in this condition, but residents of a nearby subdivision have objected to the smoke. For now the invasive plants have to be laboriously cut and hauled away and new growth controlled with Roundup (glysophate).

After lunch we climb to the crest of the ridge, where we notice a grave marker propped against some rocks. Inscribed on the stone are the words,

JACOB BOY
OF
AVONDALE
1941–1955

Is this the final resting place of a young man, tragically cut down in youth? Later we will learn the stone marks the grave of a family pet that passed away in the fullness of dog years.

Back in the boat, we pass under the footbridge and are soon in the open cattail marsh. Industrial parks mark its boundaries on the north and the south, where the land was dry enough to tempt developers. At Highway 83 the scenery and river bottom change dramatically. The marsh gives way to woods and low grassy banks. Instead of muck, the bottom consists of baseball-sized rocks, giving it a cobbled appearance. A few larger boulders appear along the shore. From here to Nagawicka Lake the river is posted as a fish refuge. Presumably the combination of high water quality and rocky bottom are good for spawning.

This is one of the loveliest and most serene reaches of the Bark. Except for an old barn on the left bank, immediately downstream from Highway 83, we see no signs of human habitation until the homes along Nagawicka Road. Nor is there any trace of the beaver dam we had to maneuver around on a previous trip. The sole sign of animal life is a doe that watches us from the edge of the woods, standing stock-still except for her outsize ears, turning like radar dishes. When the federal surveyor mapped this section in 1836, he noted an Indian trail that crossed the river between Hartland Marsh and Nagawicka Lake. It was part of a network linking Pewaukee Lake (then called Snail Lake by white settlers) with Pine and North Lakes.

Upstream from the Nagawicka Road bridge, the river turns shallow and gravelly. The riffles continue as we pass under the bridge and into a meadow that was probably once a pasture belonging to the farm on the left bank. Beyond the barn is a stand of hardwoods with orioles clearly visible in the branches. Farther back, a subdivision has sprouted from soil that formerly produced corn. The river bottom turns from gravel to sand and then silt as we approach Nagawicka Lake. An enormous willow guards the entrance, its branches draped like a bead curtain over the water. Threading our way through, we encounter our first dock with the inevitable pairing of pontoon boat and jet ski.

No silt bar blocks the channel into the lake, probably due to dredging, which has long been a way of life on Nagawicka Lake. In the natural course of things a glacial lake such as Nagawicka gradually fills with silt, becoming first a wetland and then a meadow. For the last century and a half, erosion from agriculture, quarrying, and development in the Bark River watershed has accelerated the process. On Nagawicka groups of neighbors anxious to maintain their property values regularly apply to the DNR for permits, hire a dredging contractor, and share the cost. When issuing permits the DNR must weigh the benefits of recreational use—motorboat access, for example—against damage to fragile ecosystems. In recent years residents of Delafield have looked to the city to manage dredging operations on parts of the lake, such as the Bark River delta, the channel leading to the dam, and, on the south shore of St. John's Bay, a boat launching site for the private use of Delafield and Nashotah residents.

Turning north as we enter the lake, we pass several large homes with sloping lawns before coming to a cattail marsh with willow shrubs, swamp loosestrife, and an occasional tamarack. Dredged channels lead through the marsh to homes situated on higher ground. Two channels at the northeast corner of the lake lead to docking for a condominium complex where pontoon boats line the dock. Submerged stumps and logs suggest that the lake was once lower, perhaps before the dam in Delafield stabilized its level. Though luxuriant algae carpets the surface, the water beneath is remarkably clear.

It wasn't always this clear along Nagawicka's eastern shore, where the prevailing west wind tends to deposit a "bathtub ring" of waterborne debris. In 1952 property owners in Fernwood, near the mouth of the Bark, presented a petition to the Delafield town board, asking that it seek an injunction to prevent Hartland from polluting the river. Three years later a group of sportsmen associated with the Izaak Walton League became incensed at an especially noxious accumulation of solid waste in Zastrow Bay, south of the river entrance. They collected samples, sealed them in the presence of two sheriff's deputies, and sent them to the state health lab for analysis. Residents and users of the lake generally pointed up the Bark River to Hartland as the source of the sewage. Some had seen human waste floating below the outflow pipe from the Hartland sewage treatment plant. In response, Hartland claimed that its plant released only clean effluent into the river.

Delafield, though understandably outraged at Hartland's penchant for shipping its problems downstream, had cause to examine its own conscience. A *Milwaukee Journal* reporter sniffing around the downtown area in May 1966 traced the powerful odor of sewage to effluent from several homes, businesses, and especially the grounds of St. John's Military Academy, located on the north bank of the Bark River west of Genesee Street. The academy laundry discharged wastewater into lagoons, whence it was carried by a ditch into the river. Separate septic systems, some of them failing, served other buildings. Though an academy spokesman declared its effluent "clean enough to drink," he didn't divulge whether he'd sampled it himself.

Delafield's mayor speculated that the academy was delaying corrective action because the city had, off and on, discussed construction of a treatment plant to which the school could connect. But the discussion came to nothing as evidence of serious pollution accumulated. A 1970 study conducted by Aqua-Tech of Waukesha reported high fecal coliform levels in the river below the Hartland sewage plant. The following year the DNR identified the plant as one of fifteen in the Rock River watershed that were inadequate. When Hartland requested DNR approval to discharge pollutants into the Bark

River in 1974, a Delafield citizens group calling itself CLEAN (Committee for Legislative Equity and Alliance) demanded closer DNR scrutiny of the Hartland operation.

The finger-pointing raised tempers but did little to improve the water quality. Finally Bill Moylan, the chairman of the Delafield Common Council and a resident of Nagawicka's eastern shore, brought a visual and olfactory aid to a council meeting. Placing a pail full of sludge on the table, he declared that it was time to put recriminations aside and help Hartland to build a new treatment plant. After the two municipalities formed a joint sewage district they had to agree on the location of the plant, which also proved contentious. "Not in my backyard" was the response of one neighborhood after another.

So it is all the more remarkable that in 1980 the Delafield-Hartland Water Pollution Control Commission opened a state-of-the-art facility on Butler Drive in Delafield. It could treat 2.2 million gallons of sewage per day, removing 98 to 99 percent of all solids from the water before returning it to the Bark River four miles downstream. Furthermore, the price was right. Federal funding covered all but $5.3 million of the $18 million project. Delafield and Hartland split the remaining cost. As the district's population grew over the next couple of decades, it spent another $16 million to upgrade the facility to handle 3.2 million gallons of waste per day.

~~~~~~

Cattail marsh extends across Nagawicka's northern shore, interspersed with stands of large tamaracks. Tamarack stumps, one of them eighteen inches in diameter, dot the entrance to an adjoining body of water. This is the Nagawicka Kettle Bog, fifteen acres of which have been preserved by the Waukesha Land Conservancy and are open to the public. It is home to the Blanding's turtle, a threatened species in Wisconsin. Large pilings on the east shore of the bog mark the location of an old dock. A dredged channel on the northwest leads to the base of a steep bank occupied by several houses.

Leaving the bog, we head south, cruising along the lake's western shore. On our right tamaracks give way to hardwoods. On our left low offshore islands create an ecosystem that reminds Puck of another place we've visited.

"Remember that bayou in the Florida Everglades?" she asks. "I half expect to see cypress trees and alligators."

"When the Potawatomi camped along this shore," I respond, "they probably appreciated protection from winds off the lake. They were still here in the 1860s, fishing, hunting, trapping, and living on good terms with the white settlers who owned the land."

"Even in '62?"

"Even in '62, though that summer was bad enough for relations between the two races."

Puck's question alludes to the notorious Dakota Conflict (also called the Sioux Uprising) in Minnesota, which had repercussions in this area. It began on August 17, 1862, when a hunting party of four young braves killed five white settlers in Meeker County. The murders were not premeditated, yet the next morning between two and three hundred warriors began attacking settlements, forts, and Indian agencies in the Minnesota River valley and beyond. By the time the conflict ended on September 23, hundreds more of the Dakota had taken part in the attacks, killing about 500 whites and taking 269 white and mixed-blood captives. Following the Indians' surrender, a military court condemned 303 of them to death. President Abraham Lincoln pardoned or commuted the sentences of all but thirty-eight. Their death by hanging in Mankato on December 26 remains the largest public execution in US history.

"What I don't understand," Puck muses, "is why the Dakotas didn't turn the four murderers over to US authorities rather than take their side. They were sure to lose that battle."

"Most of the Indians saw it your way. They'd given up most of their lands in treaties, but still occupied a substantial reservation served by two agencies. Though game was becoming scarce, many had taken up farming, and the federal government paid them a yearly annuity. Two bands of the Dakota refused to take part in the conflict, and several leaders in the two rebellious bands advised against it. Even Little Crow, their war chief, accepted his role reluctantly."

"But he did accept, and I've heard that his warriors went about their business with sufficient gusto."

"Granted. Frustration and anger may account for both. The annuity often arrived late, and there wasn't much left after white traders took their share for goods purchased on credit. The payment was unusually late in 1862 because Congress was preoccupied with financing the Civil War. It arrived, ironically, on the first day of Little Crow's campaign. There had been angry confrontations over food supplies in the weeks before the conflict erupted. The murder of the five settlers was the spark that touched off the powder keg.

"You're right about the Dakotas' behavior once they tasted blood," I concede. "Eyewitness accounts are full of mutilated and dismembered bodies, regardless of age or sex. Some of the women were raped and killed or claimed as wives by the warriors. It was the kind of warfare that instills abiding hatred in survivors.

"White settlers felt especially betrayed because they'd been on friendly terms with some of the attackers, even attending Christian churches with them. When a group of warriors led by the Dakota chief Cut Nose approached a group of white farmers mowing hay in a field, the chief extended his hand toward one of them as though to shake it. Then he drew his knife and killed the farmer. He left the body with the man's scythe in it."

"Considering what was happening in Minnesota," Puck observes, "I'm surprised that here on Nagawicka"—she raises her paddle and gestures toward the western shore—"the Potawatomi and white settlers managed to remain on friendly terms."

"There were few Indians in the area, and no reservations," I point out. "That may have helped the settlers sleep easier. Still, they must have regarded their Potawatomi neighbors differently after 1862, considering how hard it was to distinguish between friendly and hostile Indians in Minnesota. The Dakota bands that refused to join Little Crow were exiled to South Dakota and eventually Nebraska anyway, as were a couple of thousand Ho-Chunk who had nothing to do with the conflict. The US considered removing the Ojibwe from Minnesota, too, but that proved unfeasible."

"How strange to think that the country was fighting racially charged wars on two fronts," Puck reflects, "seeking to liberate one race in the South and subjugate another in the West. Strange and tragic."

I nod in agreement, adding, "Like Shakespearean tragedy, it had its moments of comic relief. The *New York Times* and other newspapers reported that the uprising was fomented by the 'cursed Secessionists of Missouri,' as though the Dakotas had no other reason to take to the warpath. Little Crow's fighting force was rumored to be ten thousand warriors, more than ten times the number he actually mustered for any of the attacks.

"Here's the strangest part of the story. You can understand why hundreds of Minnesotans fled the countryside for the forts and the cities. But who could have predicted that the panic would spread to southeastern Wisconsin? During the afternoon and evening of September 4 thousands of people in this part of the state fled their farms and villages for the safety of Milwaukee and Waukesha. They arrived in all manner of conveyance, including hay wagon and ox-drawn sleigh, carrying prized possessions and animals. They related tales of bloody massacres and farms put to the torch in the surrounding counties. The governor ordered the Milwaukee militia to march north to intercept the Indians. They found none, and by the next morning the burned buildings had risen miraculously from their ashes. The episode proved to be a hoax perpetrated by a bored young man from Merton with a fiendish instinct for the panic button."

We paddle halfway to Delafield between the shore and the islands before venturing onto the open lake again. The water remains quite shallow along its southwest corner, then drops off sharply where the Bark River exits the lake. Buoys mark the dredged channel. We land to the right of the dam, noticing as we do so that a good deal of water is spilling from the lake into the river below. Ordinarily, a brisk current would bode well for our next trip. But we have planned a different kind of outing for the following Saturday and are hoping for low water.

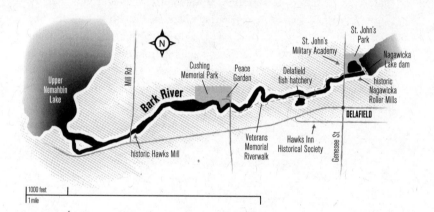

Upper
Nemahbin
Lake

Mill Rd

N

Cushing
Memorial Park

Peace
Garden

Delafield
fish hatchery

St. John's
Military Academy

St. John's
Park

Nagawicka
Lake dam

Bark River

historic
Nagawicka
Roller Mills

DELAFIELD

historic Hawks Mill

Veterans
Memorial
Riverwalk

Hawks Inn
Historical Society

Genesee St

1000 feet
1 mile

CHAPTER 6

Nagawicka Lake
to Hawks Mill

On the next-to-last Saturday of May, Puck and I arrive early at the old fish hatchery in Delafield. We have organized a group of Sierra Club volunteers to help clean up the Bark River between the Nagawicka Lake dam and Upper Nemahbin Lake. Our effort is part of a nationwide event, Outdoor America's National River Cleanup Week. We are soon joined by Nancy Hagstrom, the unofficial secretary of Fish Hatchery Limited, the group responsible for restoring the Delafield fish hatchery building, constructed in 1907 of fieldstone. The hatchery once diverted water from the river and Nagawicka Lake to a half-dozen ponds. A sportsmen's group still uses one of them to raise muskies.

Cars topped with canoes begin to arrive as the 9:30 meeting time approaches. Soon there are eighteen of us from the Sierra Club, including Kent and Gail. (Did I mention that they converted their suburban lawn to prairie years ago, to the consternation of their neighbors?) Mark Lien, a Sierra Club member who runs an auto body shop in Delafield, has managed to secure a

Dumpster from the city. There are several other volunteers from Delafield: Jim Bacon, who teaches at the Ladd Lake School; Stuart and Warren Lyman of the Cushing School Nature Club; Doug and Kathy Lyman and two of their children; and Margaret Zerwekh, a local historian who owns the old mill and millpond downstream from the hatchery.

We divide into four groups. Mark and Jim use a chain saw to remove downed trees from the channel upstream from the fish hatchery. Four canoeists clean up the section between Mill Road and Upper Nemahbin. The majority of the volunteers, working from boats in the river or on foot along the shore, tackle the section between the hatchery and the millpond. Puck and I assign ourselves along with Don and Becky Lintner to clear debris from the river between Genesee Street and the hatchery.

The water is running high and fast as we'd anticipated, so it is a challenge to maneuver our canoes around downed trees. We immediately haul in our first catch of the day, an orange plastic toboggan snagged in mid-river. Thereafter we have to work harder for less satisfying trophies, chiefly Styrofoam worm boxes and plastic soft drink bottles. I have to saw through obstructing branches to reach some of the debris, and Don wades into waist-deep water to break up a logjam. Eventually we drift down to the chain saw crew, which we find laboring over a large willow limb that blocks the channel. Jim saws sections from the limb and floats them down to volunteers who wade in and drag them ashore.

We work our way down to the hatchery just in time for lunch, donated by local grocery stores and served by Olive Brown and Julie Platz of Delafield. It is quite a spread: sloppy joe sandwiches, hot dogs, potato salad, beans, potato chips, vegetables and dip, cookies, coffee, and soft drinks. Has our morning's work merited this largesse? Our haul up to this point doesn't fill much of the Dumpster, but includes a shopping cart and a rusty drum. Boats continue to arrive, towed upstream and laden to the gunwales with junk. The group assigned to the section below Mill Road has located a graveyard for worn-out tires on an island near the entrance to Upper Nemahbin.

As we enjoy our lunch and the sunshine at picnic tables near the hatchery, a reporter from the *Waukesha Freeman* circulates, asking questions and taking notes. Earlier, a *Freeman* photographer had taken pictures, one of which will appear in Monday's paper. It shows Sierra Club member Peter Sparrow on the river with two of his sons.

After lunch Mark and Kent take a pickup truck down to get the tires. There are twenty-one of them along with other trash, which adds significantly to our collection. Several volunteers call it a day at this point, but six Sierra Club canoes continue the cleanup on the reach from Lower Nemahbin Lake to Genesee Lake Road. When we take out late in the afternoon we have three more tires, a car door, and countless soft drink and beer cans to feed the Dumpster on our way home.

~~~~~

We consider driving up to the Wolf River a week later, until we remember that it will be Memorial Day weekend and the unofficial start of the rafting season. Besides the more predictable and stationary obstacles in the rapids, we'd have to negotiate out-of-control fleets of rubber boats. Opting for solitude and serenity we decide, paradoxically, to paddle one of the more urban sections of the Bark, the same stretch that we'd cleaned up the previous Saturday. I call Margaret Zerwekh to let her know that we'll arrive at her mill on Monday around midday.

"We'll bring trash bags with us," I say. "With the water level dropping, we'll be able to reach some of the stuff that we missed on the cleanup trip. May we leave it with you for the city trash pickup?"

"You may if you promise to look for the cattle troughs I told you about. There should be two of them between the fish hatchery and the millpond."

"We'll watch for them."

On Monday we leave our minivan at a walk-in site for launching boats on Lower Nemahbin Lake. Returning to Delafield, I secure my bike and we board our canoe below the Nagawicka dam. We pass a mother and her daughter fishing just upstream from Genesee Street, then glide through the culvert, Puck using her paddle to sweep away the spider webs.

The river bends left, passing a secluded modern home located perilously in the flood plain between the Bark and a debris-choked tailrace that once carried water from the mill for which Delafield's Mill Street is named. John Heath and William Pearmain purchased the site in 1839, and Heath began work on a dam and mill. When Pearmain and his family returned to Massachusetts, Heath sold an interest in the operation to Charles Delafield and Paraclete Potter. The city and township bear Delafield's name, not because he was an original settler or especially prominent but because his name seemed "euphonious." The mill passed through several owners and was known as Nagawicka Roller Mills when it ceased milling operations and became a hardware store. Today the handsome stone structure at 627 Mill Street is a private residence.

Below the tailrace the river veers sharply right and ducks under a twelve-inch pipe that formerly carried water from the lake to three of the fish hatchery ponds. That diversion of water was a source of contention between the fish hatchery and the mill downstream. When the state of Wisconsin purchased the hatchery site in 1906, it contracted with Evan Humphrey, then the owner of the upper mill and dam, to regulate the water level for the benefit of the hatchery. George Apfelbacher, the owner of the mill that now belongs to Margaret, frequently complained about their interference in his business. He sued the state and Humphrey twice—in 1912 for releasing too much water and washing out part of his dam, and in 1916 for releasing too little water to sustain his operation. He lost the first suit, but won the second.

From the hatchery the river heads due west toward Margaret's millpond. For the next two and a half hours we drift slowly downstream, collecting trash as we go. We see plenty of birds but no other members of our own species until we come upon a man fishing from a dock.

"Having any luck?"

Leaning over, he lifts a stringer with two smallmouth bass. "I hooked a good-sized walleye too, but he got away."

Farther on, we find a couple of boys, about ten or eleven years old, catching shiners with a seine net.

"What are you going to do with all those minnows?" I ask. Thinking of the walleye that got away, I know how I would use them.

"Let them go."

Yet they will keep the best part of their catch. Long after their friends have forgotten their soccer and video games, they will remember—remember with their skin and nerves—a day on the Bark, immersed up to their knees in a force of nature.

Approaching Cushing Memorial Park, we can hear family picnics in progress but see no one due to the screen of vegetation along the bank. The park is named after three brothers who distinguished themselves in military service during the nineteenth century. They were the sons of Milton Buckingham Cushing and his second wife, Mary Barker Smith. Cushing, a native of Fredonia, New York, completed a medical degree but practiced only briefly before trying to make his livelihood as a merchant in Ohio. He lost every-thing in the financial panic of 1837 and came west to the Wisconsin Territory, hoping to recoup his losses by farming. The Cushings' first son, Milton Jr., was born in Ohio in 1837. Howard was born in Milwaukee in 1838. Alonzo and

William were born beside the Bark River in 1841 and 1842, respectively, and possibly baptized in its waters.

The family arrived in Wisconsin just before the Milwaukee and Rock River Canal Company offered land for sale along the projected route of the waterway. In 1839 Milton purchased 250 acres on the Bark between Nagawicka and Upper Nemahbin Lakes, with his brother as holder of a mortgage for the full price of the land. Milton built a log cabin—the site is marked with a stone in Cushing Park—and held positions of responsibility in the town then called Nemahbin. However, he was unable to repay his brother's loan. He sold the land and was still looking for ways to provide for his family when he died of tuberculosis in 1847. His wife, sons, and a newborn daughter returned to Fredonia, where Cushing relatives helped them make a new home. Family connections also secured appointments to military academies for two of the sons—West Point for Alonzo and Annapolis for William.

An obelisk in Cushing Park testifies to the heroism of Howard Cushing and his younger brothers, all of whom served in the Civil War. As a twenty-two-year-old artillery officer, Alonzo held his ground against Pickett's charge at Gettysburg, dying on July 3, 1863, when the Confederacy famously reached its "high water mark" at his battery. Congress awarded him the Medal of Honor posthumously, due chiefly to the efforts of Margaret Zerwekh. William Cushing was likewise a twenty-two-year-old officer in 1864, when he planned and executed a daring attack on a Confederate ironclad ram that had wreaked havoc on the Union navy. Though he succeeded in sinking the *Albemarle* in the Roanoke River, his own vessel was destroyed and most of the crew was killed, drowned, or captured. William managed to escape by shedding his bullet-riddled clothing and swimming to shore. Howard Cushing, like Alonzo, served as an artillery officer in the Civil War. He subsequently transferred to the cavalry and was killed by Apaches in Arizona in 1871. The oldest brother, Milton Jr., served as a navy paymaster during the Civil War and is not mentioned on the obelisk.

Given the Cushing brothers' extraordinary record of service, Cushing Park is an appropriate location for the Peace Garden that anchors the western end of the Veterans Memorial Riverwalk. Dedicated in 2006, the walk follows the Bark River from St. John's Park at the Nagawicka Lake dam to Cushing Park. Information panels at nine stations along the way describe major American military campaigns from the Revolutionary War to the War on Terror. Like the boardwalk and overlooks in Hartland Marsh, the riverwalk also serves as an introduction to the ecology of the Bark and its bordering marsh. The DNR contributed $183,000 to its construction.

Visitors who walk the three-quarters of a mile between the lake and Cushing Park might reflect not only on American military history and the river ecosystem but also on the ancient people who once lived here for at least part of the year. Archeologists have discovered flint projectile points and copper implements in the park, dating probably to the Middle Archaic period (5,000–2,000 BC). Indians likely fashioned the implements from float copper, chunks of the mineral transported to the area by the Wisconsin Glacier.

Besides the abundant fish and game, a fresh water source attracted native people to the Cushing Park site. They called it Mokkejeewun, or Peace Spring. The spring's precise location is uncertain, as it no longer flows above ground. Also unknown is the place where Milton and Mary Cushing buried their third child, a son who died within a few days of his birth in 1839. The Cushings sold their farm to Alfred L. Castleman and Albert Alden when they left Wisconsin. In a poignant gesture prior to leaving, Mary purchased the child's burial plot from Castleman.

Crossing Margaret's millpond, we tether our canoe to her thin ice sign and knock on the door. She invites us in for sugary crullers and shows us the photos she'd taken of our trash haul the previous weekend.

"Did you find anything today?" she asks. "There can't be much left."

Puck gestures in the general direction of the canoe. "We have a couple of bags full—mostly cans and plastic bags and bottles. Also a lawnmower wheel, a Frisbee, a pot from a camper's cooking kit, some PVC pipe, and a broken canoe paddle. Our prize catch was a big two-handled tub, but we landed that soon enough to leave it in the Dumpster behind the fish hatchery."

"How about my cattle troughs? Did you see them?"

"We spotted one of them just downstream from the bridge to Cushing Park," I answer. "It's in deep water and more than we can handle from a canoe." Borrowing a piece of paper and a pen, I sketch a map showing the location of the trough and three barrels we'd also had to pass up. Knowing Margaret, we're confident that she will move heaven and earth and the Delafield Common Council to remove them. That's the kind of person she is. Our friendship with this persistent woman began on a June afternoon in 1997, when I sought out her expertise in Delafield history. What follows is an account of that first meeting.

When I rang the doorbell at 500 Mill Road in Delafield, a friendly, energetic woman in her late seventies greeted me in a pink turtleneck, turquoise sweatshirt, chinos, and tennis shoes. Margaret had put her personal stamp on this conventional attire by wearing the sweatshirt reversed, its cheerful embroidered chickadees toward the back.

"Please come in," she said, leading the way to a couple of chairs and a table spread with maps and documents. "I have a question for you."

She didn't get around to the question until later because the papers on the table reminded her of one story after another. These tumbled out in no particular order, and if I hadn't done some preliminary reading in the history of the area I would have been lost after five minutes. Margaret told me that her late husband, Kenneth Zerwekh, purchased the mill in 1947 and refitted it to generate electric power. Prior to World War II, when he lived in Madison and managed his family's brickmaking business, he often passed the white frame structure when driving to Milwaukee on US Highway 30. He asked the owner, George Apfelbacher, to let him know if he ever decided to sell the property. Zerwekh had occasion to recall the old mill while serving in an ordnance unit in France during the war. He noticed that French millers were spared the blackouts and power shortages that were part of wartime life for their neighbors. He was also intrigued by the prospect of doing modern work with an ancient technology.

After the war he found Apfelbacher ready to sell, but the mill was in a sad state. The building leaned north toward its reflection in the millrace. The machinery had been sold for scrap metal, leaving gaping holes in the floor and ceiling of the milling floor. A shed that protected the north side of the structure had been torn down, exposing the lower level to the elements. The fourteen-inch-square support beams were rotting at their base. During the postwar housing shortage Apfelbacher had nevertheless found renters who were willing to take a chance on the two apartments he had carved out of the cavernous interior.

Delafield residents were relieved when Zerwekh bought the old eyesore, for they assumed he would tear it down and build a contemporary home on the site. Instead, drawing on his training as an engineer, he brought the mill literally back from the brink. After jacking up the floors to level them, he jury-rigged an old elevator cable from the main beam on the third floor to the base of a nearby telephone pole. Over the next five years, with the help of a chain hoist and an occasional north wind, he gradually cranked the structure upright

Courtesy of Margaret Zerwekh

Hawks Mill early in the twentieth century, when it was
known as Nemahbin Roller Mills

and shimmed the support beams. He enclosed the lower level and installed
a turbine salvaged from a mill in Plymouth, Wisconsin. He connected the
turbine to a 1920 White truck transmission and a generator, likewise salvaged.

The machinery worked more or less efficiently until 2003, when it shut
down for the last time. Water was drawn from the millpond into the upper
section of the millrace, called the headrace. The headrace conveyed the water
to a pipelike penstock set over the turbine, a metal waterwheel enclosed in a
metal casing. The penstock directed the stream of water downward, spinning
the turbine's curved vanes horizontally around the vertical hub. From the
turbine water dropped into the tailrace, which returned it to the Bark River
downstream from the dam spillway.

Once the basic system was in place, Zerwekh tinkered with its compo-
nents to wring as much energy as possible from the moving water. In 1976
he replaced the original turbine, whose wheel was 17½ inches in diameter,
with a 26½-inch wheel salvaged from the Smith Brothers Flour Mill in nearby
Monches. That waterwheel, a fifteen-horsepower Francis turbine manufactured in 1876 by the James Leffel Company, still cranked the old truck transmission at the time of my visit. Waterpower eventually supplied 90 percent of
the electricity needed by Zerwekh's family of four. But it was years before the
power could be put to full domestic use, for Zerwekh resided in Madison.

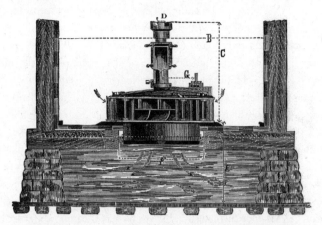

Society for the Preservation of Old Mills Archives

A Leffel turbine positioned in a millrace. Water entered at the top (D), spun the vanes of the waterwheel, and dropped (F) into the tailrace.

"He never considered this was going to be a home," Margaret recalled. "He thought it was just going to be a place to play with electricity."

The new toy required constant attention, however, and after renting the mill for a time he decided to remodel it for his own family. He and his first wife added a wing in 1953, with a kitchen on the first floor and a bedroom on the second. They turned the milling floor into a spacious living room with a limestone fireplace and large picture windows. They recycled a wooden millstone cover as a circular bench, its E. P. Allis manufacturer's plate still attached. They used pine boards from the grain chutes for wainscoting and sections of the grain elevator screw mechanism as supports for a yard light and a school bell. From the Wisconsin Brick and Block Corporation, Zerwekh's family business, they obtained the red brick with which they faced the entire south wing and the lower part of the main building.

Zerwekh's first marriage ended in divorce, and he married Margaret in March 1969. They were living in the mill when it caught fire that May. Awakened early on a Sunday morning by the barking of their dog, Blackie, they fled the building. Inspectors traced the fire to fireplace flues that hadn't been installed properly by the contractor. It spread from the wall behind the fireplace to other parts of the house, inflicting over twenty thousand dollars' worth of damage and destroying many antiques. Its effects can still be seen on a portion of the living room ceiling, where the charred log joists and planks of the second-story floor show through. Otherwise the beams and joists have been sandblasted down to sound wood and stained.

Though Kenneth Zerwekh died in 1990 at the age of seventy-nine, his desire to make the old mill a paying proposition was kept alive by his widow. In a good year Margaret generated a surplus of about fifty-eight thousand kilowatt hours of electricity, which she sold to the Wisconsin Electric Power Company (WEPCO) at the same rate that they charged their customers. Like her late husband, Margaret abhors waste and inefficiency. In 1997, contemplating the scrim of water that poured over the spillway rather than into the headrace, she remarked, "Those are dollar bills going over the spillway there. They should be going through my turbine." To harvest some of those dollars, she wanted to add another 26½-inch turbine and raise the level of the pond about six inches; but those alterations required the approval of the Public Service Commission and other state and local agencies.

Margaret knows from experience what the private dam owner is up against, financially. Her monthly WEPCO checks, which averaged about $290 in 1996, were adequate to feed the old truck transmission's appetite for grease and universal joints. But they didn't begin to offset the staggering cost of maintaining the dam. Except for the spillway, the Zerwekh dam is mostly an earthen dike about 250 feet long, and water has ways of getting around or through it.

In 1977 the DNR ordered the Zerwekhs to cut down all of the trees growing on the dam, some sixty-two of them. In 1994 the department required removal of the stumps as well. Trees blown over in a storm open holes at the top of a dike, and their roots can channel water through the structure. Trees also shade out grass that holds the topsoil in place. When Margaret first moved into the mill she could see the pond from her living room windows, framed by maples and box elders. Without those trees the pond had a starker appearance.

Still larger costs loomed in the future. Following a dam safety analysis completed at Margaret's expense in 1997, the DNR ordered her to prepare an emergency action plan in case of flooding. To prevent the dam from washing out during a flood, she also had to hire an engineer to devise ways of releasing the excess water. This might have entailed widening the spillway or installing a bypass around the north end of the dike.

Why did she persist in the face of natural hazards, state regulation, and red ink? The answer lies partly in Margaret's tenacious personality and partly in her special relationship with the past. An avid historian, she finds that the old mill connects her to the early days of Delafield, and to American pioneer history in general, in a way that books and documents cannot. On exhibit throughout the first floor of her home are paintings and photographs of old mills located in Wisconsin and elsewhere in North America. Margaret's mill is the subject of several historic photos, a couple of watercolors, and an abstract oil painting on glass, a gift from an art school graduate who used to mow her lawn. Portraits of previous owners, from Nelson Page Hawks through Kenneth Zerwekh, are also on display.

Margaret is a member of the Society for the Preservation of Old Mills, and she has offered her place as a site for one of the group's annual meetings. So far, the society has declined the offer in favor of operating sawmills and gristmills, preferably with wooden waterwheels.

"People think they have to see falling water," Margaret observed wryly. "And that's the thing that the artists like to paint."

Another offer has likewise gone begging. Her late husband's well-meaning improvements, particularly the red brick facing, disqualify the mill for the National Register of Historic Places. Beneath the brick is a white drop siding installed around 1900. Beneath that, Margaret has discovered, are red-stained boards that identify the building as the "red mill" mentioned by early settlers. Back then people usually called it Hawks Mill, after its original owner.

Nelson Page Hawks regards visitors from a framed photograph on Margaret's wall, taken five months prior to his death in June 1863. Though the crown of his head and his upper lip are hairless, a patriarchal beard cascades from his firmly set jaw, its corners unmarred in keeping with the Levitical code. A clay churchwarden's pipe depends from the left side of his mouth, and a burgherly girth displays his waistcoat to good advantage. His expression is rather severe, considering his reputation as a taproom wit and practical joker. Yet the picture projects a sense of contentment.

Hawks was the quintessential frontier figure, rising from obscure origins to a position of wealth and prominence. The *Milwaukee Sentinel* called him "one of the pioneer settlers in our state" and "a man of great energy." Hawks compiled a lengthy résumé of business ventures while moving from place to place in New York State and from New York to Wisconsin Territory. In Wisconsin he settled first in Aztalan on the Rock River, where he lived amicably in the neighborhood of three hundred Ho-Chunk Indians. Then he moved to Milwaukee, where he operated the Fountain House hotel on the corner of West Water and Second Streets.

Courtesy of Sauk County Historical Society

Nelson Page Hawks in 1863, sitting for a portrait by George Thomas

He sold the Fountain House in 1841 and came to Delafield as an innkeeper, enlarging a log cabin for the purpose until he could replace it with a grander structure in the Greek Revival style. Completed in 1846, the Delafield House, better known as Hawks Inn, was moved in 1960 from its original location on Genesee Street to its present location at 426 Wells Street. Today it serves as the headquarters of the Hawks Inn Historical Society and is open to the public for tours.

Immigrants heading west on the old Territorial Road stopped at the inn, as did wheat farmers heading east to Milwaukee with their harvest. Busy as it was, the Delafield House didn't exhaust Hawks's restless energy. Among his other business ventures in the 1840s were a Mississippi River steamboat and a 320-acre farm. He also became Albert Alden's partner in a sawmill west of the village, on the Bark River. Alden was a direct descendant of the John Alden who, as readers of Longfellow's poem recall, courted Priscilla Mullens on Miles Standish's behalf but ended up marrying her himself.

Alden had purchased sixty acres from Milton B. Cushing. In a letter of May 25, 1844, regarding the transaction, Cushing offered Alden a piece of advice: "Take care of your water rights." To emphasize the point he sketched a small hand in the margin, pointing to the sentence. Was he referring to the Milwaukee and Rock River Canal? Perhaps, though by this time it was clear that the project would never be completed. There was, however, another way that Alden could exercise his water rights. To reconstruct what he saw when he pondered his purchase, you have to go back to the time of the public land surveys.

Soon after the Potawatomi and Ho-Chunk tribes ceded their lands in southeastern Wisconsin to the United States in the early 1830s, federal surveyors went to work with chains and notebooks. They tamed the frontier in their own way, inscribing an imaginary grid of ranges, towns, and sections on the landscape in preparation for the sale of public land to squatters and speculators. Alden's purchase lay within that grid, straddling the Bark River between Nagawicka and Upper Nemahbin Lakes. When the surveyor ran the north-south line between Sections 17 and 18 in 1836, he jotted the following entry in his notebook:

Creek 30 links wide by measure
Rapid current 2½ feet deep
Stony bottom low banks WSW

The rapid current indicated a significant decline in elevation, a feature of interest to millers. In fact, Alexander M. Mitchell, the territorial engineer, told Territorial Governor Henry Dodge in 1839 that "one of the finest hydraulic powers in the Territory" could be created on the Bark River between the two lakes. John Heath had already seized the opportunity before Alden purchased his site. But with a sixteen-foot fall of water between Nagawicka and Upper Nemahbin—before Heath's dam at the Nagawicka outlet raised it another four to six feet—there was clearly room for a second waterpower downstream.

Though low, the river banks were firm, consisting probably of sedge meadow. The meadow supplied early settlers with marsh hay and inspired Delafield's original pseudo-Greek name, Hayopolis. The surveyor's notebook describes the land north of the river in Section 19 as level, with a scattering of white, black, and bur oaks. Oak savanna likewise covered the higher ground to the south, but that side would have been difficult to farm. There the Wisconsin Glacier had deposited irregular mounds of glacial till, producing a landscape that was, in the surveyor's words, "Broken & Hilly." In a day when dams were constructed of logs, rocks, and gravel, Alden's parcel must have seemed providentially appointed as a mill site.

There were no physical obstacles to building a dam with a head of ten feet or higher on the site. Nor were there significant legal obstacles. Under the Milldam Act of 1840 entrepreneurs could erect dams across non-navigable streams without seeking the approval of the Territorial Legislature or obtaining easements for the property that their millponds overflowed. Today the Bark River would be classified as a navigable stream because it floats canoes and other small boats during at least part of the year. But in the 1840s the legislature sought to encourage economic development, particularly the construction of saw- and gristmills, by reserving the "navigable" classification for rivers deep enough to carry large boats.

Alden therefore enjoyed the blessings of nature and civil authority when he began to construct a low dam and a sawmill on the land that he purchased from Cushing. Before finishing either, he took Nelson Page Hawks as his partner. They agreed in October 1846 that Hawks would complete the sawmill, using materials supplied by Alden. The latter would raise the dam to a five-foot head with the option to extend it to seven feet. At first the two were co-owners of the property, but Hawks eventually bought the mill and the land on which it was situated. Around 1847 he built a gristmill beside the sawmill and later added a turning lathe. On the 1850 census he reported grinding ten thousand bushels of wheat and sawing sixty thousand feet of lumber.

A wooden waterwheel may originally have powered the mill, for water turbines did not come into widespread use in Wisconsin until the 1850s. In a memoir written many years later, Hawks's son, Nelson Crocker Hawks, fondly recalled the overshot mill wheels of his boyhood, as though these were the norm. Apart from their aesthetic appeal, however, wooden wheels had distinct disadvantages. They required constant maintenance and iced up in the winter, whereas a turbine's metal casing protects its rotating vanes and other moving parts from the elements. Turbines are far more efficient than wooden water-wheels, a consideration that would have weighed heavily with proprietor Hawks. In 1852, if not earlier, he installed a state-of-the-art turbine.

Except for this improvement in power transmission, Hawks Mill ground wheat into flour by traditional means. The turbine drove three matching pairs, or "runs," of imported French burrstones. Each stone consisted of several smaller stones, or "burrs," that were cemented together and girdled by an iron band. The lower, or "bed," stone remained stationary. The upper, or "runner," stone was turned by a shaft that was linked by belts or gears to the turbine. Each run of stone was enclosed in a cylindrical wooden vat with a hopper on top and a spout on the side.

The wheat kernels were first cleaned of chaff and dirt, then fed through the hopper into the center, or "eye," of the stones. If the stones were properly spaced and sharpened, they sheared the outer coating of the wheat kernels, the bran, from the digestible endosperm. Furrows or grooves on the grinding faces of the stones directed the flour and bran toward the outside of the vat, where it exited from the spout. Then it was bolted—that is, sifted, usually through silk—and collected in bags or barrels. Five bushels of wheat produced one barrel of flour.

Hawks's son had warm memories of growing up around his father's mill. He recalled not only the gristmill but also the large "bull wheel" used to hoist logs from the pond into the sawmill. He enjoyed hitching a ride on the carriage that guided the logs through the jigging vertical blade, his pleasure doubtless enhanced by the peril. It must have been a noisy place, with all that sawing and grinding. Yet the summer symphony would otherwise have been incomplete, according to young Hawks's memoir:

> The mill pond was a paradise for frogs who serenaded the community every summer night, with full chorus of soprano, alto, treble and heavy bass, assisted sometimes by katydids, crickets and whippoorwills. The Mill, too, had its music by day. To the rushing sound of the water was added the tick-tack of hopper spindles, the gliding of the elevator cups and the tapping of the bolting frame—all this was music to the young-sters who played around the mill.

Hawks Mill hummed along nicely in the 1840s and 1850s, when wheat was still king in the region and flour milling a major industry. Had there been license plates in 1848 when the territory became a state, Wisconsin might have used that medium to proclaim itself America's Wheatland. Instead, the message was writ large on the landscape as settlers from New England, the Middle Atlantic states, and Europe poured into the Lake Michigan ports of Milwaukee and Chicago. Heading west in wagons, they took up 40-, 80-, or 160-acre parcels of wheat-growing land, choosing first the more desirable oak openings. Lacking sawmills in the beginning, they built log cabins and planted vegetable gardens to supply their own tables. Then they broke the prairie sod with ox-drawn plows and planted the rest of the land in wheat.

Yields remained low before midcentury, when the grain had to be planted, harvested, and threshed by hand. Thereafter, with the help of the grain drill, the McCormick reaper, and the threshing machine, the annual harvest rose steadily toward the peak of 29 million bushels in 1860, when Wisconsin ranked second only to Illinois in wheat production. Flour milling was then the state's foremost industry, accounting for 40 percent of its total industrial output.

The wheat boom might have continued indefinitely if farmers had learned from previous experience in the East or heeded the warnings in agricultural journals to diversify their crops. They did not, and by the 1870s the soil showed signs of exhaustion from monocropping. Chinch bugs and plant diseases claimed an increasing share of the annual harvest. By 1880 wheat was deposed as king, and Wisconsin was on its way to becoming America's Dairyland.

Before the boom went bust, the farmer's chief quandary was how to get his bonanza from local flour mills to the ports on Lake Michigan. The canal that might have made Delafield's fortune was never dug. Later, both the Watertown Plank Road and the railroad bypassed the village. So lucrative was the market for wheat, however, that there was still plenty of grist for Hawks Mill and its competitor upstream.

Unable to be everywhere at once, Hawks entrusted the daily operation of his mill to a succession of millers and sawyers. After 1854 he called the enterprise Twin Mills, partly in reference to its flouring and sawing operations, partly as a tribute to three sets of twins born to his millers' wives. On display in Margaret's private museum are a couple of barrel stencils with the words "Twin Mills / Extra / Family / Flour / N.P. Hawks." The syntax is intriguing. Did the "extra" apply to "flour" or to "family"? If the latter, it promised more than nutrition to the families that consumed it.

Hawks's extended family of millers included its share of black sheep. His son characterized one as a "rascal we never could get a cent from." Hawks suspected another, named Reynolds, of selling toll wheat—grain paid in return for the mill's services—for his own profit. Reynolds apparently shipped the wheat under cover of darkness to a brother-in-law in Watertown, who sold it at the going rate, over a dollar a bushel.

A fire in 1853 simultaneously confirmed Hawks's suspicions and destroyed the incriminating evidence. When Hawks checked Reynolds's books in late December, he found that there should have been about three thousand bushels of toll wheat stored on the third floor. To Hawks there appeared to be far less. He ordered the wheat to be weighed, a process that would normally have taken a couple of days to complete. The inventory never went beyond the first day, for the mill burned to the ground on the night of December 23.

Fire was never far from a miller's mind. Flour mills resembled wooden chimneys, with their three-story structure and fluelike elevators. Under certain conditions, when flour dust was suspended in the enclosed rooms, they would explode like a powder magazine if ignited. We can imagine Hawks's helplessness as he watched the mill go up in flames. Ice covered the millpond, preventing access to water that might have been used to fight the blaze. To make matters worse, Hawks had been recovering from an illness and had been unable to travel to Milwaukee to renew the insurance policy on the property. Consequently, the policy had lapsed and the mill was a total loss.

The following spring Hawks took out a loan and began to rebuild. The new Hawks Mill is the one in which Margaret lives today. Does it occupy the same site as the original mill? She has yet to find out for sure. Charred timbers were discovered along the foundation of the current mill's south wing, but these may have been dumped there as fill. Testimony in a 1916 lawsuit suggests that Hawks's first mill was located farther north on the earthen dike, perhaps on the opposite bank of the river. But remnants of the older mill have yet to be discovered.

It may be easier to unearth the original mill than to recover the real Nelson Page Hawks. By and large, the historical record paints a flattering portrait of the man. His descendants and members of the Hawks Inn Historical Society are proud to be associated with a pioneer who served Delafield not only as innkeeper and entrepreneur but also as postmaster and justice of the peace. According to records in the Waukesha County District Court, however, the life of this model citizen was clouded for several years by scandal.

On August 31, 1847, a young woman named Ophelia A. Jones (née Finch) appeared before Justice of the Peace Vernon Tichenor and alleged that Hawks had tried to rape her on August 3. Furthermore, she claimed, he "did beat, wound, and ill treat" her in the process. Judging that there was probable cause for a charge of felonious assault, Tichenor issued a warrant for Hawks's arrest. The following day Hawks pleaded not guilty and moved for an adjournment of the proceedings. He was granted that adjournment and two others during the month of September, then failed to appear in court in October, supposedly due to an accident caused by runaway horses.

On February 25, 1848, a grand jury formally indicted Hawks for "assault with intent to ravish." The case was continued several times over the next twenty-one months, on one occasion because Hawks professed to be too sick to leave his house. Finally, on November 27, 1849, the prosecution asked the court to dismiss the case. It did so, but held Hawks liable for the costs of the suit.

These are the bare facts of the court case, dots that might be connected with any number of storylines. Is this the tale of a prosperous and well-connected man in the prime of life (Hawks was in his late forties) who took advantage of a powerless young woman, possibly an employee, on the assumption that she wouldn't dare complain? Or is it the story of a calculating woman who tried to extort money from, or take revenge upon, a man who had a reputation to protect? Why did Ophelia wait four weeks before approaching the justice, by which time her injuries would no longer have been obvious? Did her family—her husband, Gilbert N. Jones, and two members of the Finch family are named in the court subpoenas—abet or discourage the suit? Did the district attorney give up because the plaintiff and witnesses had lost their will to press the suit or because he saw no way to prevent Hawks from dragging it out indefinitely? We're unlikely ever to have answers to these questions.

When Hawks died in 1863, less than half a year after sitting for the portrait on Margaret's wall, his son chose not to pursue his father's business ventures. The mill and its forty acres were sold for $5,000 (about $89,600 today), which the younger Hawks believed to be a mere third of the property's real value. The mill passed through the hands of several owners before being purchased in 1872 by William Notbohm. During Notbohm's tenure the mill came to be known as Nemahbin Roller Mills, a name that reflects a revolution in grain milling technology.

For thousands of years prior to the mid-nineteenth century, wheat was ground between stones. Because stone of sufficient hardness and porosity was difficult to find in the New World, millstones weighing up to 3,500 pounds were imported at considerable expense from quarries in France and other parts of Europe. The grinding face needed to be dressed periodically with a steel pick to sharpen the grooves radiating from the center. Two men usually required ten hours to dress a single run of stone. Then the runner stone had to be balanced over the bed stone in such a way that they did not touch, yet were close enough to shear the bran from the kernels.

If the stones were improperly dressed or spaced, the kernels would not be ground evenly. Or the bran would be crushed rather than sheared, making it harder to sift from the flour. If the layer of gluten cells immediately beneath the bran was removed along with the bran, the flour was unsuitable for baking. If the flour was ground too fine by a dull stone, it felt oily and clogged the bolting cloth. When the grinding apparatus was expertly tuned and sharpened, the flour passed the test described by Oliver Evans, an eighteenth-century miller and millwright whom Jerry Apps quotes in *Mills of Wisconsin and the Midwest*:

> Catch your hand full, and holding the palm up, shut it briskly; if the greatest quantity of the meal fly out and escape between your fingers, it shows it to be in a fine and lively state, the stones sharp, the bran thin, and that it will bolt well: but the greater the quantity that stays in the hand, the more faulty is the flour.

Achieving the desired effect with the ponderous stones was like performing surgery with an axe. There had to be an easier way, and there was added
incentive to find one as spring wheat began to replace winter wheat in the
Midwest. The harder, more brittle bran cover of the spring wheat tended to
shatter into tiny bits when passed between stones. The smaller bran particles
passed through the bolting cloth and darkened the flour. The larger particles,
when sifted out, took the gluten with them.

Roller mills were the answer to a miller's prayers. Developed chiefly in
Switzerland, the roller mill worked much like a clothes wringer. The wheat was
passed between revolving iron or steel cylinders, usually twice. Corrugated
rollers broke the kernel open on the first pass. The chaff was then sifted from
the "middlings," which were passed between smooth rollers to produce the
flour. The rollers did not need to be dressed, and their spacing could be
adjusted easily. Millers in southeastern Wisconsin were particularly fortunate
in having a manufacturer of roller mills nearby. Edward P. Allis and Company
of Milwaukee, which merged in 1901 with three other manufacturers to form
the Allis-Chalmers Company, was already producing French burrstones and
silk bolting cloth. The company began to manufacture roller mills in the 1870s
and was soon the nation's leading producer of the new machinery.

Nemahbin Roller Mills was typical of small mills in the way that it assimilated the new technology. Though William Notbohm and his successor, George
Apfelbacher, did most of their work with roller machines, they kept a run of
stone for custom flouring. According to Margaret Zerwekh, Apfelbacher was
so particular about his millstones that he dressed them weekly. Rather than
rely on the flour-in-hand test, he carried a sample to Notbohm's daughters,
who lived nearby, and had them test its quality in baking. Apfelbacher ground
eight hundred to one thousand bushels of wheat per year, some of it winter
wheat brought in from Minnesota and the Dakotas. He mixed the winter
wheat with local spring wheat and sold his proprietary blend in Milwaukee.

As dairying replaced wheat growing in Wisconsin, Nemahbin Roller Mills
did less flouring and more custom milling of corn, barley, oats, and rye for
livestock. Even this trade declined during the 1930s, when portable hammer
mills began to tour the countryside. These produced a coarse meal that was
adequate for feeding livestock and poultry, and saved farmers a trip to the mill.
Business at Nemahbin Roller Mills fell off accordingly. In 1946 Apfelbacher
retired as a miller and converted the building to apartments. The following
year he sold it to Kenneth Zerwekh.

It was sometime during the Apfelbacher regime that the last pair of French burrstones disappeared, a casualty of the flour dynasties in Minneapolis. A couple of the burrs remain in Margaret's yard, one cemented into a concrete wall at the headrace. Others may lie in the silt deposited behind the dam. In 1975, when a Delafield couple began remodeling a nearby building that had once been a grocery store, the Zerwekhs asked them to look for the missing millstones. Sure enough, the couple found three stones along the building's foundation. Margaret suspects that these are from the mill upstream rather than Hawks Mill because they are made from solid blocks of stone rather than burrs cemented together. The Zerwekhs nevertheless had a pair of the stones hauled by tractor to their current resting place beside the driveway.

At Margaret's invitation, I climbed a spiral staircase to the second floor of the mill. Then I mounted a rickety ladder to the third floor, where a flour dust collector and other odds and ends of milling equipment are stored. No country kitsch occupies her attic, just the queer, ungainly implements of pioneer labor. All was quiet save for the hum of the generator and the sound of water passing through the turbine and dropping into the tailrace. Dusk was settling in by the time I returned to the main floor, and Margaret had switched on a lamp over her table.

She had remembered the question she wanted to ask me in my capacity as a college professor. Riffling through papers on the table, she pulled out a brochure from the continuing education program at a local college campus. "Do you think that I should take this course?" she asked, her finger on an offering entitled "Embracing a Sense of Place." I hesitated, wondering how you can embrace something as volatile as a sense of place. Isn't it most authentic when you cannot grasp it, when it flies out and escapes between your fingers like expertly ground flour? I doubted that the course had anything to offer Margaret, and told her so. At Hawks Mill the sense of place was still in a fine and lively state.

～～～～～

Though Margaret continued to generate electrical power in the years following my first visit to the mill, the venture became less and less profitable. Soon she was paying more to maintain the equipment than she received from selling electricity to the power company. When a chunk of concrete from the headrace washed into the turbine in 2003, it brought to a shuddering halt the experiment that Kenneth Zerwekh had undertaken a half century earlier.

Margaret advertised two turbines and a generator in a millers trade journal and sold them to an Amish community in Pennsylvania that was restoring its old mill.

Margaret no longer needed the millpond, but she was still under pressure from the DNR to bring her dam up to current safety standards. Unable to pay for its reconstruction, she filed for abandonment of the dam in October 2004. Though far less expensive than reconstruction, abandonment can be a costly procedure. The dam owner is responsible not only for removing the structure but also for restoring the natural river channel. Yet Margaret's decision was not exclusively economic, for she shares the DNR's belief that rivers are healthier, environmentally speaking, without dams and millponds.

A group of property owners with frontage on the north and south shores of the pond saw it otherwise. They estimated their property would lose a million dollars of its value without the pond. The Delafield Common Council agreed, though it couched its objections in environmental and recreational terms. Removal of the dam would, it claimed, result in the loss of animal habitat and opportunities for fishing, boating, and skating.

When Margaret refused to sell her property to the city, the common council passed an ordinance authorizing the use of eminent domain to acquire it if she proceeded with abandonment. Delafield never exercised that authority and later rescinded the ordinance. The common council had good cause to reconsider. A consultant advised the city that the dam would have to be replaced, not merely repaired, at a cost of $650,000 to $850,000. Where would the money come from—city taxes or a special assessment on shoreline property owners? Did the millpond benefit all residents, or chiefly those with water frontage?

The DNR placed Margaret's abandonment request on hold to allow the interested parties—Margaret, the city, and the riparian landowners—to work out their differences. These escalated into a lawsuit in 2005, when the landowners sued to prevent the DNR from issuing a permit to abandon the dam. The suit proved unsuccessful.

The stalemate persisted until the late spring of 2008, when another interested party, the Bark River, declared its position. Over eight inches of rain fell on the upper Bark watershed on June 7 and 8, raising Nagawicka Lake to the top of a newly constructed dam at the river outlet. To avert a washout, the city sandbagged the earthen dike on either side of the spillway and released water downstream. The overflow flooded a private residence and a couple of commercial buildings in downtown Delafield. It damaged Margaret's millrace, tearing away boards that had blocked the headrace since 2003 and dislodging some of the stones that lined the race.

Concerned lest floodwaters breach the dike and threaten life and property downstream, the DNR ordered removal of spillway flashboards to lower the level of the pond. A contractor installed sheet metal across the headrace entrance as a temporary fix. Even so, enough of the Bark River went over the spillway to flood about thirteen homes downstream and render the west end of Main Street impassable. A man drowned when he tried to drive his car through the water.

In early July, after the immediate threat of flooding had passed, the DNR ordered that the millpond be drawn down gradually and remain in that state until the dam was either removed or reconstructed. To stabilize the exposed sediment, estimated at 52,000 cubic yards, the DNR seeded shoreline belonging to the city and several of the lawsuit plaintiffs with winter wheat (an annual grass that would not interfere with restoration of the pond) and most of the rest with wheat and wetland perennials. The department was anxious to avoid what happened when it had removed Funk's Dam from the Oconomowoc River a decade earlier. Torrential rains during drawdown had flushed thousands of pounds of sediment into North Lake.

By the end of August the pond was gone. Forlorn, stranded docks and an occasional boat overlooked twelve acres of mud flat. The Bark groped its way in shallow rivulets, searching for a channel. Weary combatants on both sides of the dam abandonment issue were likewise looking for a way out. In April 2009 a channel seemed briefly to open up. The common council considered a request by the riparian property owners to form a lake management district, which would have allowed them to borrow money to rebuild the dam. However, four of the seven Council members voted against it, fearing that the city would be liable for debts incurred by the district. Then on April 21 an administrative law judge announced his decision, based on hearings the previous December, that the DNR should issue an abandonment permit.

City officials, including some who had supported restoration of the millpond, were relieved to put the controversy behind them. However, the judge's decision merely triggered additional rounds of litigation. The millpond property owners immediately sued the state to overturn the April 2009 ruling. That suit was dismissed, but a couple of years later, when the Delafield Plan Commission issued the final permit for dismantling the dam, a half-dozen neighbors sued both the city and Margaret, again claiming that removal would diminish the value of their property and the quality of their lives. This time a county circuit court judge allowed the suit to go forward against Margaret but not against the city.

Following a jury trial in February 2012, the jurors decided unanimously that the plaintiffs are not entitled to millpond access or benefits and Margaret is not responsible for any financial loss they may have suffered. Barring a successful appeal, it appears that Margaret's dam will finally go the way of all the other privately owned dams on the Bark River. Those that remain will belong to municipalities: the village of Merton, the city of Delafield (Nagawicka Lake dam), and the town of Sullivan (Rome Pond).

Today dam removal is driven not only by familiar economic realities—the cost of repair and replacement—but also by public policy that has begun to reflect our changing relationship to natural resources. In his 1949 book *A Sand County Almanac*, Wisconsin environmentalist Aldo Leopold traced the evolution of a "land ethic" from the old human-centered notions of right and wrong. Milton B. Cushing's "Take care of your water rights" epitomized the ethic of the 1840s. Revised for the twenty-first century, his advice might be "Take care of your water's rights."

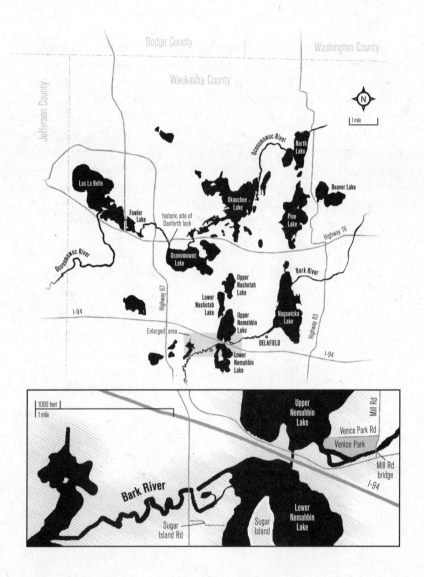

Dodge County

Washington County

Jefferson County

Waukesha County

N

1 mile

Oconomowoc River

North Lake

Lac La Belle

Beaver Lake

Fowler Lake

Okauchee Lake

historic site of Danforth lock

Pine Lake

Highway 16

Oconomowoc River

Oconomowoc Lake

Bark River

I-94

Highway 67

Upper Nashotah Lake

Lower Nashotah Lake

Upper Nemahbin Lake

Nagawicka Lake

Highway 83

Enlarged area

DELAFIELD

I-94

Lower Nemahbin Lake

1000 feet

1 mile

Upper Nemahbin Lake

Mill Rd

Venice Park Rd

Venice Park

Mill Rd bridge

I-94

Bark River

Sugar Island Rd

Sugar Island

Lower Nemahbin Lake

CHAPTER 7

Hawks Mill to
Lower Nemahbin Lake

W e are blissfully ignorant of the dam's troubled future on our Memorial Day outing. The millpond still laps at the dike and the turbine still cranks out kilowatts as we take leave of Margaret Zerwekh. We lift our canoe onto the dike and carry it to the river. Before launching we take a few minutes to scout the Mill Road bridge. On the upstream side a section of chain-link fence blocks access from the road but leaves sufficient clearance below for a canoe. A couple of Margaret's domestic geese eye us from the spillway as we step into the boat and let the river carry us under the bridge, ducking to avoid the fence. The current quickens to a sluice-like run between brushy banks, then stalls as we drop down to the cottages and docks that crowd both sides of the passage to Upper Nemahbin Lake.

Here the slack water is choked with weeds. Arriving at the island where the cleanup crew removed twenty-one tires, we veer left, following the original river channel. The water is shallow, and swamp loosestrife is doing its part to obstruct motorboat traffic. We swing right around the lower end of the island and paddle against the current to the upper end. Though man-made, the channel on this side is wider and deeper. The cottages on its north bank are set well back from the water and shaded by mature oak and hickory trees.

We are looking at Venice Park, a forty-acre parcel that Charles Cuno purchased in 1905 from heirs of Albert Alden. It was apparently Cuno who dredged the channel before platting the subdivision in 1906. The development included three lots north of Venice Park Road with frontage on Upper Nemahbin Lake, and as many as nineteen lots south of the road, fronting on the Bark River and the channel. Though deep, most of the lots are relatively narrow, with about seventy to eighty feet of shoreline. Given such proximity to their neighbors, residents could hardly expect Thoreauvian solitude. Real estate agent W. S. McDowell marketed the development as an "ideal colony of summer homes." Anticipating one obstacle to ideal harmony, McDowell assured potential buyers that no liquor would be sold in Venice Park.

Among those who found that prospect attractive was Milwaukee's health commissioner, Dr. G. A. Bading, who paid $1,200 (about $29,700 today) for a lot. Ease of transportation may also have figured in his decision, for the Milwaukee Electric Railroad had recently completed the Waukesha-Oconomowoc leg of its line to Watertown. Hourly service connected Venice Park to Milwaukee. According to McDowell, commuters could make the trip in about forty-five minutes.

McDowell's clients occupied a modest niche in the social hierarchy of Waukesha County's lake country. During the last decade of the nineteenth century, barons of industry from Chicago, Milwaukee, and St. Louis had built imposing estates on Oconomowoc Lake and two neighboring bodies of water, Lac La Belle and Fowler Lake. There, more or less aloof from the local population, they staged the rituals of fashionable society on expansive lawns. The local press and Chicago newspapers dutifully reported their annual arrivals and departures; their costly construction projects, fetes, and travels; their engagements, marriages, and scandals.

Those who summered at this "Newport of the Midwest"—a title to which Lake Geneva also lay claim—delighted in excursions aboard power launches. In an effort to extend their cruising range, residents of Lac La Belle formed a joint stock company during the 1880s to facilitate passage to Fowler Lake. Created originally as a millpond above a dam on the Oconomowoc River, Fowler was eight feet higher than La Belle. The seven-thousand-dollar project involved building locks and dredging a short section of the Oconomowoc River. There proved to be too few users to pay for maintaining the locks, however, and they were removed after five years.

In 1892 property owners on Oconomowoc Lake advanced a bolder scheme. They would link the seven lakes in the Oconomowoc River chain (La Belle, Fowler, Oconomowoc Lake, Okauchee, North, Pine, and Beaver) to the five in the Bark River chain (Upper and Lower Nashotah, Upper and Lower Nemahbin, and Nagawicka) by dredging the natural waterways between the lakes and digging two canals. A half-mile canal would cut through the marsh and a ridge separating Oconomowoc Lake from Upper Nashotah Lake. A canal of roughly the same length would connect Pine and Nagawicka Lakes.

Complicating the project was the significant variation in water levels among the lakes. Upper Nashotah was about nine feet higher than Oconomowoc, and Pine about eleven feet higher than Nagawicka, so two locks would have to be constructed on each canal. Besides the differences between the two watersheds, there were variations within each chain. The lock between La Belle and Fowler would have to be reconstructed. Upper Nashotah, at the north end of the Bark River chain, was higher than Lower Nemahbin, at the south end. Advocates of the project proposed to construct a dam at the Bark River's exit from Lower Nemahbin to bring four of the lakes in this chain—all but Nagawicka—to the same level.

At a meeting in July 1892 the Oconomowoc Lake residents formed a committee to approach landowners whose cooperation would be essential to the project. Mason M. Hill, who owned the crucial parcel between Oconomowoc and Upper Nashotah, not only offered an easement for the canal but also dug half of it at his own expense in September 1894, partly to provide water access to a marshy section of his land. He and several others incorporated as the Oconomowoc Lake Waterway and Improvement Company in January 1895. State Assemblyman Caleb C. Harris then approached the Assembly Committee on Incorporations with a bill that would authorize the company to proceed. They hoped to complete the project by the upcoming Fourth of July.

The assembly bill proved highly controversial and sheds light on the social and environmental attitudes of the era. Supporters claimed that opening the lakes to power launches would raise property values and attract tourists to the lakeside resorts, shops, and taverns. Dredging the natural river channels and constructing canals would beautify the landscape by replacing pestiferous marshes with dry banks on which homes could be built. This was a compelling argument in a day when marshes, bogs, and fens had yet to be appreciated as "wetlands." The dam at the Lower Nemahbin outlet would improve the lake's appearance by drowning the weeds in its shallower areas.

Opponents of the bill fell into several categories. Millers on the Bark River downstream from the lakes feared diversion of water to the Oconomowoc watershed through the Upper Nashotah–Oconomowoc canal. Property owners on the Nashotah and Nemahbin lakes valued privacy and a quiet retreat from the noise and bustle of the city. They dreaded invasion by an armada of power launches. Residents of the flood-prone area near the Bark's entrance into Upper Nemahbin worried about the elevated lake level. Waukesha County taxpayers were concerned about costs incidental to the project, such as the construction and maintenance of bridges where canals intersected with roads. The administration and faculty of Nashotah Mission (today's Nashotah House), an Episcopal divinity school on Upper Nashotah, expected to lose both their serenity and their picturesque shoreline. Bishop Nicholson vowed to go personally to Madison to oppose the bill.

Responding to these objections, proponents said that boat traffic on Upper Nashotah would be seasonal, when the divinity school was not in session. Regarding the loss of Bark River water, they claimed that it would be offset by Oconomowoc River water entering Nagawicka Lake through the Pine Lake canal. The dam at the Lower Nemahbin outlet would, they asserted, raise that lake only about a foot—not enough to flood shorelines farther up the chain. Finally, with $20,000 in declared assets (about $536,000 today) the Oconomowoc Lake Waterway and Improvement Company felt prepared to cover all costs of the project.

Lurking behind the technical, fiscal, and environmental concerns, but left mostly unspoken, were social, cultural, and political issues. Many people suspected that Philip D. Armour, the Chicago meat-packing millionaire who owned a large estate on Oconomowoc Lake, had originated the scheme and directed one of his own attorneys to draft the bill. Though the bill proposed ostensibly "to increase the attractions of the lakes as a summer resort," its chief beneficiaries would be the Oconomowoc-Fowler-La Belle plutocrats. Their private corporation was asking the state of Wisconsin to allow them to seize property by eminent domain and collect tolls from all users of the canals and locks.

In the days leading up to consideration of the bill, the *Milwaukee Sentinel* and the *Waukesha Daily Freeman* published letters pro and con. On the Sunday preceding the vote the *Sentinel* ran an editorial that must have gladdened the hearts of cottage owners on the Nashotah and Nemahbin lakes. It said, in part,

> An instance of the crude power of money in our American life, of the manner in which it seeks to over-ride private rights . . . is afforded by the proposed confiscation of riparian property and disregard of the wishes of small property owners in a bill now pending before the legislature. . . . The wealthy sojourners at Oconomowoc, not content with three extensive sheets of water for their pleasuring, any one of which would hold the little chain of four with ample room to spare, are clamorous to annex the small lakes to their waterway, that they may enjoy a new diversion for an idle hour.

The bill faced heavy opposition when it came before the assembly committee on March 13, and Assemblyman Harris withdrew it from consideration.

For several years thereafter, the scheme to connect the Waukesha County lakes appeared moribund, if not dead. Though water links within the Oconomowoc-Fowler-La Belle chain became an issue in the local elections of 1898, the high cost of obtaining easements thwarted any progress. But if property owners on the Bark River lakes had begun to feel secure from attack by the Oconomowoc navy, they were proven wrong by events that unfolded rapidly during the spring and summer of 1899.

In July the newspapers broke an astonishing story of legal stealth. Following their defeat in 1895 the Oconomowoc group had formed a secret company. They raised the money to hire a Milwaukee lawyer, Lynn S. Pease, and send him to Green Lake in Green Lake County. There Pease agitated among wealthy lake residents for a canal connection to the Fox River. The Green Lake association petitioned the legislature for authority to condemn property in the canal right-of-way, modeled on similar legislation for railroad companies. On April 28 the legislature passed Chapter 288 of the Wisconsin statutes, allowing for such a procedure anywhere in the state.

Armed with the new bill, Pease wasted no time getting to Waukesha to search the titles of land for purchase or condemnation by the Oconomowoc group. Their secret association went public and sold shares as the Oconomowoc Waterways Company. This time they laid out their plans like a military campaign. During its first phase the company would connect Lac La Belle to Fowler and then Oconomowoc. By 1900 they hoped to begin work on the canal to Upper Nashotah and the other lakes in the Nashotah-Nemahbin group. Though they did not plan initially to dig a canal between Pine Lake and Nagawicka, they suggested that the network might ultimately include not only those lakes but also Pewaukee Lake, well to the east.

The venture would require substantial capital. Rather than construct a lock at the eight-foot rise from La Belle to Fowler, they planned to build a narrow-gauge railway to carry boats up to thirty-five feet long across the isthmus between the two lakes, a distance of about two hundred feet. They would build four locks during the first phase—one between Fowler and Oconomowoc, two between Oconomowoc and Upper Nashotah, and one between the two Nemahbins. Beside the railway and each lock they would construct a keeper's cottage in a small, attractively landscaped park.

The tone of the 1899 campaign differed markedly from that of 1895. This time there was no pretense of generating business for the lake resorts or enhancing scenery for the common weal. Now, according to the *Wisconsin State Journal*, company investors sought frankly "to increase their opportunities for pleasure." Boaters who had formerly used natural waterways and portages to travel from lake to lake could expect to pay a toll on future excursions. A rowboat passing through a lock could be charged up to twenty-five cents for the boat (equivalent to slightly under seven dollars today) and five cents for each passenger. Philip D. Armour, who had remained discreetly in the background in 1895, offered to contribute liberally to the project.

Faced with this display of bare-knuckled capitalism backed by state law, opponents of the waterway scheme might well have resigned themselves to defeat. In August 1899 the Waterways Company began work on the marine railway. During the following summer it built a keeper's cottage at the Fowler terminus and remodeled a building across the street as a station—the Loiterers' Club, it was called—where passengers could wait in comfort while their launches were transported. At the Oconomowoc Lake terminus the Armour family constructed a lock and a keeper's cottage where the Oconomowoc River exited the lake. In June 1901 a mail boat inaugurated regular delivery to residents of the three lakes. For twenty-five cents passengers could also enjoy a twelve-mile excursion aboard the boat.

Mysteriously, though, the grander scheme of connecting the two lake systems never materialized. Mason Hill had sold one of the parcels between Oconomowoc and Upper Nashotah Lakes to E. J. Lindsay. Rather than extend Hill's canal toward Upper Nashotah, Lindsay began dredging the marsh to create

CAN BE
CHARTERED
FOR
EXCURSIONS
ON
Oconomowoc
Fowler and
La Belle
Lakes.

RATES
For Parties
of 15 or less
$1.50 per hour.
10c per hour
for each
additional
person

LEAVES
Ernst &
Thompson's
Dock
Daily at
7 a. m. and
6:45 p. m.
Sundays at
9 a. m.

Fare for
Round
Trip
25c

U. S. MAIL AND EXCURSION STEAMER "OCONOMOWOC."
PLYING THE OCONOMOWOC WATERWAYS, THROUGH THE CANAL, LOCK, OCONOMOWOC AND FOWLER LAKES,
DISTANCE 12 MILES.

Great Lakes Marine Collection of the Milwaukee Public Library / Wisconsin Marine Historical Society
The Oconomowoc *mail and excursion boat, about 1901*

firm land for building. In mid-October 1899 the *Milwaukee Sentinel* reported the abandonment of the projected Oconomowoc-Upper Nashotah canal without citing a reason. The Oconomowoc Waterways Company remained in business to maintain the Oconomowoc-Fowler-La Belle improvements until 1908, when the company forfeited its rights and privileges for failure to file annual reports. Though the forfeiture was rescinded in 1911 because the company claimed to own real estate, it reported no actual business between 1911 and 1930. The state finally drove a stake through its corporate heart in 1932, long after the company's original officers and shareholders had passed away.

Why did the Oconomowoc Waterways Company give up on the more ambitious plan? Did the project cost more than the company was able to raise through the sale of stock? Or was it unable to acquire the necessary rights-of-way? According to the 1899 statute, at least three-fourths of property owners in a canal right-of-way had to agree to the canal before the company could initiate condemnation proceedings against holdouts. Philip D. Armour's absence may also have made a difference at this critical juncture. He was away for much of the time in Europe, seeking a cure for the health problems that would cause his death in January 1901. Whatever the reason, the Bark and Oconomowoc Rivers, arising within three miles of one another in the glacial terrain of Washington County, would continue to take their separate ways to the Rock River.

A few draw strokes at bow and stern serve to pivot our canoe in the Venice Park channel, and we drop down to Upper Nemahbin Lake. Here we enter not merely another waterway but another era. Traffic on the interstate combines with the revving of motorcycles at a lakeside tavern, the buzz-saw whine of motorboats and jet skis, and a portable radio on a nearby dock, producing a high-decibel din. As we paddle toward the channel to Lower Nemahbin, a young man roars by in a 145-horsepower outboard, oblivious not only of us but also of a white boat bumper float that marks the site of DNR research into zebra mussel infestation of the lake. Clearly all is not well with Nemahbin, which is under assault by more than one invasive species.

It is hard not to feel nostalgia for the days of the steam launches, though that period was by no means free of mayhem, especially as the Gilded Age faded into Prohibition. Our bow points toward the southern shore of Upper Nemahbin, where the mobster Jack Zuta met his end. A Jew born in Poland, Zuta came to the United States and eventually became chief of vice operations for George "Bugs" Moran on Chicago's North Side. In that capacity he planned the murder of Alfred Lingle, a *Chicago Tribune* crime reporter who may have tried to shake him down for protection money. Lingle was friendly with Al Capone, whose gang had taken out five members of the Moran-Aiello gang, together with a couple of nonmembers, in the Saint Valentine's Day Massacre of 1929. Feeling the Chicago heat, Zuta reacted as many Chicagoans still do. He lit out for Wisconsin's lake country.

On the evening of August 1, 1930, members of the Capone gang caught up with Zuta at the Lake View Hotel on Upper Nemahbin. The mobster was in the hotel dance pavilion, dropping coins in the player piano and watching couples dance, when several men walked in and opened up with machine guns and a pistol. The death certificate recorded eleven bullet wounds in the victim's torso, mouth, and brain. The mortician who prepared the body for viewing thought-fully left Zuta's chest exposed so that curious visitors could count the hits for themselves. Though it was little consolation to the dead man, prosecutors found in his warehouse and safety deposit boxes sufficient evidence to indict dozens of corrupt politicians.

The Lake View Hotel was torn down in the 1960s to make way for Interstate 94. A piece of the Bark River disappeared then, too. Old postcards show a sunlit stream connecting the two Nemahbins, bordered on the east by wetland and on the west by wooded higher ground. Rowboats are tethered on the downstream side of a low bridge across the river. Today a busy public boat landing occupies the space between the east- and westbound lanes of the interstate. It is a relief to emerge from the labyrinth of concrete pylons and see, directly ahead, the familiar profile of Sugar Island. We marvel for the hundredth time—an exaggeration, but not by much—at its serene presence in the midst of a highly developed and heavily used lake.

"Wouldn't it be fun to live there?" Puck asks, gesturing toward houses barely visible on the island's wooded ridge. "But how do people get to their homes?"

"A man named Harvey Kuhlman deserves the prize for the most original solution to that challenge. He drove an amphibious car to the island in 1977."

"Really?"

"Really. He was the developer who built the first homes on Sugar Island in the 1950s. Until then it had remained more or less in its natural state since the Potawatomi came each spring to tap its trees for maple sugar. The early settlers followed their example. Remember Nelson Crocker Hawks, the son of the Delafield innkeeper? He had fond memories of maple-sugaring expeditions to the island in the mid-nineteenth century. Later it acquired a reputation as the place to find rare wildflowers."

Puck has stopped paddling. She shades her eyes with one hand for a clearer view of the island shoreline. "So all those people used boats to get out there?"

"You can walk across when the lake is frozen, as Hawks and his friends did. You can also wade and swim. Otherwise, yes, boats are the only way. You saw all those signs at the end of the road, saying that the landing is reserved for the use of Sugar Island residents."

"Why not extend Sugar Island Road out to the island? It can't be more than two hundred yards."

"A plausible solution, and one that has pitted owners of island property against various other groups and agencies since at least 1907." I tell Puck the story of Lorenz Wagner, a Milwaukee real estate developer who bought the island, platted forty-four lots on its twenty-eight acres, and began construction of a causeway linking it to the lake's western shore in 1921. The State Railroad Commission halted the project because it would have obstructed navigation. Wagner bided his time until 1923, when he hoped that a turnover in the state legislature would favor an appeal to the Joint Highway Committee. Without road access, he claimed, the island lacked commercial value. To make matters worse, it was attracting back-to-nature types. He told the committee that he once found twenty-six rowboats pulled up on shore. "I got on the island," he testified, "and it looked like a Garden of Eden. I never saw so many naked people in my life, both men and women."

"What did he do?" Puck asks. "Banish them from the Garden and post an angel with a flaming sword?"

"Alas, there is no record of his response. But he persisted in trying to build the road, even when lakeshore residents claimed that it would cause stagnation and silting on that side of the lake. When a circuit court found in their favor, Wagner took the matter to the State Supreme Court and lost again. In May 1925 the court ordered him to cease construction and remove the section he'd already built, all four hundred feet of it."

"I'll bet he was one angry fella."

"Angry? Hell hath no fury like a developer scorned. This is where it gets ugly. Shortly after the court decision Wagner called a meeting of lakeshore property owners and presented an ultimatum. He claimed to have paid $32,000 for the island, though it was assessed at only $6,000, and to have spent $4,000 on the road. He would sell it to them, road and all, for the bargain price of $28,000."

"Or else? You said it was an ultimatum."

"If they didn't take him up on the offer by mid-July, he would sell the island to a group of African Americans. It would become a summer colony for a couple of hundred families from Chicago or Milwaukee."

"What a provoking man! Weren't there still lynchings in the South in the 1920s? Good thing that this was Wisconsin, not Mississippi."

"The Midwest had its Mississippi moments, too. You know that Billie Holiday song 'Strange Fruit'? It was based on the lynching of two black teenagers in 1930—in Indiana. A few people reminded Wagner that the Ku Klux Klan had burned crosses in Delafield when a landlord tried to rent a home to a black family. Were the cross burners really Klansmen, or guys in KKK drag? Who knows? Anyway, the residents repeated their threat during the ensuing weeks, while organizing an NPA—Nemahbin Protective Association."

"That must have given Wagner pause."

"Not for a moment. He scoffed at their threat to bring out the 'men in white nighties.' He poked another stick in their eye by hiring an African American contractor to dismantle the road. He spent the rest of the summer negotiating with black realtors in Milwaukee and Chicago, taking prospective buyers on tours of the island in full view of lakeshore residents. The colony began to take definite shape. Members would build on waterfront lots and share a clubhouse on the south end of the island. They might eventually acquire land nearby for a golf course and tennis courts."

"Sounds rather tony to me."

"The *Milwaukee Journal* characterized the interested parties as 'the cream of Ethiopia's aristocracy.' Their affluence merely added fuel to the fire. The chairman of the protective association told the *Journal* that black people from Milwaukee would be 'jerked up short' if they didn't stay within bounds."

"So what happened when 'Ethiopia' invaded Nemahbin? Was there any violence?"

"The invasion never materialized. Black investors apparently lost interest in Sugar Island for the same reason as white investors: there was no road access to the property. Wagner held onto the island till 1927, hoping for a state legislature that would allow him to rebuild the road. Finally, he sold it to Jacob Held."

"So it all ended peacefully?"

"Of course not. Held was a developer too, and he planned to sell home sites on the island. Guess what? He wanted to build a road from the lakeshore to the lots. It was *déjà vu* all over again. For a while it looked as though he would succeed where Wagner had failed. The town of Summit approved his design for a causeway with several bridges to facilitate navigation and circulation of lake water."

"Let me guess. The lake association didn't like that idea, either."

"Hardly. Their secretary issued a call to arms on the front page of the *Waukesha Freeman*, asking for public support in the Second Battle of Sugar Island. The letter took a preservationist approach, arguing that the island was a refuge for birds, animals, and stressed-out city dwellers."

"Stressed-out city dwellers?"

"If they weren't stressed out before they purchased their lots, they were soon after, when Held failed to build a road. Some tried unsuccessfully to sue him for not honoring his promise. From then until the 1960s Sugar Island property passed from hand to hand, its history consisting of suit and countersuit over construction of a roadway. People eventually built homes on the island. As you can see, however, there is still no road to obstruct our navigation."

We steer to the right of the island. Halfway down its length we spot our destination, a wooden dock in the cattails bordering the lake's western shore. A path leads from the dock to the fenced-in parking area where I've left our minivan. We are almost to the dock when a green heron flushes from the cattails and flies toward Sugar Island. About the birds, at least, the lake association secretary was right.

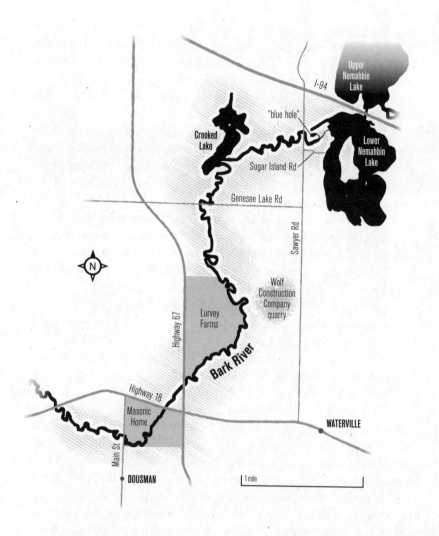

CHAPTER 8

Lower Nemahbin Lake
to Dousman

everal weeks pass before we resume, in late June, our rediscovery and exploration of the Bark River. Driving west on Interstate 94, we cross the channel linking the two Nemahbins and take the exit to Sawyer Road. Turning south on Sawyer, we cross the Bark, stopping briefly to check the water level. A low dam just upstream from the bridge maintains the lake level, so there is little variation on that side. The downstream side is a better gauge of recent precipitation.

Continuing south, we turn east onto Sugar Island Road, which ends in a private gravel boat landing on Lower Nemahbin. Here we turn left into the parking lot for users of the public boat-launching site. We unload our gear and carry it down a path to a dock that extends into cattail marsh. Leaving Puck with the canoe, I drive to our take-out in Dousman and park at a small wayside downstream from the Main Street bridge. Twenty minutes after pulling my bike from the rear of the minivan, I am back at the launching site. I secure my shuttle vehicle to a tree and stroll down the path.

Puck is standing on the dock, observing red-winged blackbirds through binoculars. Several have staked out their favorite cattails and are swaying like metronomes in the breeze.

We push off and paddle north. The lake remains shallow until we reach an opening in the marsh where the Bark exits Lower Nemahbin. The current has scoured out a deeper basin at the entrance, where we have practiced rolling our whitewater kayaks. If you miscalculate and roll in water that is too shallow, your head strikes cushiony silt rather than rock or hard-packed sand. The bottom changes from silt to sand as we enter the channel, and the current quickens. Floating mats of cattail form the banks on either side, providing cover for small fish. Occasionally the river tears off an island of cattail mat and sends it downstream.

Halfway between the lake and Sawyer Road a side channel leads north to a small pond in the midst of the marsh, where I've taken our children to fish for perch and sunfish. Known locally as the "blue hole," the pond is surprisingly deep—indeed, artificially so. It was gouged out by miners in pursuit of marl, also called bog limestone. Marl deposits form in the shallower glacial lakes and swamps when calcium carbonate precipitates out of solution and mixes with bottom clay and the fossil shells of clams and snails.

Iron smelters sometimes used marl rather than crushed limestone as flux to remove impurities from the molten metal. Chiefly, though, farmers used it to enrich depleted soils. Increase Lapham, the canal engineer, archeologist, and all-around scientist, wrote in 1851 that southern Wisconsin's marl beds "constitute a great bank, not likely to be broken or to suspend payment, from which to draw future supplies of the food of plants, whenever our present soils shall exhibit signs of exhaustion." There's not likely to be a run on the great marl bank any time soon, however. A marl mining operation based in Dousman, our destination today, failed after a few years due to the cost of processing and transporting its product.

For the Potawatomi and the native people who preceded them on Lower Nemahbin, the lake itself was the great food bank. Evidence of their camps is particularly abundant along the northwest shore. A place so prolific in the elements that sustained life—fish, waterfowl, fur-bearing animals, deer, edible plants, maple sugar, and of course water—must have seemed a good place to lie down for eternity. Around 1900 archeologists reported a string of seven Woodland period conical mounds along the northwest shore of the lake and the north bank of the Bark River. They contained the remains of seven adults and one child. The largest mound had been destroyed during construction of a cottage. Today, despite a state tax exemption program to protect archeologically significant sites, ever-larger homes rise on the graves of the ancient lake dwellers.

After carrying us due west for another fifty yards beyond the "blue hole," the Bark bends sharply right at a high bank occupied by small cottages. Then it parallels Sawyer Road for about thirty yards, running fast and clear over the skeleton of a sunken rowboat. Small bass sunning themselves in the main channel scoot into the cattails at our approach. Just upstream from the Sawyer Road bridge is a low concrete dam that the Nemahbin-Nashotah Lakes Protective Association built in 1931. When the State Public Service Commission approved the association's request, it recommended construction of a walkway around the dam and rollers to facilitate portaging boats.

If the walkway and rollers were ever built, they no longer remain, and the dam can be tricky to negotiate. We take out on the right and secure our gear in the boat. Uncoiling the bow painter, we lower the canoe carefully, stern first, into the turbulent water below the dam. Then, paddle in hand, I step from the bridge abutment into the bow and work my way to the stern. Puck tosses the rope into the boat, crosses the road, and re-embarks on the other side.

In years past, when our children joined us on these excursions, the Sawyer Road bridge was a place to linger. The water is clean enough to swim in and not too cold. The backroller beneath the dam offers limitless possibilities for surfing on inner tubes and other flotation devices, provided the current isn't overly strong and no one is fishing from the bridge.

Today, though, we yield to the river's leisurely meander through cattail marsh to Crooked Lake. Here and there we encounter evidence of human habitation. The first dock below the bridge juts from property once owned by C. P. ("Chappie") Fox, the circus historian and entrepreneur who brought the annual circus parade to Milwaukee for many years. Near another dock on the left, a short distance downstream, is an especially deep pool where we once spied an outboard motor, its engine on the bottom and its propeller swaying in the current like some exotic species of water plant.

A wooden bridge serves as portal to a marsh inhabited chiefly by muskrats, ducks, red-winged blackbirds, carp, and suckers. Deer find refuge and acorns in the oak woods that crown the islands of higher ground. Bill Hibbard, the *Milwaukee Journal*'s distinguished outdoors writer, once described this area, a state wildlife refuge, as "a small segment of such wilderness as might have greeted the first white men to venture into what is now southeastern Wisconsin."

This afternoon the marsh provides us with entertainment as well as a connection with the frontier past. A smallish duck—we eventually recognize it as a blue-winged teal—flushes from the cattails on our right and launches into her crippled-wing decoy act. Though we've witnessed countless examples of the genre, this one is special. The little trouper really gets into it, weaving back and forth a mere five yards in front of our bow. Each melodramatic spasm looks as though it could be her last. A hundred yards downstream she lifts off with a final plaintive cry and returns to her nest, leaving us to wonder whether we should set our paddles aside and applaud. Are there Tony Awards for ducks? If so, she is a contender for Best Performance by a Featured Hen of the Anatidae Family.

Two-thirds of the way to Crooked Lake, where the river bends left, a man-made channel leads straight ahead to the lake's attractive and undeveloped northeastern shore. We let our boat follow its nose downstream and soon arrive on Crooked Lake. In 1845 Indian camps, most likely Potawatomi, occupied the north shore of the lake. The extensive mound groups of Summit Township are only a half mile farther north. Ruined duck blinds mark the river entrance to the lake. More substantial structures, including an especially grand estate, are sprinkled along the shore to the west and south.

Keeping to the channel to avoid a sediment bar, we make the horseshoe turn to the left, where the river leaves the lake. Above a low rock dam at the outlet a couple of bass cruise the shoreline. A thirty-inch northern pike holds steady in the middle until it detects our approach and moves reluctantly off. On the right, at the end of a ridge that extends all the way to Genesee Lake Road, is a new dock with a PRIVATE PROPERTY sign. It replaces an enormous fallen tree that was once our regular lunch stop.

The place is full of memories for Puck. "Remember," she asks, "how our kids used to bring their masks and snorkels so they could swim in the pool above the rocks?"

"I do. But on the outing I remember best it was too cold for swimming."

"I know which one you mean. That was the Friday in October when we did a canoe picnic." As soon as our son and daughter came home from school we had left for Lower Nemahbin with a supper of cold chicken. By the time we finished eating, perched on the old tree trunk, it was getting dark. We'd forgotten to take the shorter fall days into account. Luckily, it was a clear, moonlit night.

"Whenever I recall that evening," Puck says, "I see a full moon behind a great blue heron, perched on a dead snag. Did we really see that, or have I mixed it up with a Japanese print?"

"We really saw it. There's the dead tree, still standing." We have maneuvered through a slot in the rock dam and drifted down to what we call the *Wind in the Willows* section of the river. Here the channel narrows and the current quickens as it passes through reeds on either side, recalling the E. H. Shepard illustrations in Kenneth Grahame's book. Somewhere Puck managed to find us matching t-shirts with a Shepard drawing and Ratty's immortal words: "There is nothing—absolutely nothing—half so much worth doing as simply messing about in boats."

Absolutely nothing, unless it's messing about on a crisp moonlit October night, when you can hear raccoons and muskrats rustling through the dry cattails. Grahame did his boating on the Thames River in England, where he could choose between rowing and punting. Puck and I have tried punting on the Cherwell River in Oxford, with decidedly mixed results. Though the Cherwell resembles the Bark, punting does not resemble canoeing. We never got the hang of poling a square-nosed boat upstream—or down, for that matter—while balancing on the stern deck. England once floated the most formidable navy in the world. When it comes to boat design for small rivers, however, the American woodland Indians left the Brits in their wake.

It would be hard to imagine a watercraft more perfectly suited to its environment than the canoe. Its hydrodynamic, fish-shaped hull is fast and streamlined yet stable, even in turbulent water. Unlike the kayak, it can haul a heavy load and is easy to step into and out of, yet remains relatively dry. The paddlers face forward, an advantage in negotiating obstacles and observing wildlife. It is light enough to portage overland for a moderate distance. The American Indian prototype, constructed of birch bark sewn to a wooden frame, could be repaired with materials available along the river.

The real genius of the canoe, however, lies in its mode of locomotion. Both the forward thrust and the steering are divided between bow and stern. With a combination of forward and backward strokes, sweeps, braces, pries, and draws, paddlers can move the boat virtually anywhere on the water, often using the current to assist muscle power. Observing a pair of paddlers who have mastered the full repertoire of strokes and know how to read the river is a rare aesthetic experience, not to be compared with our performance on the Cherwell.

We manage not to embarrass ourselves while passing under a farm bridge and riding a couple of crack-the-whip meanders up to Genesee Lake Road. The vegetation on the left bank has been cropped close by sheep and goats belonging to a farmer on that side. Downstream on the right we spot another grazing animal. A magnificent buck with a full rack of antlers lifts his head and trots into the trees as we drift down the gravelly riffles toward a handsome farmhouse.

The river veers sharply left at the farmhouse and carries us under the Genesee Lake Road bridge. We've often used the access downstream from the bridge to take out when doing a short trip from Lower Nemahbin. From here it's an easy walk or jog back to the parking area on the lake. In the winter you can launch a canoe at the bridge and paddle down to Dousman, thereby avoiding the frozen lakes. Except for a ledge of ice along each bank, the Bark remains open during much of the winter. In December the muskrats and beavers are especially active and not particularly shy.

Today we steer around a couple of turns and pull over for lunch beside a relatively straight section with a sand and gravel bottom. Lacking a convenient tree trunk on which to eat our sandwiches, we sit sidesaddle on the caned canoe seats, our feet in the river. An ebony jewelwing, a species of damselfly, is perched before us on a twig protruding from the water. With its paper-thin wings and needlelike thorax, it appears fragile until another jewelwing approaches. Both must be males, to judge from the way the twig squatter drives the intruder from its claim. Back on its perch, waiting for a damsel to impregnate, it puts on a display. Its four black wings flare out from the body in an asterisk pattern, fold into a single blade on its back, then flare out again.

Since taking a course called "Bark River Ecology via Canoe" offered by the University of Wisconsin Extension, I can't help but think of the river from here to Highway 67 as a combination of classroom and laboratory. Marlin Johnson, who coordinated the preservation of Hartland Marsh, regularly taught the course.

Our group assembled in a more conventional classroom, the University of Wisconsin–Waukesha Field Station in Waterville. There Professor Johnson, in academic apparel appropriate for the occasion—baseball cap, t-shirt with dragonfly image, shorts, and sneakers—showed us a map of the section we were about to study and passed out copies of George K. Reid's *Pond Life*, a young person's field guide to aquatic species. Then we formed a caravan of seven canoe-topped cars to the Genesee Lake Road bridge. Five minutes later we arrived at this spot for our first lesson, equipped with seine and dip nets for gathering specimens.

Puck gets right to the point when I tell her about that Saturday morning in August. "Did you pass the course? It would be pretty embarrassing if you didn't."

"It was a non-credit course, so we didn't have to write any essays or take a final exam. If it will make you feel better, I'll give myself the exam right now."

"What kind of school allows students to write their own exams? But go ahead."

Exam question 1: How did this section of riverbed acquire its distinctive composition?

"It was part of a glacial outwash plain, with the sorting—that is, distribution of till—characteristic of such places. Gravel was deposited here, sand a bit farther along."

"Not bad for a start. And the next question is—?"

Exam question 2: What kinds of aquatic life did you find in this section?

"Fish, to begin with: bluntnose minnows, with a black dot at the base of their tails; shiner minnows; blackstripe topminnows, with their mouths located toward the top of their heads so they can feed on surface insects; stonerollers, with a 'scraper' on their bottom lip to graze algae from rocks; and some kind of darter—I forget which. Its name comes from the way it moves from rock to rock in the streambed rather than swim against the current—"

"Minus five points for not knowing the type of darter."

"—Now I remember. It was a Johnny darter. But I have to tell you about the most remarkable critter we found. It was a freshwater sponge, which in this location is bright green due to the algae that it attaches to itself. Sponges don't tolerate silt because it clogs their gills and suffocates them. So their presence is a sign of high water quality, much as some lichens signal high air quality."

Exam question 3: What kinds of insects did you find?

"Damselflies, of course, like our ebony jewelwing. Also water scorpions, dragonfly larvae, and whirligig beetles. The beetles carry a tiny silver air bubble as an oxygen source, like a scuba diver's tank. The little dervishes

Milton J. Bates

Marlin Johnson (foreground) with students in the Bark River ecology class in 1997

have one advantage over scuba divers: with two pairs of eyes, they can watch the sky and the river bottom simultaneously, a real advantage in avoiding predators while hunting for food."

Exam question 4: What kinds of plants did you identify growing in the riverbed?

"Cattails of both the narrow- and the broadleaf variety, bulrushes, and broad-leaved arrowhead. American Indians ate the tuberous root of the arrowhead plant."

"I'll give you a pass on the exam so far," Puck concedes. "But you said 'first lesson.' There were others?"

"There were. The second was a short distance downriver. I'll show you where."

We pack the remains of our lunch in a waterproof bag, guide the boat into the current, and get under way. Where the channel narrows and passes under a large willow, we see a pair of longnose gars sculling upstream. Their prehistoric appearance suggests that nature doesn't tamper with a proven design. The gars are also a reminder that many species eluded our nets during the Bark River ecology class. We saw neither of the two endangered species believed to be in the river, the starhead topminnow and a catfish called the slender madtom, and only a fraction of the twenty species identified in DNR surveys of this section between 1972 and 2002.

We come to an oxbow where Professor Johnson had directed our attention to a plant community that looked, to our unpracticed eyes, like the wetland bordering the rest of the river.

Exam question 5: What is special about this particular wetland?
"It is a fen, which botanists define as grassland on a wet, springy site. Unlike a bog, which is acidic, a fen is saturated with alkaline-rich water."

Professor Johnson attributed the alkalinity of this spot to dolomitic rocks in the underlying glacial outwash. A fen lacks trees but abounds in grasses and shrubby cinquefoil or potentilla.

Below the fen Puck and I approach the expansive cultivated fields belonging to Lurvey Farms, locally famous for its late spring strawberries. Four bridges span the river between here and Highway 67. The first allows plenty of clearance at any water level. The second and third can be run in low water, though paddlers should approach them cautiously. We've seen more than one canoe jammed between the water and the bridge, unable to move forward or back. The fourth bridge, located in view of the old farmhouse, always requires a carry-around.

Just downstream from the second bridge, on the left bank, is a small picnic area with a scattering of juniper trees. It was formerly equipped with a pair of wooden outhouses that flushed, so to speak, directly into the river. These have been removed.

The third bridge links Highway 67 to a quarry operated by Wolf Construction Company. It was downstream from this bridge that Professor Johnson invited us to disembark and wade the river. The bottom was covered with rocks about the size of baseballs. Virtually indistinguishable from the rocks, and furred with the same algae, were numerous shellfish.

Exam question 6: What kinds of clams did you find in the Bark River?
"None. This is a trick question. What we lifted from the river and passed from hand to hand were freshwater mussels. One, called the three-ridge mussel, has indentations like those on an oyster. Another, the black sand shell, has a shell with a purple lining. We searched in vain for the ellipse mussel, which is on the state's list of threatened species."

Exam question 7: How do freshwater mussels propagate?

"They depend on fish to nurture their larvae. The ingenious dwarf wedge-mussel, for example, waves a flap of skin to attract passing fish, then sprays them with eggs. Other species produce a pack of eggs that the fish ingest. Some of the eggs evade the fish's gullet and attach themselves to its gills. The larvae feed on blood in the gills until they're ready to cut loose and claim a spot on the riverbed. The little vampires are particular when it comes to host species, and will die out if the right kinds of fish aren't available. Consequently, dams that interfere with the movement of fish may also interfere with the propagation of mussels."

Professor Johnson's lesson recalls the conflict that arose between environmental and historical interests during restoration of the Wade House in Greenbush. Built as a stagecoach inn on the plank road between Sheboygan and Fond du Lac, the Wade property included a blacksmith shop, a carriage house, and a sawmill on the Mullet River. The original sawmill was built by Charles Robinson in 1847 and burned in 1853. A couple of years later Theodor Herrling, a German immigrant, rebuilt the mill. His family operated it until 1910, when they dismantled it.

Members of the Kohler plumbing fixture family wanted to rebuild the dam and sawmill while refurbishing the inn in the 1950s. The sawmill didn't open until decades later due to—here I quote from an independent review of the episode—"the failure of two bureaucracies (the DNR and the State Historical Society) to communicate with each other." At first, neither agency had the expertise to construct an authentic sawmill of the type that produced lumber for the Wade House, the plank road, and other local construction. Following research and archeological excavations, the State Historical Society drew up plans for the mill. It also had $2.2 million in funding, most of it from Herbert V. Kohler Jr. and the Kohler Trust for Preservation.

By this time, however, the DNR had discovered that the ellipse mussel and another threatened species, the slippershell, depend on Johnny darters and sculpins to carry their eggs up and down the river. A dam would block access to upper reaches of the Mullet. Fortunately, the DNR and the Historical Society were able to come up with a design that is historically accurate, for the most part, without destroying mussel populations above the dam.

The grand opening of the Robinson-Herrling Sawmill on June 16, 2001, was a fascinating event for the adults and children who attended. Volunteers dressed in period costume served as interpreters and sawyers. When they engaged the enormous leather belts linking the waterwheel to the mill machinery, a carriage guided a log through the reciprocating saw blade. Meanwhile, unobserved, the darters and sculpins put on a demonstration of their own, bypassing the dam and millpond in a separate channel.

Below the mussel beds Puck and I come to one of our favorite spots in this section of the river. The main channel turns sharply right past a stand of mature tamaracks. A shallow side channel loops to the left around the island of feathery trees, then rejoins the mainstream. If you didn't know better, you would think that you had paddled into one of the boggy rivers of northern Wisconsin. Unfortunately, the tamaracks appear distressed and are beginning to die off.

A quarter mile below the tamarack island, on the left, is a ditch that releases effluent from the Delafield-Hartland Sewage Treatment Plant into the river. It has traveled about four miles by pipeline to get here, bypassing several lakes. Professor Johnson chose this spot for the final lesson in his open-air classroom. Maneuvering his canoe into position beside the outfall, he waited patiently for the student canoes to fan out in front of him. Then he pointed with his paddle at the green carpet of vegetation around us.

Exam question 8 (for extra credit): What was that green stuff, and why does it matter?

We were looking at duckweed and filamentous algae. Lacking roots into the riverbed, these plants depend entirely on waterborne nutrients. Their location suggests that they find something delectable in the Dela-Hart effluent.

Initially, according to Professor Johnson, the Dela-Hart plant didn't treat its wastewater for phosphorus, which stimulates plant growth as effectively in lakes and rivers as it does on urban lawns. A decade after the plant opened, it continued to discharge enough phosphorus, much of it from laundry detergents sold illegally, to sustain a flourishing growth of water star-grass. Dela-Hart effluent also raises the temperature of the water to a level that some aquatic animals cannot tolerate. Our class saw few mussels and no sponges between the outfall and Highway 67. These canaries in the coal mine suggest that the sewage plant, though it has done much to upgrade the lower Bark from a sewer to a functioning ecosystem, has not fixed all of its problems. Like many other river communities, Delafield and Hartland pass their problems on to the next community downstream. Due largely to its high level of phosphorus, the Bark has remained on the DNR's list of impaired waters, "impaired" being a euphemism for polluted.

Puck awards me a pass on the exam, and we continue downstream, mesmerized by the luxuriant fronds of star-grass. Watching the plants undulate like feather boas in the current, we wish that they were as benign as they are beautiful. After a carry-around at the last Lurvey Farms bridge, we shortcut an oxbow and arrive at the Highway 67 bridge, where the professor had dismissed our class. The bridge can be an obstacle to navigation when the river is running high. On those occasions we take our mothers' advice to look both ways, then sprint across the pavement with our canoe. Today is more typical. We duck below the gunwales and allow the current to carry us beneath the highway and down a pleasant cattail-lined stretch to Highway 18.

Between the two highways the river clips a corner of land that was once farmed by Elisha W. Edgerton. It had a reputation as a model farm. In June 1860 a correspondent for the *Milwaukee Sentinel* passed it on a walking tour with several friends. Praising the Edgerton place as "the handsomest and best arranged farm we ever saw," he added, "it consists of three hundred and twenty acres of 'burr oak opening land,' and as it is very level, and nearly all the trees and stumps removed, it can scarcely be distinguished from prairie. The Bark river, a stream of chrystal clearness, runs along near the barn, and crosses the road, affording a grand watering place for the stock. The owner of the farm, with two or three men, were washing sheep by the bridge when we passed." The river was presumably less crystalline after its encounter with Edgerton's barnyard and livestock.

Replacing the 1860 bridge is a modern structure that allows a bit more clearance than the Highway 67 bridge. Taking advantage of the headroom, we use our paddles to steer around the exposed rocks that mark the beginning of a lively little rapids. They also mark the boundary of the Masonic Home grounds. Originally part of Edgerton's farm, this acreage was subsequently farmed and operated as a resort by the van Brunt family, which donated it to the Masons as a home for elderly members. On the right are the original buildings, set among mature hardwoods. On the left, linked to the older section by an arching footbridge, is an attractively landscaped cluster of modern buildings. These must offer compelling indoor entertainment, to judge from the deserted benches along the riverbank. Prior to the new development we often exchanged greetings with residents enjoying front-row seats on the Bark.

Below the riffles, the river slows to a series of meanders. The high ground gives way to bog studded with tamaracks. These will turn from green to gold in the fall before dropping their needles. Today one of them holds a great blue heron. It emits a croaking noise at our approach and launches clumsily into the air.

Leaving the tamarack bog in our wake, we come within sight of the Main Street bridge in Dousman. The river allows us one last view of the Masonic Home's stately oak woods on the right before carrying us under the bridge. We take out on the left. Less than four hours have elapsed since we slid the canoe into Lower Nemahbin, less than four miles away. Yet we feel as though we've traveled long and far. In the midst of suburban sprawl and commuter traffic, the Bark remains a place apart.

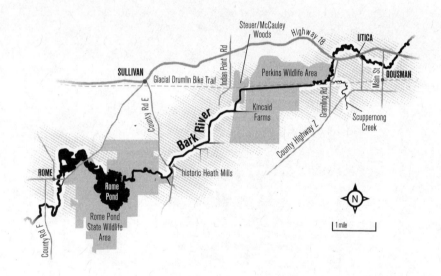

CHAPTER 9

Dousman to Rome

W e are back at the Main Street landing in Dousman on the
following Saturday, which happens to be part of the Fourth
of July weekend. The air is thick with humidity, and we try to
ignore several rain-swollen clouds as we load the canoe and maneuver it into
the current. We're on the water early, hoping to make it all the way to the town
of Rome. As a precaution we've left the bicycle at the County Road E bridge in
Sullivan, upstream from the vast Rome Pond. We don't want to be caught out
in the open if a thunderstorm materializes.

From Dousman to the Glacial Drumlin Bike Trail, located on the former
Chicago and Northwestern right-of-way, the Bark is in no hurry to get
anywhere. It ranges freely from side to side, like a hound sniffing out a cold
trail. We once made the mistake of inviting a couple of novice paddlers to join
us for this section. Despite a preliminary seminar in draw and pry strokes, they
ricocheted from bank to bank, accumulating a canoe full of leaves and twigs
until the channel finally straightened out beside the old railroad bed.

Between Dousman and the first Highway 18 bridge, in the village of Utica,
the Bark is in places a backyard river. Especially today, when people are setting

up lawn chairs and readying charcoal grills for a holiday cookout, we feel as though we're invading their dining rooms. Passing under a steel-frame pedestrian bridge and then the highway bridge, we enter one of the more rewarding reaches of the river. During the next forty-five minutes at least two dozen deer flush from cover. One is a large buck that lumbers into the underbrush; the others are mostly does with fawns. Once we surprise a doe standing up to her belly in the river. Mature trees line both banks. A deer hunting stand in one of them suggests that we're not the first to notice the concentration of game in this out-of-the-way pocket.

The wayside downstream from the second Highway 18 bridge used to be a popular picnicking and fishing spot, not to mention a convenient place to launch canoes. Now it is closed, and weeds almost hide the warped gray boards of the picnic tables. Less than a mile below the wayside a sandy delta marks the spot where Scuppernong Creek enters on the left. The creek travels a circuitous route from its headwaters near Lapham Peak to Waterville, where it was dammed to create Waterville Lake. The section between the dam and Dutchman Lake supports a trout population, thanks to infusions of cold water from natural springs. We've paddled the lower end of the creek from County Highway Z to the Bark.

Below Scuppernong Creek we hear what sounds like hornets—very large hornets, and very angry. The noise issues from a go-cart track located on Gramling Road. Fortunately, the track is out of sight on the other side of the railroad right-of-way. The railroad bed rises almost vertically from the waters of the Bark at this point, and as the engine drone fades we hear, high above our heads, snatches of conversation and the crunch of bike tires on gravel. Not until the river swings away from the bank and into a marsh meadow can we see the Glacial Drumlin Trail itself.

"I don't know about you," I tell Puck, "but I could use a dip in some cool water, preferably where there are no mosquitoes to take advantage of the situation."

"There's a breeze here in the open to keep them away. Let's look for deeper water. Remember, no weeds—excuse me, aquatic plants."

Just upstream from the railroad bridge we find a spot where the current has scooped out a deeper channel and the bottom is firm sand and fine gravel, with no vegetation to tickle her ladyship's toes. We've had the foresight to wear swimming suits under clothes chosen for their protection from insects, sun, and brush. Cyclists slow down as they cross the bridge and catch sight of this unusual species of water mammal ("Look, Jennifer—otters!"). As we dry ourselves off and climb back into the boat, we notice one couple dismount and park their bikes. They are making their way down to the water's edge as the current carries us between the wooden bridge pilings.

South of the bike path, the horizon expands considerably. As far as the eye can see in the direction of the city of Palmyra, the land lies like a great black table, etched at this season with green rows of vegetables. We're entering the basin of Glacial Lake Scuppernong, named not for Scuppernong Creek but for the Scuppernong River, another tributary of the Bark. As the two lobes of the Wisconsin Glacier retreated to the north and east, the Bark and other streams carried their meltwater to this part of Ottawa Township, where it backed up behind a dolomite sill near Janesville. Eventually the sill eroded, allowing the lake to drain south into the Rock River. But for hundreds of years—in some places perhaps thousands of years—the lake bottom accumulated deposits of decaying animal and vegetable matter.

The great Scuppernong Marsh has teemed with animal life since the days of woolly mammoths, mastodons, and giant beavers. Farmers occasionally turn up bones and tusks while plowing or ditching. Where there is wild game there will be hunters. David Overstreet and other archeologists have excavated sites near Kenosha where Paleo-Indians were butchering mammoths at least thirteen thousand years ago, some two thousand years before humans were previously thought to have entered the area. Analysis of the animal bone collagen, together with radiocarbon dating of organic material found with the bones, suggests that people were living and hunting virtually in the shadow of the glacier's Michigan Lobe.

After the native hunters came the white farmers. Though the first white settlers sought out the higher ground of the oak openings on which to plant their corn and wheat, they turned to the marsh for hay to feed and bed their livestock. Later they found that marsh hay was easier to handle than sawdust when insulating the ice harvest for storage or shipment. The hay eventually became an important cash crop that could be cut and baled several times over the course of a summer. Farmers purchased marshland, otherwise deemed useless for cultivation or grazing, solely for the hay. Local newspapers regularly reported on the crop, rejoicing in its abundance one year and lamenting its loss to fire or flood the next.

After nibbling at the fringe of the marshes, farms went on to swallow them whole. In some cases they did so with the blessing of the federal government. A series of Swamp Land Acts in 1849, 1850, and 1860 granted almost 65 million acres of wetland to the states, including over 3.3 million acres in Wisconsin. The states transferred the parcels at little or no cost to farmers who agreed to "reclaim" them. A few people regretted the loss, including a cranberry farmer in Ottawa Township. "All over Wisconsin and Minnesota," he told a newspaper correspondent in 1884, "the finest natural marshes have already perished, because, in many instances, man has destroyed nature and cultivation is rendered impossible." On the same page of the newspaper, however, is an article applauding a Hartford landowner who converted 180 acres of marsh into valuable farmland by laying drain tile. "Now the whole extent has the appearance of a garden," the article boasts, "and a very fertile one at that." Those who preferred gardens to swamps and cranberry bogs were clearly in the majority.

In 1937 Aldo Leopold mourned the loss of the state's wetlands in an essay entitled "Marshland Elegy." For Leopold the marsh's *genius loci* was the sandhill crane, believed to be the oldest species of bird still living. "When we hear his call," Leopold wrote, "we hear no mere bird. He is the symbol of our untamable past, of that incredible sweep of millennia which underlies and conditions the daily affairs of birds and men." There was a period, he observed, when cranes and farmers were able to coexist. Farmers had their seasons for cutting and gathering hay; the cranes had theirs for breeding and raising their young. Gradually, however, the farmers came to resent the crane's appetite for corn, especially when newly sprouted. They also discovered that an investment in drain tile and ditching paid large dividends in tillable soil.

Leopold predicted that the crane's wild bugling, which he regarded as the trumpet call of the Pleistocene, would soon be heard for the last time. He considered himself lucky to have observed a pair of cranes near the Endeavor marsh in 1934, when he believed there were no more than twenty breeding pairs in the state. Fortunately, his elegy has proved premature for *Grus canadensis*. Due partly to the efforts of the International Crane Foundation, located a few miles from the played-out farm where Leopold gathered the material for his environmental classic, *A Sand County Almanac*, Wisconsin is now home to about fifteen thousand sandhills. As some farmers and hunters see it, the numbers warrant a hunting season of the kind already allowed in a few western states.

Leopold's elegy was by no means premature for the crane's habitat, however. Wisconsin had over ten million acres of wetland when white settlers arrived, but has lost half of them to ditching and draining. The same year that Leopold saw the Endeavor cranes, he prepared a survey of the state's wetlands for the

Conservation Department, the forerunner to the DNR. As professor of game management at the University of Wisconsin, he was especially interested in marshes that might be preserved as wildlife breeding habitat. Among these was the Bark River Marsh, which he described as "the best we have—much better than further north where soil is poor, marshes more acidic, black flies (hence duck disease) bad. Prairie chickens can be re-established on this marsh."

The farmers who owned property in the marsh weighed its value on a different scale, the economic. A few years after Leopold's report, they drained nearly a thousand acres to create "muck farms," large tracts of rich, peaty soil devoted to celery, spinach, corn, mint, soybeans, and root crops such as carrots, onions, potatoes, and beets. During the 1940s and 1950s two brothers with muck farming experience in Michigan, Dean and Richard Kincaid, bought parcels of land south of the Bark River and consolidated them into large-scale agribusinesses. Though they managed their holdings separately, their enterprise was known locally as Kincaid Farms. So it will be known, for a while at least, as the property passes to other owners.

Muck farms altered not only the glacial lake bottom but also the course of the Bark River in Ottawa Township. When Deputy Surveyor Robert Clark Jr. and his crew (two chainmen and an axman) came to this part of the marsh in 1836, they found themselves wading through a couple of feet of water and using tamaracks as "witness trees" to mark the section corners. Sections 5, 6, 7, and 8 came together squarely in the middle of the Bark, leaving them no place to set the corner post. From this point the river looped a quarter mile south in a lazy oxbow, then north to the east-west line between Sections 6 and 7 before resuming its westerly course into Jefferson County.

Surveyors' notebooks are rather laconic documents, as a rule. They record distances in chains and links (100 links to a chain, eighty chains to a mile) and identify witness trees by species (for example, "W.O." for white oak) and diameter. They usually devote a phrase or two to description of the terrain and its commercial value, for example, "hilly with first-rate timber." Clark's entry for the section line across the oxbow is therefore remarkable for its prolixity. "This line was not run," his full-page disquisition begins. "At the time I was there the water was high and the stream could not be approached nearer than within 10 to 20 chains [660 to 1,320 feet] the shores being the worst kind of bog and then all afloat—The mile is all an open marsh—no timber. . . . I regreted the necessity of leaving this line thus, the more as it is I think the first I was ever compelled to leave in surveying several thousand miles—I am sure it was the most difficult that ever came in my way. For the omission I mainly plead the impossibility of the case. . . ."

Now the Bark runs straight as a section line between the railroad bridge and the Waukesha-Jefferson county line. In 1951 the Wisconsin Public Service Commission allowed Emery Owens to block off the oxbow and relocate the river north of his muck farm. Dean Kincaid straightened the channel after he acquired the property from Owens. Today Clark's survey crew could set a corner post—in a patch of onions, say, or soybeans—without getting their britches wet. Machines have erased not only the oxbow but also a tributary stream that once linked School Section Lake to the Bark River.

A channelized river is unfortunately a dead river. Puck and I never look forward to this part of the trip, particularly at this time of year, when the channel is shallow, weed choked, and stagnant. On hot days there is nowhere to escape from the sun. When the prevailing west wind is up, we have little choice but to grit our teeth and tow the canoe for much of the mile and three-quarters. Luckily, the bottom is sandy and firm.

Today, as we alternate between paddling and slogging down the channel, I notice that the river is more alive than it appears from a distance. One of Aldo Leopold's sons, Luna, devoted a long and distinguished career to hydrology, particularly the phenomenon of river meandering. In collaboration with a colleague he developed elegant mathematical formulas to describe how rivers use (to speak anthropomorphically) meanders to discharge, in a uniform and efficient way, the energy generated by downward flow. Straight reaches of river alternate between pools and riffles, the vertical movement accomplishing the same purpose as lateral movement. At low levels of flow on a straight reach, the current also ranges from side to side within the channel, mimicking the movement of a meandered reach.

Coming to the first grove of trees on the left bank of the channel, we stop for lunch. For some time we've been hearing the otherworldly chortling of cranes on the left, but the bank is too high to see any distance. Climbing to the top of the bank, we can barely make them out, a pair of stately birds stepping across the field far to the southeast. They probably built a nest in the Perkins Wildlife Area north of the bike trail when they returned in March from their wintering grounds near the Gulf of Mexico. Today they're checking out the lunch menu on the muck farm.

Spreading our life jackets as cushions on the bank, we pull out our sandwiches and a pair of binoculars. With their help we can see a young crane, called a colt, with the adults. It is about two months old, nearly ready to fly. The three appear as spectral gray presences, shimmering in the heat waves above the black soil. For farmers the birds are merely another nuisance, like deer and cutworms. Yet it is easy to understand why they figure prominently in the art and folklore of many cultures, especially in Asia. During the half year that Puck and I lived in China we frequently saw images of red-crowned cranes paired with pine boughs, the combination symbolizing happiness and longevity. In China's Yellow River valley archeologists have unearthed flutes that were fashioned nine thousand years ago from the bones of red-crowned cranes. One of them can still be played.

Settling into our sandwiches, we scan the wooded bank across the channel. In the spring the trees and shrubs are alive with warblers—more species than we can identify, though we're sure of the redstarts and the black-and-whites. The warblers remain hidden today, but tree swallows are putting on a spectacular air show above the channel, tracing intricate patterns that never quite intersect. Even the fish are giving it a try. One especially large specimen, probably a carp, goes briefly airborne, then splashes back into its native element.

It is feeding time for the mosquitoes, too, so we don't dawdle over lunch. Soon we are back in the canoe, making the sharp left turn that takes us from the ditched section of the river to its naturally meandering channel. On our right is a 16½-acre parcel known as the Steuer/McCauley Woods, which the Waukesha Land Conservancy purchased in 1993 as a buffer for the Perkins Wildlife Area. The DNR contributed nearly seven thousand dollars toward the purchase. It was on this higher ground that in 1836 the federal surveyor noticed a trail crossing the river, possibly used by Indians seeking a dry route through pockets of wetland.

On our left soon after, we pass the intake for the muck farm's irrigation system. A good deal of water is needed to replace what was drained from the marsh. People living downstream from the muck farms have occasionally complained about diversion of Bark River water for this purpose. In 1959, for example, the property owners association on Rome Pond filed a complaint with the State Public Service Commission against Emery Owens. Owens denied diverting the water from the Bark, but said that he might eventually irrigate with water from Scuppernong Creek, which would have the same effect.

Downstream from the irrigation intake an extensive marsh spreads to the south, suggesting how this basin might have looked for many millennia after Glacial Lake Scuppernong drained into the Rock River. Signs on both sides of the river indicate that the property is a state game farm. There are several plywood observation platforms, apparently for watching waterfowl. On the north bank the terrain climbs eighty feet from cattail marsh to an attractive wooded knoll at the end of Indian Point Road. Though much of this high ground has been converted from farms to a modern subdivision, the homes are out of sight and the river valley retains its wild appearance. Where a path comes down to the water we see a hen turkey. Shortly after, a deer splashes through the marshy border on the right, flushing several ducks, and disappears into the woods.

The open vistas of marsh and hilltop contract to a brushy tunnel as we approach our next landmark, a steel girder farm bridge. Below the steel bridge on both sides of the river are low dams, possibly to control the water level for waterfowl. Beavers have improved on one of these, raising the wetland about eight inches above the river. Considering the marshy terrain, we are surprised to find a newly built home on the right bank, a mere thirty yards from the water. Though rocks line the shore and the yard is attractively landscaped, a scrim of silt on the lawn marks a recent rise in the river. From the bank a hose leads to a throbbing intake pump. Some of the water is going to potted plants near the house, tended by a man who resembles Wilfred Brimley, the actor known best for his Quaker Oats and Liberty Medical commercials. He gives no indication that he has seen us.

Below the Brimley place we encounter a series of downfalls. It is slow going, though we are able to lift over all but one of the trees. During the sole carry-around we alternate between hauling the canoe and slapping mosquitoes. Fortunately, we are able to float under a couple of farm bridges farther along. In an oak tree beside one of them a great horned owl blinks in the daylight, beset by unhappy blackbirds. County Road E comes into sight soon after, and we pull ashore on the right, downstream from the bridge.

Four hours have elapsed since we launched our canoe in Dousman, and we must decide whether to extend our voyage to Rome Pond. Except for the last quarter mile it has been an easy trip, and the threatening clouds have dissolved into hazy sunlight. We decide to go for it. First, though, I have to shuttle our car to the pond. I unlock the cable on my bike, climb aboard, and pedal north on County E to the Glacial Drumlin Bike Trail. Spinning east along the former railroad grade, I see many of the same places—Indian Point, Steuer/McCauley Woods, Kincaid Farms, the Perkins Wildlife Area—from a different angle. Though I traverse the distance in a fraction of the time, I can't help but notice the decline in sensory richness. The bike trail is a single instrument, whereas the river is an orchestra.

The reshuttle takes about an hour, so it is late afternoon when I coast down County E to the river bottom. Puck has put the interval to good use, exploring the vicinity of the bridge.

"Have you ever noticed the foundations of the old bridge?" she asks, pointing first across the river and then downstream on our side. I haven't, though I can make out the ruins now, all but covered with vines and branches.

"And notice how far apart they are." She's right. The channel washes against the old foundation on the left bank, but the one on the right is set well back from the water.

"Do you suppose that the river was wider when it was built?" she wonders.

"Who knows? So much has changed in this spot. The old bridge carried southbound travelers into the thriving community of Heath's Mill. Remember Stephen Warren, who was one of the first settlers of Hartland? In 1844 his father, Sylvanus, bought 160 acres on this stretch of the Bark River. That same year, John Heath—"

"The man who built the mill in Delafield?"

"Same guy. No sooner did he finish the dam and mill on Nagawicka Lake than he moved his family here and bought the quarter section from Warren. He must have been part beaver, because he went right to work on another dam just about where the new bridge crosses the river. The millpond extended a half mile upstream. Heath built a sawmill and a gristmill, one on either side of the dam."

"I noticed some pieces of limestone beside the river," Puck says. "Nice old-gold color. Do you suppose they came from one of the mill foundations?"

"Could be. There were plenty of buildings they might have supported. Heath's mills had 'quite a business appearance,' I've read in a Milwaukee newspaper, and they soon attracted other businesses. There was a cider press, a blacksmith shop, a wagon shop, a reaper and mower works, a general store, a couple of shoe-maker's shops, and even a schoolhouse. Heath had it surveyed and laid out in eighty-three lots. In 1856 it became officially the village of Sullivan."

"Isn't Sullivan north of here, on Highway 18?"

"Today, yes. But that Sullivan was called Winfield then. This Sullivan had other names, too: Heath's Mill, Heath Mills, Heathsburg, and—don't ask me why—Erfurt."

"It's hard to imagine such a lively spot, looking at it today. What happened to—whatever it was called?"

"The railroad decided its fate in 1881, when it laid track through Winfield. Seven or eight trains stopped there daily. Winfield became Sullivan, and Heath's

Mill became a ghost town. Remember that old anthology chestnut, Oliver Goldsmith's 'The Deserted Village'?"

"Sweet Auburn! loveliest village of the plain, / Where health and plenty cheer'd the labouring swain . . .'"

"That's the one. I can tell you were an English major. It came to mind when I ran across a memoir by Edward Hainke. He spent his boyhood in Heath's Mill, where he enjoyed long summer days fishing in the millpond. His family left the village a half-dozen years after the railroad came to Winfield. Hainke brought fishing tackle when he returned in 1916, only to discover that the dam had washed out and the mill was in disrepair. Having nothing better to do, he wrote a melancholy reminiscence for the *Sullivan News*. You know the genre: 'Gone are the carefree days of childhood.' I'll show you a copy when we get home."

"You can't go home again."

"Today you can't even get to Sullivan, if you insist on going by rail. The train station was razed in 1966. Anyway, let me cable my bike to a tree and we'll be on our way."

We step into the boat and steer for the liveliest current. The first quarter mile is heavily wooded, and any dallying exposes us to death by a million mosquito bites. Then we enter the Rome Pond State Wildlife Area, several square miles of cattail marsh dotted with hummocks of high wooded ground, much like the Hartland Marsh. Though only a mile separates the border of the marsh from the pond, we must paddle half again that distance because the river noses this way and that through the cattails. It requires an act of scientific faith to believe, as Luna Leopold did, that there is a logic to these twists and turns. He compared a river to a strip of steel. When the strip is grasped at each end and bent, it distributes the force of bending equally over the span of the strip. Meanders, which approximate sine-generated curves, dissipate energy efficiently over the length of the river.

Silt and bits of vegetation in the water enable us to observe another phenomenon that Leopold studied. Where the river enters a bend, centrifugal force tugs harder on the fast water near the surface, moving it toward the outside of the bend, along with our canoe. This causes the slower water near the bottom to rotate toward the inside of the bend, creating a helical movement. The water helix scours material from the outside of the bend and deposits it on the inside. When the river bends the other way, the helix reverses the direction of its rotation. Like a sidewinder snake, the river sidles from side to side within its floodplain.

We paddle quietly, not talking, scanning the cattails for cranes. It was on this section the previous fall that we flushed a flock of twenty-one sandhills, stopping on their way south. Never had we been so close to so many. Halfway through the marsh the river swings close to an island of high ground, densely forested with oak, maple, and basswood trees. The DNR designated it a "community of special concern"—something short of endangered or threatened—partly because each spring it is densely carpeted with trilliums. We have yet to witness the trillium display on this side of the pond, but we've seen the flowers on the west shore, where a trail leads from a parking area on County Road F to a high ridge over-looking the whole marsh.

The Bark traces one last oxbow in the cattails and delivers us to the pond. We are relieved to find four inches of water over the bar of silt deposited at the entrance. Occasionally the silt bar forms a dam, causing the river to overflow its banks upstream. For some distance into the pond our paddles churn more silt than water. Then the pond deepens, and we can appreciate the display of water lilies without wondering whether we'll have to spend the night with them. The pond's depth, which is maintained by a dam in the village of Rome, has always been a source of contention among mill operators, shoreline residents, recreational users, and farmers. A succession of state agencies—the Railroad Commission, the Public Service Commission, the Conservation Department, and finally the DNR—has had to deal with complaints and lawsuits.

Today the town of Sullivan establishes the water level with DNR oversight. The township acquired the dam in 1974 from a private owner who had filed an application to abandon it rather than undertake costly repairs. The circum-stances were similar in some respects to those of Margaret Zerwekh's dam in Delafield, except that here more people had a stake in maintaining the structure. At 446 acres, Rome Pond is the largest impoundment of its kind in the state. It is actually two ponds, separated by County Road F. Small homes and seasonal cottages line the shore of the lower pond. The upper, surrounded by the state wilderness area, is a destination for hunters and fishermen. Though shallow and warm as bath water, the pond still supports a population of panfish, largemouth bass, and northern pike in addition to carp.

We paddle toward the parking area west of the County F bridge, giving wide berth to a couple of fishermen's bobbers. On my way to the car I peek into the five-gallon pail that serves as their live well. A century ago, according to one account, fishermen routinely filled gunnysacks or milk cans with their catch and loaded them onto wagons. This pair will have fewer to clean, but enough for a Fourth of July fish fry. Thirteen thousand years after ice-out, Glacial Lake Scuppernong still provides.

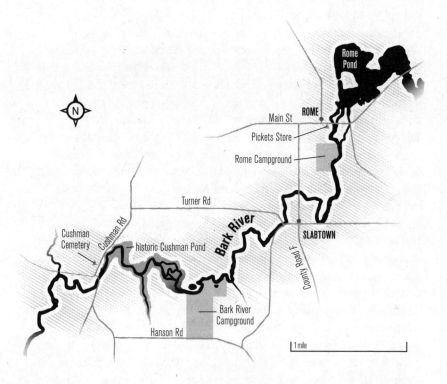

N

Rome
Pond

Main St — ROME
Pickets Store
Rome Campground

Turner Rd

Bark River

SLABTOWN

County Road F

Cushman Rd

Cushman
Cemetery

historic Cushman Pond

Bark River
Campground

Hanson Rd

1 mile

CHAPTER 10

Rome to Cushman Road

O n this relatively cool morning in mid-August the proprietor of Pickets Store seems happy to be outdoors. We ask permission to use his parking lot whenever we launch our canoe below the dam in Rome. He always says yes, and always reminds us not to block access to a small pond near the river, where fire trucks refill their tanks. Then we buy snacks or drinks to supplement our lunch, whether we need them or not. Today, with no other customers to attend to, he follows us out the door and lingers in the sunshine to chat.

"Weren't you folks here last year, with a bunch of other people?"

"We were," Puck replies. "That was a Sierra Club cleanup trip. We planned to cover the whole section between here and Hebron, but there was so much stuff that we called it a day at Cushman Pond. The Cushmans let us leave the trash bags with them for their weekly pickup."

"Some of that stuff probably came from this store. Whenever I sell a bottle of soda or a box of worms I wonder whether it will end up in the river. It's fishermen on the pond, mainly. City people. The locals don't use the river much. When I want to fish I drive over to the Rock. With these dams coming out there'll be still fewer fishermen on the Bark. I know Bill Cushman is worried about his dam, and I gather that the folks in Hebron are having second thoughts about allowing the DNR to take theirs out. Not that they had much choice. There won't be any water left in the river when the dams are gone. What brings you back today? Fishing?"

"Not today," I answer. "We're planning to canoe the whole river this year, from Bark Lake to the Rock River. We cruised around Rome Pond a couple of years ago, so we're skipping the lower part of the pond this time. But we wouldn't pass up this section of the Bark. It's one of our favorites."

A pickup truck turns off Main Street and crunches across the gravel of the parking lot. The proprietor wishes us luck, greets the man stepping from the truck, and precedes him into the store. Too late, I realize that I've forgotten to ask the question that occurred to me during our last trip: is Picket his last name or an allusion to *Picket Fences*, the television series that ran from 1992 through 1996?

Set in Rome, Wisconsin, the series notoriously combined small-town values with bizarre episodes and characters. Cows gave birth to human babies, and a woman froze to death when she fell into her own freezer. The actress Marlee Matlin played a bank robber who performed a little dance after each heist. When caught and convicted, she was sentenced to complete three thousand hours of community service. The town allowed her to discharge the obligation by serving as its mayor. Like a Shakespearean comedy, the show concluded with multiple weddings and the reconciliation of its main characters, played by Tom Skerritt and Kathy Baker.

The series won fourteen Emmys and a Golden Globe. Though it never achieved high ratings, it had a loyal following. Fans kept the flame alive on web pages and blogs for eleven years between the final episode and the first DVD release. Reruns of the series are popular in Europe, which may not please Wisconsin Romans who value the good opinion of, say, Italian Romans. Of course *Picket Fences* was no more about Rome, Wisconsin, than *Laverne & Shirley* and *Happy Days* were about Milwaukee. This brainchild of David E. Kelley was filmed in Monrovia, California, and located fictionally somewhere near Green Bay.

Jefferson County's Rome, named after the city in New York State from which some of its first settlers came, has had its whimsical moments, too. When Silas Sears built its first hotel in 1848, he named it Live and Let Live. It lived, but apparently didn't thrive. The next owner tried a more businesslike name, the Rome Exchange. It was still the Exchange, and apparently still struggling, when the third owner put it up for sale in 1857. The newspaper advertisement described Rome as a "flourishing village" of sixty families with three sawmills, a flour mill, a chair factory, a bedstead factory, and a wood-turning shop.

As these enterprises suggest, the village's prosperity depended on the Bark River for power and the surrounding countryside for timber and grain crops. The community began with a dam and sawmill in 1842. The mill was located on a race that paralleled the east bank of the river and rejoined it just above Main Street. Several mills occupied the same site over the years, sawing lumber, grinding grain, and even, for a couple of decades in the early twentieth century, generating electricity. In 1856 Dempster Seely built a steam-powered sawmill on the west bank of the river, beside the dam. He used the Bark not for power but for transportation, to raft his lumber downstream. Two of his brothers dug another race to the east of the first. It carried water a quarter of a mile from the millpond to a sawmill south of the village.

There are few remnants of Rome's past as a milling center. The sole extant mill is a substantial concrete block building on Main Street, located near the site of the original sawmill. The Globe Milling Company of Watertown used it as a feed mill from the 1940s through the 1960s, when it applied to transfer ownership of the dam to the Rome Lake Improvement Association. Though the State Public Service Commission did not approve the transfer then, it allowed the town of Sullivan to take over the dam in 1974.

The flood of June 2008 tore off a gate section at the powerhouse, prompting the DNR to issue a repair or abandon order. Though the township elected to repair the structure, it continues to weigh the cost of maintaining an aging dam. Could it be made to pay its way by generating electricity? Even if that proves feasible, which is unlikely, the pond will remain the chief reason for preserving the dam. Today Rome is a place of residence and recreation rather than industry, a place to live and let live.

"How did they manage to raft lumber down the river?" Puck asks as we step into our boat and draw it into the main channel. "It's less than a foot deep."

"Maybe they saved their shipments for high water in the spring. But even then they would have had to negotiate three dams between here and Fort Atkinson."

"Not to mention this turn." Puck points to a high bank straight ahead, which deflects the river sharply to the left. "Remember the Petersons?"

How could I forget the father and son whose canoe overturned here, less than five minutes into our cleanup trip? In their care to avoid the Scylla of the right bank they got tangled in the Charybdis of willow branches on the left. We considered ourselves lucky, that morning, to be able to run the turn at all. It tends to collect uprooted trees and branches, becoming entirely blocked at times. Then we have little choice but to carry around on the right, hauling our canoe partway up the steep bank.

Below the willows the channel straightens and the current slows. What remains of the Seely brothers' millrace enters on the left. When a subsequent owner began to fill it in, the State Bureau of Water and Shoreline Management issued an order to desist, reminding him that millraces are considered public waterways.

The Rome Campground occupies the right bank of this tranquil stretch. For paddlers who have taken an unplanned swim, it is a good place to regroup. Those who are still upright can exchange greetings with people fishing or basking in the sunlight on campground docks. Today a couple of kids are wading in the river, trying to catch minnows with nets. Farther on are several large bur oaks, the remnant of an oak savanna, their lower branches festooned with monofilament fishing line. A kingfisher issues its ratcheting call and flies from one oak to another.

After a shallow, quick-stepping riffle and a lazy loop to the south, the river passes through a cattail marsh. A flock of redwing blackbirds rustles among the stalks. Their gathering has the feel of a family reunion. None wants to be left behind when the signal comes to fly south. We ride a tongue of fast water under the County Road F bridge and pass a corral on the right, attracting the attention of a couple of ponies.

"See that bridge up ahead?" I ask Puck. "A German immigrant named George Senz built a dam just this side of it. We've been paddling the basin of his millpond for the last quarter mile. His sawmill was the seed of a flourishing little German community. Eventually it had a gristmill, a blacksmith shop, a cider press, a turning shop, a grocery, and an icehouse for storing blocks harvested from the millpond. It even had a church where Senz served as a lay preacher."

"Is this the place called Slabtown in our gazetteer?"

"That's the name that finally stuck. When Senz cut the side slabs from his logs he used to stack them beside the mill. He couldn't use them for lumber, but they made good fuel. The settlement was also called Senz's Mill or Sanses Mill."

"Another Bark River ghost town, like Heath's Mill. What happened to it? We can't blame the railroad for this one."

"After Senz the mill belonged to several owners with German surnames, including Henry Notbohm Sr. It was Henry's son William who operated the former Hawks Mill in Delafield from the 1870s through the 1890s. A man from Chicago, Frank Neitzel, eventually dismantled most of the buildings in Slabtown after he bought the dam and shoreline property in the 1940s and 1950s."

"Was he the one who removed the dam?" Puck asks. "Nothing seems to be left of it."

"Neitzel kept the dam during his lifetime for the sake of the pond, and it remained more or less functional until 1969, when a spring flood swept part of it away. The owner at the time, R. Winfield Scott, lived in Atlanta. When the Public Service Commission couldn't contact him, it declared the dam abandoned. The remnant was removed in the early 1970s. That home on the left is all that remains of Slabtown."

Approaching a sharp drop in the riverbed above Turner Road, we steer to the left of center and follow the deeper water to a pool below the bridge. Here the river widens, leaving exposed bars of silt in the middle. Looming directly ahead is one of the more attractive glacial features along the Bark River. From this vantage point it looks like a perfectly symmetrical kame, a place where meltwater drilled a hole vertically through the ice sheet, depositing sand and gravel in a cone-shaped mound, much like the bottom half of an hourglass. From other angles the landform appears more elongated, like a drumlin. Whatever its technical name, it provides a dramatic backdrop for the dairy farm at its base.

The river loops around the right side of the farm. Where a barn opens onto a cattle pen, we hug the deep water along the left bank. A monstrous snapping turtle rises almost to the surface, then fades into the depths.

"Did you see that?" Puck asks.

"I'm not sure. It was like a ghost. Or a water spirit, like the turtle effigy mounds."

We continue our circuit of the dairy farm, with fenced-in pasture on the left and a wooded drumlin on the right, then enter a low-lying woods where downfalls require maneuvering and an occasional carry-around. It's a bit of a shock to emerge from this hardwood jungle into the parklike grounds of the Bark River Campground.

People who enter the campground from Hanson Road and never venture onto the river miss seeing the place from an intriguing perspective. The right bank has been left in its natural state, sedge meadow and woods, except for a picnic area and playing field cleared at a bend in the river. A footbridge connects the playing field to the left bank, where small trailers with decks and picnic tables hug the edge of a high bluff overlooking the Bark. Jury-rigged steps lead from several of the campsites to the water. A couple of overturned canoes and a paddleboat lie beached and tethered on the steep incline, defying gravity and all but the most nimble boaters. Several campers wave when they catch sight of our canoe. Otherwise we remain eerily detached from the scene, like explorers happening upon an isolated tribe along the Amazon.

We should probably study their culture before it vanishes. But that project will have to wait, for the current carries us past the campground and into a vast cattail marsh. We startle a couple of deer on the left, where the marsh meets the woods. The channel swings right, straightens out beside a large pondlike opening in the cattails, and then veers left along a field of ripe corn. Here the river divides. The main channel loops back toward the woods while a secondary channel continues along the cornfield. We consult.

"Which way shall we go today?"

"The right channel is shorter."

"But there's hardly any current, and it may not be deep enough at this time of year."

Seeing a great blue heron on the right, stalking the shallows, we go left to avoid disturbing it.

The channels converge as we leave the cattail marsh and cross the invisible boundary between the towns of Sullivan and Hebron. When the federal surveyor ran this line in the fall of 1836, he described the higher ground as "level first rate," forested with sugar maples, elms, oaks, and ironwoods. The Bark measured about forty feet wide and moved with a rapid current. Though its pace is no longer so brisk, it does quicken where the river bends sharply left (south) into another marshy expanse.

Cows graze the woodlot at the bend. One, appearing more curious than belligerent, stands knee-deep in the water and watches us negotiate the turn. Places like these, where livestock has trampled the bank into a mud pudding, are a source of concern to the DNR. Runoff from the pasture, loaded with nitrogen from the chemical fertilizer and manure, not to mention *E. coli* bacteria, flows unimpeded into the Bark. As a result, the marsh downstream is considered "eutrophic," a DNR euphemism for a soup of algae and duckweed. Though the algae disburse oxygen generously during the day, they take it back with interest at night. Few species of fish besides carp can survive in the deoxygenated water.

Still, turtles seem to like it here. We often see painted turtles and occasionally a giant snapper. Today an unusual reptile has hauled itself onto a log, and doesn't seem to mind our closer scrutiny.

"This one looks as though he forgot to put on his shell this morning," Puck says. "Let me check the field guide."

She rummages in the waterproof bag for our reptile book. When she locates the turtle section, I tick off several field markings.

"About fourteen inches long. Flat head. Pointed nose. Brown skin—or shell, if that's what it is."

"Got it! He's an eastern spiny softshell. I should probably say 'she.' It says here that the males top out at about nine inches, just over half the length of the largest females."

Leaving Ms. Softshell to her sunbath, we arrive at another fork in the watery road. The left branch is actually a small inlet stream that drains an extensive marsh to the south. It is worth exploring, though you won't get far before you have to turn around. The main branch carries us right, toward Cushman Pond. To get there we pass through a narrow defile bordered on both sides by drumlins. These are oriented north and south in the direction of the glacier's retreat and rise abruptly to an elevation of about nine hundred feet.

Conspicuously situated at the entrance to the narrows, halfway up a drumlin on the left bank, is a small shanty. With the Cushmans' permission we've sometimes stopped there for lunch and fantasized about making it our permanent residence. Dreams are cheaper than real estate. What the shanty lacks in creature comforts—plumbing, for example, and electricity—it makes up for in perspective. From its perch on the bluff you can survey the river and marsh, observe a redtail hawk soaring above or a kingfisher diving from a dead snag on the opposite bank. The hillside is studded with trilliums in the spring. Later in the season, its profusion of wildflowers includes a few showy lady's slippers.

It must have been a place like this, perhaps this very spot, that seduced Cyrus Cushman. Around 1840, according to a family historian, the young pioneer from Tunbridge, Vermont, built a log cabin "on a high bank above a bend in Bark River." It was of course the cheap land rather than rustic solitude that lured him here. That, plus the profitable combination of timber and water-power where the river descended between thickly forested hills. Cushman had worked at a store in Ohio before arriving in the Wisconsin Territory in the fall of 1837. The twenty-six-year-old stayed over the winter in Sullivan Township in a home built by a relative, Cyrus Curtis. Then he made his claim and built a cabin on the Bark. By 1842 he owned 920 acres and was ready to build a frame house befitting the owner of an estate that extended all the way to the village of Rome.

In 1843 Cushman hired a crew to construct a log-crib dam and a sawmill. Raising the sawmill was itself a major project, requiring the effort of fifty men for two days. Before the crew could fit the logs together they had to chop freezing rain out of the mortises. With the sawmill up and running, Cushman cut lumber for the frame of the house. For the foundation he hauled fieldstone and bricks fashioned in a brickyard on Duck Creek, a tributary that joins the Bark a half mile downstream from the house. The Cushman house was rather grand for its time and place, a two-story Vermont-style colonial with a ballroom on the second floor. Endowed with a parlor, sitting room, dining room, and extra bedrooms, it became a natural way station for people traveling the coach road between Milwaukee and Janesville or Madison.

The sawmill was the nucleus of the enterprises that gave Cushman's Mills its name. Much of the year, the Bark was too shallow to float rafts of lumber to markets downstream on the Rock River. But Cushman took advantage of the occasional rise to sell lumber as far away as Rockford, Illinois. He added a gristmill to the sawing operation, replacing the grinding stones with roller mills when the new technology became available. He also built a turning shop to manufacture axe handles and furniture, particularly bedsteads. A creamery, blacksmith shop, and schoolhouse filled out the cluster of buildings around the mill. Not the least of Cushman's enterprises was his farm, remarkable for its substantial annual production of butter and maple sugar as well as its Ayrshire cattle and Berkshire hogs.

For a moment it appeared that Cushman would put his personal stamp on the name of the township as well as the landscape. When the town of Bark River was subdivided into smaller towns, he managed to have one of them named Tunbridge after his hometown. In 1846 there was even a town meeting in the Cushman home. But the name disappeared a year later, when the adjoining towns of Jefferson and Hebron assimilated Tunbridge.

According to an oft-quoted passage in Jane Austen's *Pride and Prejudice*, a single man in possession of a good fortune must be in want of a wife.

Such seems to have been the case with Cushman, for at the age of forty-nine the bachelor landlord married his housekeeper, a young widow and former schoolteacher named Cynthia Molthrop Dibble. The marriage apparently required adjustments on both sides. According to family legend, this daughter of a Methodist Episcopal minister disapproved of dancing and insisted that the second-floor ballroom be converted into bedrooms. Their growing family—ultimately five daughters and a son—required the conversion in any case.

For her part, Cynthia discovered that life with Cyrus wasn't always "easy," in the discreet phrasing of a family historian. The qualities of character that make a successful entrepreneur aren't always conducive to cozy personal relationships, and Cushman could be a stern disciplinarian. On one occasion he whipped his son, also named Cyrus, with a buggy whip. When the young man proposed to join his cousins in a sawmill venture in Oregon, the patriarch threatened to disown him. In temperament and dynastic aspirations, Cyrus was apparently cast in the mold of William Faulkner's Thomas Sutpen rather than Austen's Charles Bingley.

As the Cushman daughters married, Cyrus provided each with a dowry of land on the condition that it not be sold outside the family. Consequently, federal census records show a steady decline in his own acreage, from the original 920 acres to 640 in 1870 and 395 in 1880. What remained was nonetheless valuable. The land and improvements were worth $16,000 in 1880, equivalent to about $352,000 today.

~~~~~~~

After threading the narrows between forested drumlins, we turn left into the main part of Cushman Pond. On the left shore a doe and a fawn from this spring hoist their white flags and bound up the hillside. They are one reason that this was a favorite hunting and fishing grounds of the Ho-Chunk and Potawatomi Indians. In the days before tractors replaced horses, farmhands regularly turned up arrowheads and other projectile points while plowing fields to the south and west of the pond. When Cynthia Cushman glanced out her kitchen window, she frequently saw Indians following a trail beside the river.

Charlie Schumacher, a hired hand who operated the mills for Cyrus, remembered an Indian camp on the hill west of the river, across Cushman Road from the millpond. Cushman Cemetery currently occupies the ground, though it now belongs to the township. Clearly visible from the pond is the stone monument that marks Cyrus Cushman's grave. You have to get much closer to read the inscription below his name and the dates of his birth and death: "HE WAS OF THE 8 GENERATION/FROM REV. ROBERT CUSHMAN/ THE PILGRIM."

Cushman had reason to be proud of his descent from this Pilgrim father, even if the "Reverend" isn't quite accurate. Robert Cushman was a wool carder by trade and a deacon in the Separatist congregation in Leiden, Holland. Though he joined his brethren in the New World for only about a month, he played a crucial role in founding Plymouth Plantation. Miles Standish called him "ye stay & life of ye whole bussiness."

What did he do to deserve such praise? In 1617 the Leiden congregation delegated Cushman and John Carver, later the first governor of the colony, to obtain a patent from the Virginia Company and the permission of James I of England to settle in Virginia. They secured the necessary permissions, but the Virginia Company was unfortunately bankrupt. After negotiating briefly with another company, the Separatists came to terms with a group of London merchant "adventurers"—we would call them venture capitalists today— organized by Thomas Weston.

As they worked out the details of the contract, their proposed destination shifted north from settlements dominated by Anglicans to the part of Virginia known as New England. There, remote from an ecclesiastical influence that they abhorred, the Separatists hoped to live and practice their religion more freely. This shift provoked some controversy within the Leiden group, but not nearly as much as a couple of changes in the contract.

According to the revised articles of agreement the colony would be run as a joint stock company for seven years. During that period, the investors were to supply the necessary capital, while all profits from timber, furs, fishing, and so forth would go into a joint account or common store. From that store the settlers would receive their daily necessities. At the end of seven years, all goods and profits would be divided among the settlers and investors according to the number of shares they held in the company. In this quasi-socialist arrangement a settler had little incentive to work harder than his neighbor, for he received an equal portion during the first seven years and a portion based on shares thereafter. Clauses in the original agreement allowed settlers to accumulate personal capital apart from the general store, but these were struck from the final version.

Cushman, as the congregation's chief agent in negotiating the agreement, came under sharp attack for agreeing to the revisions. When the *Mayflower* sailed from Southampton, England, in August 1620, the Pilgrims had not signed the articles of agreement and were uncertain whether Weston's company would back them. To make matters worse their second ship, the *Speedwell*, leaked badly, forcing both vessels to return to port. When the *Mayflower* finally got off in September, it carried about 102 passengers, most of whom were "Strangers," that is, good Anglicans seeking economic opportunity rather than religious freedom in the New World. Though the ship was able to accommodate some passengers from the woefully misnamed *Speedwell*, it had to leave about twenty behind, including Cushman.

Cushman therefore missed that first difficult winter in Plymouth, when about half of the colony died. He finally arrived in November 1621 with his fourteen-year-old son, Thomas, and some bad news: Weston, who had not dared to tell his investors about the unsigned agreement, now insisted that the leaders of the colony comply with its terms. That, or forgo further supplies. Plymouth's leading citizens signed reluctantly, anticipating resistance from their fellow settlers, especially the Strangers.

To help them swallow this bitter pill and head off mutiny, Cushman mustered his oratorical skills for a sermon delivered in the Plymouth Common House on December 9. He took as his text a passage from Paul's first epistle to the Corinthians: "Let no man seeke his owne, But every man anothers wealth" (I Cor. 10:24). He opened by invoking Divine authority for his message: much as God had sent Paul to admonish the people of Corinth, He had now sent Cushman to correct whatever was "amisse" in Plymouth. Cushman's sermon was no "sinners in the hands of an angry God" harangue. That was the style of a later generation. Rather, like the typical Puritan preacher of his day, Cushman argued his case point by point, taking objections into account and working toward practical applications of the biblical principles.

After giving due consideration to the standard arguments in favor of immediately distributing the common land and goods among individuals, Cushman argued that they were obliged to repay their investors first: "Wee also have beene very chargeable to many of our loving friends, which helped us hither, and now againe supplyed us, so that before we thinke of gathering riches, we must even in Conscience thinke of requiting their charge, love, and labour, and cursed be that profit and gaine which aymeth not at this."

In case simple justice proved unconvincing, he went on to cite biblical precedent for the terms imposed by the articles of agreement. The Israelites, too, had lived in Canaan for seven years before dividing the Promised Land among tribes, and still longer before the tribes parceled it out to families. The temptation to divide the common wealth prematurely could come, Cushman maintained, from only one source: "Who, I pray thee, brought this particularizing first into the world? Did not Sathan, who was not content to keepe that equall state with his fellowes, but would set his throne above the Starres?"

Powerful as this ethical and theological appeal was, it was probably self-interest that ultimately moved the colonists to abide by the original contract for another year and a half. In the spring of 1623 they took the first step away from that agreement by allowing families to set aside acreage for their own use, though they did not actually own the land. By the time Cushman died in 1625, well before the seven-year term expired, the original scheme was honored more in the breach than the observance.

Cushman never returned to Plymouth, where today a monument memorializes his address. It was the first extant sermon to be preached on American soil, preceding John Winthrop's "A Modell of Christian Charity" by nine years. The latter is better known and has become the classic text on American exceptionalism. Nothing in Cushman's performance is as memorable as Winthrop's comparison of the Massachusetts Bay Colony to a "Citty upon a Hill." It may nevertheless have the better claim to being the keynote address for New World civil and economic order. Released abruptly from the old caste system and its hereditary distribution of property, many of the first settlers became intoxicated with opportunity. In his sermon Cushman cited the example of the Virginia colonists to the south, who were reputedly people of sound moral and religious character until they came to the New World. Thereupon they became, in his estimation, "meere worldlings."

Cushman conceded that self-interest and acquisitiveness are ingrained in human nature and can be forces for good. But he sought to balance entrepreneurship with concern for the common weal and plain old-fashioned Christian charity. Thus he put his finger on a conflict that would trouble the raw new country at every level of human interaction, from government and commerce to the domestic necessities of the frontier.

In fact Cushman regarded frontier neighborliness as a model for mutual aid in other spheres of activity: "When men are come together, to lift some weighty peece of tymber or vessell; if one stand still and doe not lift, shall not the rest be weakned and dishartned?" Two centuries later, when Cyrus Cushman and his crew fashioned sleet-glazed logs into a sawmill, they were carrying on a tradition that had Robert Cushman's—and presumably God's—blessing.

~~~~~

Approaching the dam at the south end of Cushman Pond, we take out on the left, next to a dock that doubles as a diving board. The bank rises sharply at this point, so we have to strain against gravity and slippery mud to haul our canoe to the top of the earthen dike. From there it is an easy downhill carry or slide to the put-in below the dam. A steel-sided building on the left bank houses a US Geological Survey water level gauge. Leaving our boat at the put-in, we take a water bottle and our lunch back uphill to the dam.

"Is this where Cyrus Cushman built the original sawmill?" Puck asks, making herself comfortable on the high bank.

"Just about," I answer, taking a seat beside her. "A succession of other buildings followed, the last of which succumbed to fire in 1954. The sagging old structure was for decades a favorite subject of Sunday artists."

"Think of all those canvases gathering dust in attics."

"Most probably are, but not all. The Hoard Historical Museum in Fort Atkinson has several, including one by Mary Cunningham Hoard. She was the wife of William Dempster Hoard Jr. and an avid local historian."

"We'll have to go and see them. Not that I can't predict what they'll look like: weathered gray boards, a wooden waterwheel, and a Currier and Ives title like *Old Country Mill*. Am I right?"

"I forget the titles. You're right about the weathered siding, but not about the waterwheel. If Cyrus ever used a wooden overshot wheel, he soon replaced it with a turbine."

The dam has likewise followed a trajectory of improvement followed by picturesque if potentially dangerous decay. Either Cyrus or his son replaced the original log-crib dam with another of the same type. The son, who got to Oregon after all following his father's death, died relatively young of tuberculosis, aggravated by work in the dusty mill. His son, Cyrus Leland (called Leland by the family), replaced the log structure with a concrete dam in 1913, when he was only twenty years old. That dam became the responsibility of William Leland Cushman, the fourth generation of his family to occupy the land.

~~~~~

Courtesy of Hoard Historical Museum, Fort Atkinson, Wisconsin

The Cushman mill in the early 1950s

I met Bill Cushman in March 1997, as he was coming out of his barn. A hale and hearty man of 73, he still enjoyed bow hunting for turkey. A bow and a quiver hung in the summer kitchen through which we passed on our way into the house. He introduced me to his wife, Joanne, and the three of us sat at the kitchen table, talking about Cushmans past and present.

Bill professed not to be especially interested in family history, and contrasted himself in this respect with a neighbor, also descended from Robert Cushman, who wanted him to join what Bill called a "Pilgrim Club." Somewhere in the house is an old footlocker containing documents relating to Cyrus Cushman's sawmill, but he had lost the key to the locker and lacked the curiosity to force the lock. Despite his show of indifference, Bill is well versed in the anecdotal history of the Cushmans and occasionally finds other keys to their lives. While helping his father lay drain tile he once unearthed logs from the old corduroy stage road. He knows where the brickyard and creamery were located, and regularly comes across remnants of cellars and wells belonging to the cluster of dwellings formerly known as Cushman's Mills.

His father's dam was another relic from those days. Bill doubted that he could save it from the DNR, especially since it no longer served any purpose. After the mill burned down, the dam still backed up water for the fishpond used by vacationers who rented the tiny cottages on the east shore. Built in the 1930s, these once provided Bill with supplemental income. But he no longer maintained the cottages or stocked the pond with fish.

Like Margaret Zerwekh and other owners of deteriorating small dams, he was faced with the choice between repair and removal, both of which are costly. After inspecting the Cushman dam in 1988, William Sturtevant of the DNR drew up a list of urgent repairs that could be performed by a contractor for about $9,500. Even as he approved the repairs, however, Sturtevant noted that the dam's spillway capacity was, at 216 cubic feet per second, far short of the 929 cfs stipulated by Wisconsin Administrative Code for a dam of its size and hazard rating. Following a dam failure analysis, Bill Cushman estimated that he would have to pay $240,000 to bring the dam up to state safety standards. Or he could spend $40,000 to $45,000 to remove it, a figure based on comparable dam removals upstream in Slabtown and downstream in Hebron.

During the 1990s the DNR occasionally drew on a Small and Abandoned Dam fund to pay for all or part of removals. Generally, though, it holds dam owners accountable for repairs. As a state agency, it must use taxpayers' money for the public good. When the DNR determines that a dam is unsafe, it sets a deadline for repair or removal, usually five years. If an owner fails to undertake required work before the deadline, as happened with the Cushman dam in 1988 and again in 1993, the DNR generally avoids bullying tactics. Its wait-and-see approach, though potentially risky, is meant to be humane. Contrary to the folklore of some Wisconsin sportsmen, farmers, and manufacturers, DNR employees do not, as a rule, reek of sulfur and brimstone.

Take Bill Sturtevant, for example. In a conversation with Bill in Madison, I found him to be an engaging and compassionate man. Though he takes seriously his role as a custodian of state resources, he prefers to remain on friendly terms with people who are not happy to find him on their doorstep.

He believes that a dam safety inspector should still be able to sit down to dinner with a dam owner after showing him how to comply with state code. Sturtevant expressed concern about Cushman's health and hoped that the dam issue could be resolved in a reasonable period of time—more than five years, if necessary—without hard feelings or financial distress.

Bill Cushman felt less cordial toward the DNR. Indulging in bitter humor, he reflected that if the dam were removed and the millpond drained he would have another twenty-eight acres to plant in the spring. "I'd like to plant some of those DNR fellows," he said. "It's a crop I hope would fail." But that dark cloud blew over the horizon as he pondered the greater challenges his ancestors had faced and overcome on the Wisconsin frontier. He stands in awe of what they accomplished under difficult conditions. He is also amazed at their spirit of cooperation, citing an instance when a wing of the dam washed out and neighbors pitched in to sandbag it, thereby saving the rest of the structure.

Sitting in Bill's kitchen, listening to this story, I reflected that Robert Cushman might have used it in his sermon, had he foreseen it, as an example of mutual aid. America is no longer a joint stock company, to be sure, and the fear of God is even less a deterrent today than it was in 1621. But who knows? Perhaps in today's freewheeling entrepreneurial world the old Separatist would have approved of the DNR as a protector of community resources.

Except for a parcel of land that he leases to a couple from Illinois, Bill has managed to hold onto all of the property that he inherited from his father. He would like to pass it on, still intact, to his son. "If you let it go," he told Lee Cushman, "you're out of your mind. It's a helluva livable place." But Lee resides in town and works in a bank. He may not have the time or the inclination to keep a large farm functioning.

When it was time for me to leave, Bill followed me out the door. He was on his way back to the barn, where a new crankshaft lay in pieces on the floor. Like his family, it had come from England. His job was to put it all together, install it in his tractor, and get started on the spring plowing, as Cushmans have been doing for many decades.

~~~~~~

The same heavy rains and flooding that damaged Margaret Zerwekh's millrace and prompted the DNR to drain her pond in June 2008 had a more decisive impact on Cushman Pond. The dam spillway was unable to handle the volume of water, and on June 9 the torrent breached the earthen dike on the right side

Reproduced with permission of the Wisconsin Department of Natural Resources

The Cushman dam after it washed out in a June 2008 flood

of the spillway, draining the pond. Fortunately, the bridge and road below the dam were not damaged, nor were any of the Cushman buildings.

What happened in the aftermath of this event stands in stark contrast to Delafield's prolonged agonizing over the Zerwekh millpond. On June 30 the DNR issued an order to reconstruct or remove the dam. At a public hearing on October 9 only two people besides the DNR representatives showed up to express their views—Bill Cushman and a friend. Both supported removal of the dam, which sprawled like a toppled colossus beside the free-flowing river.

The DNR declared the dam formally abandoned in March 2009 and removed it in the spring. Though the Small and Abandoned Dam fund had been used up, the fund had generated sufficient bond revenue to pay the total cost—less than eight thousand dollars—of removing the dam, burying the concrete debris on Cushman property, and stabilizing the river banks with annual ryegrass and erosion mats. Across the road from the cemetery where Cyrus Cushman lies in his grave, waiting for Judgment Day, the Bark is already undergoing a resurrection, resuming life as the river that Cyrus first encountered in the 1830s.

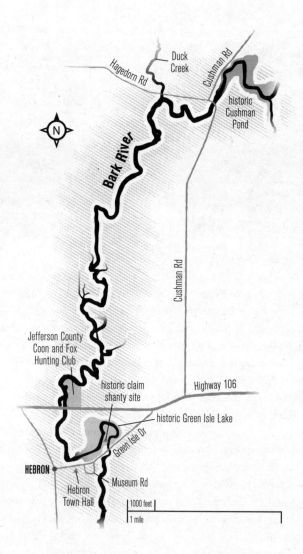

N

Duck
Creek

Hagedorn Rd

Cushman Rd

historic
Cushman
Pond

Bark River

Cushman Rd

Jefferson County
Coon and Fox
Hunting Club

historic claim
shanty site

Highway 106

historic Green Isle Lake

Green Isle Dr

HEBRON

Museum Rd

Hebron
Town Hall

1000 feet

1 mile

CHAPTER 11

Cushman Road
to Hebron

The Bark's spring 2008 rampage is still in the future as Puck and I finish our lunch beside the Cushman Pond dam and return to the canoe. We take our paddling stations, push off at an angle upstream, and swing the bow downstream to thread the eye of a bridge culvert. Just below Cushman Road, on the left, is a modern ranch-style house. Leland Cushman, the builder of the 1913 dam, constructed it as a retirement home for himself and his wife, Flora Zuill Cushman, leaving the colonial frame house to be occupied first by a hired man with a family, then by Bill Cushman's family.

Flora was the family laureate. A member and for a time the president of the Pen Women of Wisconsin, she frequently gave lectures and read her poetry. Her elegy "The River and I" records an intimate personal relationship with the Bark, which she concedes is "just an unsung river, / Not a mighty Amazon." The poem's forty-eight lines reflect a sense of stewardship grounded in religious faith. Doubtless recalling the heyday of Cushman's Mills, she addresses the river as follows:

You turned their water wheels for power
And rafted their logs down stream,
Until erosion glutted you—
Quite contrary to God's scheme.

We pass the old house, its original clapboard siding now clad in white vinyl, and ride the swift current into a sharp right turn. Here the water is deep and dark, the channel obstructed by fallen tree branches. We nevertheless study the bottom for a telltale glint of aluminum. Joanne Cushman asked us to keep our eyes open for a large two-handled pot that got the urge to travel, like the gingerbread man in the children's story. After using it to boil potatoes for a supper at the Masonic lodge in Whitewater, she had taken it out to their dog so he could lick it clean. The pot slipped from her hands and rolled down the hill to the river. It was still floating upright when she last saw it. Most likely, it bumped into a branch and sank in the first turn. Until we learn otherwise, though, we are free to imagine it jauntily riding the Gulf Stream.

Paddle, paddle with all you've got!
You can't catch me,
I'm the two-handled pot!

Shallow riffles ahead mark a place where the river is bordered by pasture. We scan this section carefully, from side to side.

"Remember the first time we paddled this?" Puck asks.

"How can I forget? Our boat still bears the scar." We were so intent on dodging rocks that we didn't notice a steel cable stretched across the river, presumably to keep cows from escaping to New Orleans. It struck the brass cap on our bow with enough force to leave a dent in the metal. Considering the alternative, vivisection by cable, we got off easy.

Duck Creek joins the Bark from the right about a half mile below Cushman Road. You can paddle under the Hagedorn Road bridge and some distance up the creek before it becomes impassible. It is hard to believe that this waterway, with its debris-choked channel and sluggish current, once powered saw- and gristmills. Before the land was cleared and ditched for agriculture, there was plenty of raw material to be sawed into lumber. The federal surveyor noted the "first rate timber land" around the mouth of the creek and an Indian sugar bush nearby, on the east bank of the Bark.

From Duck Creek to Highway 106, a distance of about three miles by water, the river meanders through a low area lying west of a string of drumlins. Silver maples and willows populate the flood plain. Here the river looks much as it did at the time of the survey, except for the occasional drainage ditch and a rusty steel bridge. We backpaddle as we approach the bridge, preferring not to be wedged under the deck or skewered on one of its broken bolts or support rods. Today there is adequate clearance, and we don't have to carry around the old wreck.

Halfway to Highway 106 the river meanders through a pleasant sedge meadow. The marsh hay, no longer harvested, is tall enough to engulf a scattering of hawthorne trees on the right. On the left a grassy meadow ascends eastward to Cushman Road. Paddling this section, we can't help but recall an uncanny episode from the previous year's cleanup trip. By the time we reached Cushman Pond we had filled a half-dozen large plastic bags with trash. We left our treasure with the Cushmans, who offered to dispose of it with their weekly pickup. The day was getting on, and we needed to reach Hebron by about five o'clock, so we paddled the rest of way at a faster clip.

Unlike today, it was broiling hot. By the time we reached this meadow we had drained the last of the lukewarm water from our water bottles. We were tired and sweaty. Perhaps the sun had addled my brain, for I began to hallucinate out loud about the cold beer in our refrigerator at home. Just then, as though on cue, a beer can materialized beside the boat. Plucking it from the river, I discovered that it was unopened. Apparently it contained enough air to keep it afloat. I rinsed off the top, dried it with my shirttail, and paused to consider the incurable diseases I might contract from a stray can of beer. Then I popped the top and took a sip. Praised be the water spirit for answering a paddler's prayer! From our boat the can passed all the way to the last canoe before joining the empties in a trash bag.

No trash bags would have been large enough for the empties we encountered next, a couple of junked vehicles from the 1930s. Riddled with hunters' bullets, they looked like getaway cars that John Dillinger might have used for a bank robbery. Today we notice they're gone. Had the property owner finally noticed the visual blight? Had Hollywood come looking for props? Or had the price of scrap metal gone up?

The Bark takes a westerly swing before dropping down to the highway, allowing an unobstructed view of pasture and hilltop on the right bank. In one place it doubles back on itself, forming an oxbow. Until the mid-1980s a dilapidated outhouse occupied a channel that cut across the oxbow. The river itself provided the plumbing. I thought of similar accommodations I had seen in Southeast Asia, where toilets are sometimes suspended over carp ponds. Why was this one located here, far from any house, in a meadow that is often flooded and unapproachable? We weren't privy to the privy's secret. Perhaps it belonged to an upscale duck blind. This part of the river, with easy access to the adjoining cornfields, is still a magnet for migrating waterfowl.

Nearly as bizarre as the stranded outhouse is a field of enormous tree trunks standing upright on our starboard side. Someone went to a good deal of trouble to move these here, possibly after deciding the trunks had no value as lumber and couldn't easily be cut into firewood. Approaching this cemetery of the giants, we feel some of the same awe and mystery that we experienced at Stonehenge in England. Until someone comes up with a better name for this place, we'll call it Woodhenge.

We hear the next attraction before we see it. The property on the left, extending all the way to the highway, belongs to a hunting club. We catch a glimpse of the clubhouse through the trees, along with vehicles belonging to the members. Then we notice a commotion in the shrubbery along the bank and find ourselves eyeball to eyeball with a couple of hounds. Apparently we aren't what they are looking for, because they disappear quickly, adding their voices to the general pandemonium. To our merely human ears, they sound aggrieved and forlorn. But on this August afternoon, with its hint of autumn in the air, they are probably having the time of their brief lives.

The chorus of hunting hounds fades as we approach the Highway 106 bridge, the first paved crossing since Cushman Road. At this point the highway marks the seam where two older townships were stitched together in 1846 to form the town of Hebron. From the creation of Jefferson County in 1839 until 1843, the entire southeast quarter of Jefferson County was designated Bark River Township. Amid sectarian squabbling over the next three years, the town was subdivided and its original name was dropped altogether. The portion of Hebron Township upstream from Highway 106, I have mentioned, was briefly called Tunbridge in tribute to Cyrus Cushman's hometown in Vermont. The portion downstream from the highway belonged briefly to a smaller Bark River Township that extended south to include today's Cold Spring. What emerged from all of this patching and realignment is a Hebron Township that remains six sections shy of the standard thirty-six.

Hebron came by its name in an equally haphazard fashion. It rained on the evening in 1846 when the board of supervisors met to choose a new name for the downsized Bark River Township, and only three supervisors showed up at the Munro schoolhouse on Highway 106. On the desks lay songbooks used by a singing class that met weekly in the same room. While waiting for others to appear, the supervisors tried out their voices on several selections. Supervisor Samuel T. Clothier took a fancy to "Hebron," composed by Lowell Mason in 1830, and suggested that the township adopt its title. His fellow supervisors approved. Local legend has not preserved which lyrics they sang to Mason's melody, those by Isaac Watts ("So let our lips and lives express . . .") or Henry H. Milman ("Ride on, ride on, in majesty!"). This Hebron differs in one respect from the contentious Middle Eastern city where Abraham, Isaac, and Jacob are buried. To avoid identifying yourself as an outsider, you must pronounce the town's name with a long *e*: HEE-bron.

Passing under the highway, we greet a fisherman who has claimed a spot next to the bridge, where there is room to park a car. Soon after, our boat is gripped by that quickening of the current that attracted early speculators in search of waterpower sites. The river pitches downward toward the base of a steep bank, then veers sharply left before passing under a light-duty steel bridge and entering a meadow that was once the first millpond on the Bark River.

"I appreciate not having to duck under the gunwales to avoid those girders," Puck says from her station in the bow. "Look! With the dam out, I can barely reach them with my paddle."

The current continues to quicken as the river drops into the meadow, waving miniature flags of whitewater wherever it encounters an obstacle.

"These are strange-looking rocks," Puck says over her shoulder, deftly shifting the bow left or right to avoid hitting the weathered gray objects. In fast water the bow paddler does most of the steering. The stern paddler follows the bow's lead, aligning the back of the boat with the front.

"That's because they're made of wood," I respond. "You're looking at the stumps of trees that were felled by some of the first white men to visit this part of Wisconsin."

"Trees growing in the middle of the river? Not likely."

"Think of the Bark as a squirrel that buried a nut 170 years ago and can't remember where it is."

"That's a really old squirrel. No wonder it can't remember."

"So the river rummages through the sediment in search of its old bed. Now and then it miscalculates and carves a new channel through soil that once formed the riverbank. With time enough and a shovel, we could probably locate the stumps that mark the original channel."

"But not today, if it's all right with you."

Today the former millpond is a textbook case of plant succession, as young trees and woody shrubs replace the weeds that first colonized the muck. Looking to our left, toward the northwest corner of the meadow, we notice a hump of higher ground topped with larger trees and shrubs. That little dollop of glacial debris gave the millpond its name, Green Isle Lake. On our right is a more signifi-cant land feature, a promontory that once extended into the pond and still bears the forlorn remains of a wooden dock. It was on this finger of high ground that a group of speculators from Milwaukee built a claim shanty in December 1835.

Milwaukee was then a settlement of five log cabins and thirty people in the vicinity of Solomon Juneau's fur-trading post. Juneau had traded with his beloved Potawatomi and Menominee for two decades, until they ceded their lands to the federal government in the 1830s. Adapting to the times, he began to trade in land rather than pelts, joining Elisha W. Edgerton (whose model farm became the Masonic Home on Highway 18), Jonas Folts, Thomas A. Holmes, Henry Hosmer, Milo Jones, and Henry Miller in a venture called the Rock River Land and Claim Company. Anticipating the public land sales of 1836, the company sought to identify and claim what Jones called "mill sites and other desirable locations."

Desirable to whom and for what? The Rock River Land and Claim Company included members who also had an interest in the Byron Kilbourn project described in a previous chronicle, the Milwaukee and Rock River Canal (see chapter 4). By enabling farmers and manufacturers to transport their products easily between the Great Lakes and the Mississippi River, the canal would have promoted development of the region and increased the value of land in the canal strip. Increase Lapham, Kilbourn's surveyor, had identified two sites on the Rock River as likely western terminals, one at the mouth of the Bark River, the other at the mouth of the Oconomowoc River.

Milo Jones, who had worked on a federal survey crew in the eastern part of the Wisconsin Territory, was in a position to identify the best waterpower sites along the proposed canal routes. In December 1835 he and a French guide named LaTonde led members of the Rock River Land and Claim Company to one site at the confluence of the Rock and Crawfish Rivers and three on the Bark River: at its junction with the Whitewater River, at its junction with the Rock River, and here at Hebron.

The Hebron site was especially attractive because it combined power for a sawmill with an apparently inexhaustible supply of sawmill fodder. For decades the area was known as Bark River Woods. Much of the land west of Prairieville (now Waukesha) consisted of oak openings, rolling grassland dotted with a variety of oak trees. According to Lucien B. Caswell, who arrived in Milwaukee with his mother and stepfather in 1836 and traveled overland to Lake Koshkonong, the landscape looked "more like an orchard than like timberland." He recalled that Indians set fire to the prairie each fall after the first frost to prevent the intrusion of woody undergrowth. The bur oaks, with their thick, wide-wale bark, are especially resistant to fire.

To protect their buildings farmers had to create firebreaks, often by plowing parallel furrows around their property and burning the vegetation between them. The Bark River served as a natural firebreak, allowing a variety of hardwoods to flourish on its east bank, downwind of the prevailing winds. Joel Bailey, who surveyed the area in September 1836, referred frequently in his notes to "first rate timber land," qualified occasionally by the phrase "except for marsh." Large tracts of Bark River Woods remained federal property, and early settlers helped themselves freely to the resource they called "Uncle Sam's timber."

Because the combination of woods, oak openings, and prairie was ideal elk and deer habitat, it attracted wolves as well. Early settlers frequently mentioned the predators in their memoirs, sometimes distinguishing between timber wolves and what they called prairie wolves (coyotes). Though there is no verifiable record of anyone being killed by wolves, pioneers feared them and recounted stories of lone travelers beset by hungry packs, especially at night, and compelled to build a fire to fend them off. As settlers hunted down or drove away the wolves' natural quarry, the animals adapted by preying on livestock, giving rise to numerous anecdotes of wolves venturing boldly into barnyards to snatch a pig or a chicken or even, on one occasion, the stirring stick from a kettle of soap. Despite the farmers' relentless efforts to eradicate them, wolves persisted in the area until the early twentieth century.

The wolves of Bark River Woods doubtless entertained David Sargent with their oratorios throughout the winter of 1835–1836. The Rock River Land and Claim Company hastily constructed a shanty for Sargent and pressed on to their other claims, leaving him alone to occupy the site. The following spring a work party arrived and built a dam about 440 yards upstream from today's concrete remnant. The first Hebron dam was a crib of large timbers filled with rocks and gravel. Its composition remained basically the same for almost a century, though it had to be rebuilt occasionally and was eventually faced with concrete. In 1933 a concrete dam replaced the crib structure.

The work party also dug a millrace to carry water some 330 yards from the pond to the projected site of the sawmill. For its construction and operation the company required more specialized skills, so it hired two men from Oneida, New York. Alvin Foster would serve as the millwright and foreman of the work crew. His brother-in-law, Rufus Dodge, would be the smith and cook. Sargent came to Milwaukee in August 1836 to meet Foster and Dodge. After an exploratory trip to the mill site with a packhorse, the three men returned with an ox team and a wagon loaded with the heavy equipment.

~~~~~~~~~~

Puck and I have circumnavigated the peninsula where Sargent spent the winter in his claim shanty. Looking downstream, we see where the river collects itself for a plunge over the low sill of concrete that remains after most of the dam was removed in 1996. We disembark on the right to scout the small drop and decide it could probably be run safely. Sufficient water pours over the jagged concrete to provide clearance. More important, the outflow is irregular and therefore less likely to trap a boat than the dangerously symmetrical hydraulic below an intact dam. However, we decide to play it safe and line the boat. With painter ropes tied to bow and stern, we guide the empty canoe into the channel, over the concrete remnant, and into an eddy.

From our position on the west bank of the Bark we look across at the spot where Sargent, Foster, and Dodge must have pulled up in their ox-drawn wagon that August evening in 1836. Their wagon was loaded with the gear needed to build a sawmill on the frontier, far from hardware and building supply stores. Their load would have included a muley saw, miscellaneous iron fixtures, and huge leather belts to transmit power from the waterwheel to the pulleys that would drive the saw and the log cradle. For his smithy Dodge would have needed an anvil, a leather apron, and an assortment of tongs and hammers. Somewhere in the wagon, probably at the top of the load where it was most accessible, was the leather bellows that Dodge would use to fan the coals to a working heat. We are sure about the bellows because it figures in his account of that evening.

Their journey by wagon had been far more arduous than the scouting run with a packhorse. From Prairieville to the Bark River they had to cut a road where before there had been only an Indian trail. It had taken them four days to cover a mere forty-five miles, and they were probably bone tired when they pulled up across from the claim shanty. Rather than ford the river with all their gear in the waning light, they decided to leave the team and wagon on the east bank. Then they waded across the river and made camp near the shanty under an old oak tree. We can imagine their dismay when they were roused during the night by the sound of wolves snarling and tearing at their baggage less than forty-five yards away. In the morning they surveyed the damage. Dodge found his precious leather bellows in tatters, whole sections missing and presumably devoured by the animals. Fortunately, the oxen were unharmed. The wolves knew better than to attack leather on the hoof.

Dodge eventually replaced his bellows, and the crew was working on the sawmill by early September. The dam and mill were notable landmarks for travelers in the area. Jonas Folts and S. C. Leavitt encountered the dam in 1836, while canoeing the Bark River from Folts's home in Summit (Waukesha County) to the mouth of Whitewater Creek. Folts, a member of the Rock River Land and Claim Company, claimed land in Hebron and subsequently held numerous political offices in the town.

Another traveler, Robert Masters, belonged to a party of six who set out from Milwaukee in the deep snow and subzero cold of late December 1836 to explore claims near the confluence of the Rock and Crawfish Rivers. The place came to be known as Masters Rapids or Jefferson Rapids, then simply as Jefferson. They arrived at Sargent's claim shanty after 1:00 a.m. on Christmas Eve and found it already full of sleeping men. After baiting their horses they squeezed into the remaining places on the floor and resumed their journey in the morning.

By February 1837 the work crew had completed the first mill to be erected in the entire Rock River watershed above Dixon's Crossing, some ninety miles to the south in Illinois. The Rock River Land and Claim Company hired Enoch G. Darling as the first sawyer. Later it hired Horace Churchill and Darling's half-brother, Alonzo Brown, to haul supplies for the sawmill crew. Brown was not impressed by the accommodations in Bark River Mills, as the settlement was known during the first decade of its existence. When he arrived in June 1837 he partook, he recalled wryly, "of a sumptuous breakfast at the Hotel Bark River, which consisted of musty pork and a few slices of stale bread and molasses."

Its cuisine aside, the place was beginning to look like a real village. Besides the sawmill and hotel, which was known by various names, Brown noticed a new frame building under construction. The first permanent resident, William Reynolds, had recently arrived and would serve the community as schoolmaster. Sadly, Reynolds's son was the first resident to be buried in the town, in 1838. That September the men of Bark River Township, all seven of them, gathered in the millhouse to choose James Duane Doty as their delegate to Congress. They might not have voted for Doty had they known that he would persuade the legislature to scuttle the Milwaukee and Rock River Canal when he became territorial governor in 1841, thereby devaluing their property.

In 1837 the Rock River Land and Claim Company still had reason to believe that the sawmill would repay their investment many times over. The lumber needed to build the communities known later as Fort Atkinson and Jefferson had to come from Bark River Mills, as there was no competing sawmill on the Rock River until the 1840s. During the late 1830s and early 1840s a man could make good money by felling trees on the public land in Bark River Woods, sawing the logs into boards at the mill, bundling the lumber into rafts, and poling the rafts eight miles down the Bark to Fort Atkinson. Myron Smith, who helped to build the first sawmills at Rome and Cushman's Mills, recalled doing just that during the summer of 1843. He earned twelve dollars per day—about $365 per day today.

Lucien B. Caswell likewise testified to heavy logging in Bark River Woods. The rafts of lumber went down the Bark and Rock Rivers, passed his cabin on Lake Koshkonong, and continued downstream to Janesville and Beloit. "I could see these rafts as they came through the lake in large numbers," Caswell recalled. "Sometimes they became windbound in the lake and were driven off into the bays. I was called in to help them out. This I greatly enjoyed, for at times we slept on the rafts over night, and sometimes on the bank, waiting for the wind to go down or change, so we could pole the raft out. The rafts often were broken by the heavy waves, and the lumber scattered to the four winds."

Like the lumber rafts, the men who were instrumental in establishing Bark River Mills tended to drift downstream. David Sargent moved to Jefferson, as did Enoch Darling. In August 1837 Darling loaded his household goods and those of his half-sisters and half-brother onto a scow and traveled down the Bark and up the Rock to Jefferson. As if this weren't sufficient freight for low-water shipping, the scow also carried the frame of a substantial building, crafted at the sawmill. Darling erected the building, apparently also a Rock

River Land and Claim Company venture, on the site of today's county court-house. It served as the Jefferson House tavern, the first courthouse, and the trading post. Darling settled in as the new community's postmaster.

Other principals moved to Fort Atkinson. Alvin Foster joined his brother Dwight, who had built a cabin near the remains of Fort Koshkonong, a military outpost whose construction figures in another chronicle (see chapter 14). Rufus Dodge returned to New York to get his family and set up as the village's first blacksmith, then its first brickmaker. Milo Jones, the surveyor-turned-entrepreneur, became the first mayor and the first president of the Jefferson County Dairymen's Association. He also built Fort Atkinson's first major hotel. A loyal Vermonter like Cyrus Cushman, he named it the Green Mountain House.

Within a decade or two, these men metamorphosed from frontiersmen and speculators into founding fathers and leading citizens. Their stories, and the intricate ways in which they interweave, suggest that the key pioneer virtue was not self-reliance—however indispensable that quality was at times—but the mutual aid recommended by Puritan deacon Robert Cushman. In this respect the cultural ecology of the frontier mirrored its natural ecology. Natural selection favors people, plants, and animals that work together to achieve individual and collective benefits. Far away in the Galapagos Islands, Darwin was just then formulating the doctrine that these men and women lived by, though his notion of fitness would be misconstrued, distorted by romantics and barons of industry alike into a myth of rugged individualism.

~~~~~~

Resuming our places in the canoe, Puck and I tack up the eddy at the dam site and into the main channel, using the current to pivot the bow downstream. The pool below the dam has long been a favorite fishing spot. Northern pike, walleye, and other species, obeying commands imprinted in their genes, continued to spawn up the Bark from Lake Koshkonong and the Rock River. Balked by the dam after 1836, they stacked up in the pool.

Today we encounter a family with a good-sized largemouth and a smaller walleye on their stringer, plus a variety of panfish. In 1893 a fisherman caught a more exotic creature near here, a 2½-pound "silver eel," presumably an American eel. Several years previously, his son had landed an even larger one. A May 1898 issue of the *Jefferson County Union* reported that in a twenty-four-hour period anglers caught a ton of fish, many of them no doubt northern pike, often called pickerel locally. Some weighed as much as ten pounds. Netting was still legal, and a man with a dip net caught forty-three fish in a single haul.

No wonder that the state had to step in, first to regulate the harvest and then to restore the depleted fishery. The private home located on the west bank of the river, just below the dam, was once the operations office of a state fish hatchery. The hatchery itself was located downstream from the Green Isle Drive bridge. Built in 1910, it remained in operation until the water quality deteriorated in the 1940s.

Our canoe bounces through the riffles and under the bridge. Fallen trees block the main channel where it veers right, so we carry around the obstacle, wading through shallow water in the woods. Back in the boat, we enter a deep pool where the river veers close to the road before heading south to Prince's Point. Our take-out is a fishermen's path on the right bank. We pull over, lift our boat onto the shore, and carry it uphill to the shoulder of the road. I retrieve our minivan from a parking lot nearby, and we're soon loaded up and ready to go.

But not just yet. From our vantage point on Green Isle Drive we study the river basin below the bridge, trying to imagine what the Rock River Land and Claim Company sawmill looked like. Nothing remains to tell us where it was located. Early plat maps and DNR records suggest that its millrace left the pond at the waste gate immediately west of the promontory on which the claim shanty was situated. After Enoch Darling moved to Jefferson, Horace Churchill managed the company sawmill for a while. Then it passed through various hands and out of company ownership until it came to John T. Fields, who sold it in 1845 to Joseph Powers.

Around 1852 Powers rebuilt the sawmill on the site it would occupy for the rest of its days, on the corner of Green Isle Drive and Museum Road. He built a flour mill beside the sawmill and dug a longer millrace a short distance west of the original race to power both operations. When the flour mill burned down in 1855, he rebuilt the mill and eventually sold it to Lyman Doud. Under Doud's management it took in sufficient grist to keep three runs of stone operating. The *Jefferson County Union* attributed its success partly to its reliable source of power. "The water power on Bark river," the newspaper proclaimed, "is one of the best in the country, with a head of 13 feet and abundantly supplied with water."

What the river gave, it could also take away. In April 1870 the *Union* reported that the Bark had become "a full grown Mississippi." That November it washed out fifty feet of the dam, then owned jointly by Powers and Doud. Subsequent reconstructions and repairs didn't stave off significant damage in a March 1943 flood. Notwithstanding such setbacks, the mill remained in operation until the 1950s, undergoing the typical metamorphosis from flour mill to livestock feed mill. By 1949 it had converted from water-driven turbines to electric motors for power.

Eventually it ceased to grind altogether. In the 1970s Robert and Joyce Shipley purchased the adjoining flour and sawmills and converted them into a comfortable home. The building has remained a stable element in the village despite changes in ownership, function, and appearance over the years.

Meanwhile, the rest of the community has seen boom and bust, mirroring the fortunes of the man who built the mill, Joseph Powers. Characterized by a local historian as "a man of energy and indomitable perseverance," Powers made Hebron a company town with himself as the company. Besides the flour and sawmills, he built a furniture factory, likewise powered by the Bark River, that stood two stories high and one hundred feet long. Drawing on the ready supply of maple, oak, walnut, and hickory in Bark River Woods, the factory turned out bedsteads, kitchen chairs, and other inexpensive furniture.

In 1849 Powers built a home one block west of the factory, using yellow bricks from a brickyard located on the river near Museum Road. Like his flour and sawmills, Powers's home has been restored and modernized. The furniture factory was not destined for such immortality. Its destruction by fire in 1866 marked the turning point in Hebron's fortunes. The factory was worth about $10,000—approximately $142,000 today. At first Powers was not disposed to rebuild, but Lucien Caswell and a group of Fort Atkinson investors raised $30,000 in capital as an incentive to relocate the factory in their city. He accepted the offer and took thirty to forty laborers and their families with him. His business thrived in its new location on the Rock River, where it evolved into the Northwestern Manufacturing Company, known for its high-quality wagons, buggies, and sleighs as well as fine furniture.

Hebron became a decidedly quieter place after Powers took his factory to Fort Atkinson. Following a population boom in the 1840s and 1850s, Hebron had become the second-largest town in the county. The federal census of 1860 tallied 1,068 people in the township. Their number probably increased steadily until the fire of 1866, then declined to the 1,372 residents recorded in the 1870 census. The exodus might have been reversed during the 1870s, when a railroad company proposed to locate a depot in Hebron on its route from

Milwaukee to Fort Atkinson. But Joseph Powers, fearing that those steel rails would point to other mills where farmers might take their trade, persuaded residents to vote against the proposal.

Hebron's status as a sleepy hamlet was confirmed when railroads bypassed the town. Yet it found a way to remain productive. Even before the railroad proposal, in 1871, the *Jefferson County Union* foresaw a bright future for Hebron in an emerging industry: "Surrounding it on all sides lies some of the finest grazing country in the west, watered by Bark river and confluent streams. The dairy will yet become in the hands of the enterprising farmers who reside here a splendid industrial interest, and in no section can be made finer butter or cheese."

William Dempster Hoard, the editor of the *Union*, probably wrote this encomium, and he knew whereof he spoke. Six months previously he had helped to found the county's first dairymen's association, with Milo Jones as president and himself as secretary. By 1878 Hebron was producing five hundred thousand pounds of cheese annually. By 1900 there were five factories devoted to dairy products, including Hoard's Creamery, managed by the editor's son Arthur. A butter factory occupied the site where the Rock River Land and Claim Company had built its shanty, symbolizing the economic revolution that had taken place in less than four decades.

The Hebron dam continued to play a role in the local economy for another half-dozen decades. Dairy cattle and other livestock have to be fed, and water power drove the gristmill until the 1940s. The dam also assured the fish hatchery of a regular flow of water, regardless of the season. Gradually, however, its function shifted, as did that of most milldams in the state, from commercial to recreational use. That evolution is reflected in the sequence of dam owners between 1914 and 1952: the Bark River Milling Company, the Haagen-Brown Lumber Company, the Sullivan Lumber & Fuel Company, the Jefferson County Co-op, and finally the Hebron Rod and Gun Club.

It is also reflected in the sequence of state agencies charged with the oversight of dams during the same period. Responsibility passed from the state legislature to the Railroad Commission (1917), the Public Service Commission (during the 1920s), and finally the Conservation Department (1969), which became the Department of Natural Resources. By the 1980s the DNR had established safety criteria for dams and was inspecting them regularly, a precaution that led to the removal of nineteen dams between 1990 and 1995. As the official steward of the state's natural resources, some of which are compromised by dams, the DNR is philosophically more disposed to remove dams than to repair them. But most dam owners—155 of those who were faced with the choice between 1990 and 1995—chose repair, often at great expense.

By the time that the DNR assumed oversight of dam safety, the Hebron dam was an obvious candidate for removal. The concrete structure built by Haagen-Brown in 1933 and repaired in 1943 needed additional work. Among other problems, the cable-controlled flashboards used to adjust the pond level had disappeared from atop the dam. The DNR recorded its deteriorating condition during inspections in 1977 and 1984. When the department discovered a broken waste gate upstream from the dam in 1988 and calculated the potential damage to property downstream, it assigned the dam its highest hazard rating.

But who would make the necessary repairs? Legally, the dam still belonged to the Hebron Rod and Gun Club, which had tried unsuccessfully to sell it to the town for one dollar. When the DNR tried in 1993 to correspond with the club's last president, he denied even being a member. The club had in fact disbanded. According to local rumor, former members transferred the titles of their homes and farms to their wives in case they would be held liable for repairs to the dam or damage caused by its failure.

In 1993 the DNR opened the spillway gates to lower the pond and relieve pressure on the dam. When someone briefly closed the gates, a gesture interpreted as a show of opposition, the department removed the gates completely. Having failed to locate an owner, the DNR prepared a dam failure analysis at state expense and determined that the Hebron dam would have to be repaired at a cost of at least $250,000 or removed for about $50,000, an estimate later reduced to $30,000. If no owner stepped forward, the state would pay for removal with money from its Small and Abandoned Dam fund.

Repair or remove: these were the alternatives that a DNR dam safety engineer presented to about forty Hebron residents at an informational meeting on October 11, 1994. Some of those in attendance expressed concern about the consequences of a dam failure. Most, however, were reluctant to lose the structure that had created their community in 1836 and continued to define it. One man, a schoolteacher who had grown up in Hebron and was familiar with the history of the dam and millpond, articulated how many residents felt about Green Isle Lake: "That lake is this community. These people have a great deal at stake here. They should feel very strongly about this and I think they do."

His sentiment is typical. Shortly before the Hebron dam was removed, a professor and a group of graduate students in the Department of Urban and Regional Planning at the University of Wisconsin–Madison published a study of fourteen small dams removed during the years 1965 through 1995, including the one in Slabtown. In every case the removal was initiated by the responsible state agency and accepted by the owner (when the owner was not a state agency) only because repair would have been prohibitively expensive. Though all of the dams had outlived their commercial value as a source of waterpower, the communities wanted to preserve their millponds for a variety of reasons, particularly recreation, property values, historic significance, and aesthetic beauty.

Nostalgia, too, was frequently mentioned. A respondent who lived near a millpond on the Kickapoo River, for example, recalled it as the site where "most of us had our first kiss, first swim, first fish, etc." Few were willing to trade known benefits for potential improvements in environmental quality. "In general," the UW–Madison researchers found, "most of the communities in this study valued the recreational and aesthetic benefits of impoundments more than those associated with free-flowing rivers."

Unable to pay a quarter of a million dollars for repairs to their dam, the people of Hebron had no choice but to allow its removal. On August 7, 1996, a DNR contractor drew down the waters of Green Isle Lake. A couple of days later a tracked power shovel chugged into position below the dam and bit away chunks of concrete, working methodically from the top down. It stopped about three feet above the streambed, leaving a fragment of the dam in place to protect the private residence (the former DNR hatchery office) on the west bank from flooding. This precaution proved inadequate the following February, when ice and debris lodged against the Green Isle Drive bridge, causing the river to back up and inundate the property. To some residents the cure seemed worse than the illness.

Certainly it looked and smelled worse. Where a sheet of water had once mirrored the sky and clouds there was now a twenty-eight-acre expanse of smelly, boot-sucking mud. True, the Bark River was running free for the first time since 1836. It was convalescing as a watershed, and in its healthy state it may eventually reclaim the affection of Hebron residents. In the meantime, though, many feel loss rather than exhilaration—the loss not only of recreation and beauty but also of their past. Regarded from the perspective of cosmic time, the impoundment known as Green Isle Lake lasted no longer than a blink of the

Buddha's eyelid. What we call history, though, begins at the point where human culture converges with natural process. For Hebron, history began in 1835.

~~~~~~~~~

The Bark River Woods Historical Society is the official custodian of Hebron's historical memory. The society's name is itself an act of historical recovery, reaching back to the frontier community that grew up around a sawmill. The society meets in the Hebron Town Hall, across Green Isle Drive from the drained millpond. Built in 1902, the hall is on the National Register of Historic Places. Stamped metal completely sheathes its interior walls and ceilings, so that it resembles an old-fashioned pie safe. This is appropriate, considering how the society raises money for its projects. Once a year, on the first Sunday of May, the society holds a pie social in the town hall. Members donate pies, most of them homemade, which are then auctioned off to the highest bidders.

On the spring afternoon when Puck and I attended the annual event, the weather was almost too pleasant for fund-raising. Village residents were taking advantage of the sunshine and warmth to stay outdoors and groom their yards. One woman hardly broke stride as she ducked into the town hall, offered twenty dollars for a pie, picked it up, and returned to weeding her lawn. The auctioneer's "Go back and get more like you" trailed after her. The rest of us were disposed to linger, enjoying the process as much as the products up for bid.

Before the auctioneer got going, volunteers arranged wedges of crusty confection on a table while an accordion player worked through his repertoire of polkas, prompting several couples to take a turn on the wooden floor.

Then the auctioneer took charge, his machine-gun delivery and repartee identifying him as a pro. A young woman held each slice aloft as he started the bidding, usually at one dollar. There was pie for every palate—apple, cherry, cherry cream, raspberry, pumpkin, sweet potato, strawberry, peach, blueberry, rhubarb, pecan, hickory nut, mincemeat, and fudge nut. The strawberry and hickory nut pies drew the highest bids, up to five dollars per slice. A winning bid entitled you to all the ice cream and coffee you needed to get the pie down.

The auction proceeded in a spirit of good humor, maintained in part by the auctioneer's hard and fast rule that married couples could not bid against one another. The banter between audience and auctioneer increased in proportion to the bids. "Do you finance?" one man asked when prodded to go for a whole pie rather than the smaller portion he wanted. Toward the end of the two-hour event, the law of supply and demand took over. There was just too much pie and too few people—a total of twenty-five, including volunteers. Whole pies were going for bids that had previously bought just a slice.

At last the auctioneer surrendered his place to the accordion player, who squeezed out one last polka. We pushed back from the table, filed up to settle accounts with the treasurer, and packed up the leftover dessert.

As volunteers folded the tables and chairs and stacked them against the wall, we paused to chat with Olive Gross, the society president. She was a bit disappointed at the turnout and the profits, both of which were about half the usual. The event nevertheless brought the society three hundred dollars closer to buying a shed in which to store the larger items in its collection of farm implements. The discussion of expenses reminded her of another that was still pending.

"I suppose we'll have to replace that eventually," she said, nodding toward a banner on the front wall. It bore the logo of the Bark River Woods Historical Society, depicting the oak opening where the Rock River Land and Claim Company made its claim in 1835. No claim shanty or other sign of human presence can be seen, with one exception. On the banner, as in the minds of many residents, the Bark still spread laterally before dropping over a concrete spillway.

Before leaving the hall, we asked whether we could see the society's museum on the second floor. "No problem," Olive responded. Though she was busy cleaning up, her husband would unlock the door for us. A few minutes later Don Gross admitted us to the spacious upper hall. The stamped metal on its walls and ceilings echoed our footsteps as we strolled past exhibits of farm tools, household implements, schoolroom furnishings, and Indian artifacts.

Near a stage at the far end of the room we came upon a glass-topped wooden case whose contents seemed out of place in a collection devoted chiefly to the workaday struggle for subsistence. A hand-carved marionette dressed in a red and white striped clown suit occupied the case, along with an animal trainer's whip, a fez with tassel, two juggler's Indian clubs shaped like bowling pins, an aerialist's harness, several big-top tent stakes, a circus handbill, and an assortment of photos and newspaper clippings.

The museum display case, smaller than a coffin, is the last resting place of a circus that once required fifteen wagons to haul its wonders from one Midwestern community to another. The people who used these items are buried, most of them, in a hilltop cemetery a half mile south of the Hebron Town Hall. The next chapter tells their story.

CHAPTER 12

The Wintermutes'
Gigantic Little Circus

The marionette in the Bark River Woods Historical Society museum in Hebron is at rest now in its display case. The stripes on its clown suit have faded. A century ago, when they were still a vivid red, the little wooden figure held the attention of several hundred men, women, and children seated on bleachers beneath the billowing roof of a great tent. A steady undercurrent of sound rose from excited children and shushing parents, animals in harness and candy vendors, luffing tent walls and straining guy ropes. A heady bouquet of canvas, sawdust, animal dung, popcorn, and sweat suffused the air. Despite these distractions, all eyes were focused on the center ring, where the miniature clown gamboled on a miniature stage. Laughing at his physical antics and cheeky repartee, the audience almost forgot the slim, dark-haired young man with a mustache who loomed over the stage, manipulating the marionette's strings.

John Harry Wintermute was the man's name. Known as Harry to his family and friends, he was the driving force behind this circus and a man of many

Bark River Woods Historical Society;
Photo by Joel Heiman

*The hand-carved marionette used in
the Wintermute Circus*

talents. Besides the marionette show, his repertoire included a ventriloquist act, an "Irish turn" (probably a humorous ethnic impersonation), a magic show in which he appeared as "Ching Ling Foo, the famous Chinese conjurer," a balancing act with spinning plates, and a "philosophical fan trick" wherein he transformed a single sheet of paper into more than fifty objects. He was the ringmaster and played an alto horn in the band. His more prosaic roles included ticket seller, boss canvasman, and master of transportation.

To another performer it seemed as though Harry was "pretty nearly the whole show himself." But he got plenty of help from his younger brothers, Thomas and Halsey. Thomas spelled his brother in the center ring with a show featuring trained dogs, ponies, and goats. He even trained a dog to play (sort of) a scaled-down piano. Thomas was also the troupe's juggler and acrobat. Halsey worked behind the scenes as the show's publicist, its "crackerjack advance agent." While his older brothers diverted the people in one community, he was already in another, distributing handbills (called "couriers" or "heralds," depending on their format) and hanging posters on fences, walls, barns, and billboards.

What magnificent posters they were! Nothing captures the spirit of the circus as effectively as these colorful exercises in hyperbole, calculated to raise anticipation to a fever pitch by promising the biggest and the best, the shortest and the tallest, the most dangerous and the most daring. A writer for *McClure's Magazine* described the bill poster as "a member of the Santa Claus family—coming from nowhere and vanishing into nothing, but leaving the glowing traces of his visit in highly colored pictorial illustrations that covered the dead walls in town and along the country roads." Halsey played Santa on behalf of the Wintermute circus. He and his elves posted about fifty lithographs in the larger show towns, ten to fifteen in the smaller villages.

Besides announcing the marvels about to unfold, the posters imprinted the

Circus World Museum, Baraboo, Wisconsin

Wintermute Circus lithograph poster, about 1908

show's "brand name" in the public mind. The Wintermute brothers tried on several labels over the years. Starting out around 1884, they called their circus the Wintermute Bros. Show. They retained that name through the 1900 season with variations on the word *Show*, including "Colossal Shows," "Five Big United Shows," "Circus," "Museum and Menagerie," "Gigantic Shows," "New Gigantic Shows," and "Wagon Shows." Like other businesses, circuses used the word *Brothers* to project an image of solid management and deep pockets. In 1901, after the Wintermutes were well established, they began to call their circus the Great Melbourne United Shows, perhaps counting on the association with an Australian port to lend their enterprise a touch of exoticism. This was the name emblazoned on their posters through 1909, again with variations and sometimes without the final *e* in Melbourne.

Apart from the posters, a calculated extravagance, the brothers kept their expenses low by making the most of family talent. Thomas, the acrobat, trained his son, Thomas Clarence, as a wire walker and hurdler. Halsey's wife, Maggie, was an aerialist. They filled out the program with acts drawn from the pool of regional, largely anonymous talent. Reflecting on the Wintermute rosters in *Badger State Showmen*, their authoritative survey of Wisconsin circuses, Fred Dahlinger Jr. and Stuart Thayer observed that "name after name appears that just as quickly disappears. Even a seasoned researcher finds none that have any future in the business. It is as if their one bright moment of fame came in their listing with this obscure wagon show."

True enough. But at least one bright star emerged from the obscurity. Bird Millman, whom a contemporary described as "the most clever and beautiful performer on the tight wire who has ever lived," performed with her parents in the Wintermute circus before going on to fame with the Ringling Bros. Circus and the Ziegfeld Follies. Millman achieved international celebrity and a place in the Circus Hall of Fame. Though understandably hazy about dates and details from her childhood, she spoke fondly of Harry Wintermute and the circus "from a wee little town called Heburn or Hepbourne in Wisconsin." She was referring, of course, to Hebron, where Harry and his brothers grew up on a farm that served for many years as their circus headquarters.

Unlike Bird Millman, who followed her parents on the sawdust trail, the young Wintermutes were born into a family of farmers. What enticed them into circus work? We lack a definitive answer to this question because the Wintermute brothers, unlike P. T. Barnum and other voluble showmen, left no personal memoirs apart from scattered remarks in newspaper interviews. In a 1927 interview Harry Wintermute recalled the thrill of attending a circus in 1870, when he was nine years old. His excitement proved contagious. In 1884 he recruited his brothers and other young men from Hebron for a show made up entirely of local talent.

James Wintermute, one of Halsey's grandsons, speculates that the brothers grew tired of farm life and hankered after adventure. Harry listed his occupation as "pedler" on the 1880 federal census, which suggests that as a young man of nineteen he was restless and looking for the opportunity that materialized four years later. The legendary circus figure George W. Hall may have served as a role model close to home. In 1880 Hall purchased a twenty-acre farm in Evansville, thirty-two miles southwest of Hebron, and made it the headquarters of his show. Known as "Popcorn" from his boyhood days as a "candy butcher" (refreshment vendor) with the circus, Hall had already acquired considerable show experience. His circus dynasty lasted for several generations and eventually drew the Wintermutes into its orbit through business transactions and marriage.

James Wintermute believes that the boys' interest was further whetted by their parents' tales of circuses based in the East. This is plausible, considering that the parents came to Wisconsin around 1860 from an area just across the Hudson River from Westchester and Putnam Counties in New York State. Those counties are known as the "cradle of the American circus" because so many shows originated there. John and Sarah Conklin Wintermute may therefore have told the boys about circuses before taking them to their first show. John Wintermute later supported his sons in an enterprise that most farmers would have considered frivolous at best, disreputable at worst. Returning home after one unsuccessful season, the brothers fully expected a lecture on the folly of circus life. Instead, their father told them, "Never mind, boys. You've got to take bumps in every business. You're young yet and you can stand it. Get some more horses and go ahead again."

Their youth was no small asset, for circus troupers lived a hard life, especially those who relied on horse-drawn wagons for transportation. Prior to the Civil War, Wisconsin became the headquarters of many circuses because the state provided cheap land, abundant pasture and water for livestock, and proximity to a growing population that the eastern shows could not reach by wagon. By the 1880s, however, when the brothers first set out from Hebron with their show, both the eastern circuses and the premier Wisconsin shows headquartered in Delavan and Baraboo had become large multi-ring extravaganzas that traveled by rail from one major city to another.

The Wintermute circus was thus an anachronism, a throwback to the early shows that traveled overland in wagons, featured a one-ring show, and charged a quarter (increased to thirty-five cents in 1914) admission. At the height of their success, around the turn of the century, the brothers toured with fifteen wagons in the main group plus two advance wagons. They performed in a tent that measured 80 by 140 feet. Smaller menagerie, sideshow, dressing, and cook tents completed their canvas outfitting.

From early May through late September, sometimes beginning earlier or finishing later, the Wintermutes followed much the same routine. Before the season opened they hired performers and crew and planned their route. Their itinerary took them through small towns in Wisconsin, Minnesota, Iowa, Illinois, Nebraska, Kansas, and South Dakota, though not all of these in a given year. Their route for the beginning of the 1907 season is typical: they were scheduled to play thirteen Wisconsin communities—Whitewater, Edgerton, Stoughton, Brooklyn, Belleville, New Glarus, Blanchardville, Argyle, South Wayne, Gratiot, Shullsburg, Cuba City, and Hazel Green—in fifteen days, covering a distance of 164 miles.

They avoided scheduling a performance too soon after a competing circus had emptied the townspeople's pockets. They favored communities that were known or reputed to be friendly to circuses, avoiding those that charged excessive licensing fees or gouged on lodging for performers and feed for animals. They also avoided places where local riffraff and petty criminals made life difficult for themselves and their audience.

A week or two before an engagement, the troupe's advance man—Halsey, in the case of the Wintermute circus—visited the community to pay fees, secure lodging and livestock feed, hang posters, distribute handbills, and arrange for advertising in the local newspaper. Meanwhile, some distance in his wake, the main company followed a predictable daily schedule. They usually rose between 2:00 and 5:00 a.m., depending on how far they had to travel to the next town on their itinerary. On reaching the outskirts of the community, they sent the work crews ahead to raise the tents and set up the "blues," or bleacher seats, while the staff and performers changed into their costumes.

The circus arrived with a flourish, its bandwagon leading a parade of wagons and animals down the main street. They put on a matinee show at two o'clock and an evening show at eight, each preceded by a half-hour musical entertainment. Before the sun rose the next morning they were back on the road, traveling to the next venue. This was the routine virtually every day but Sunday, when they observed their day of rest by repairing equipment and laundering costumes.

The life was demanding, both physically and emotionally. The roads were poorly maintained and apt to turn into a quagmire during spring rains. In 1892 the Wintermutes had to close the show after five weeks of steady rain strained all but nine of their thirty-four draft horses. The 1902 season proved almost as bad. "For the first 63 days," they reported to the entertainment trade magazine *Billboard*, "we had rain every day but nine, and so far have had no dry week." On uphill hauls the performers often dismounted from the wagons to reduce the strain on draft animals. The routes were poorly marked, and a mistake could cost them dearly. In 1901 three Great Melbourne wagons took a wrong turn between Cambridge and Edgerton in relatively familiar territory, causing that day's show to be canceled.

However early they rose, however frazzled by their journey, the company had to be in tiptop form for the afternoon and evening performances. Under these conditions, and surrounded by distractions, the aerialists performed feats in which less than perfect timing could result in serious injury or death. Though infrequent, such accidents happened often enough that in 1881 the *Milwaukee Sentinel* called for legislation barring women and children from aerial acts. After the evening show the troupers considered themselves lucky to get a few hours' sleep in a local hotel or, failing that, on the ground beneath a circus wagon. The next day the show went on in another town, regardless of fatigue and minor injuries.

Such was life in a small wagon show under ordinary conditions, where routine could turn to catastrophe in a heartbeat. The huge canvas tents that had liberated circuses from large halls in big cities were vulnerable to fire, storm, and wind. Tent manufacturers treated the canvas with a mixture of naphtha and paraffin, rendering it waterproof but vulnerable to carelessly tossed matches and—prior to electrical lighting—open-flame methods of illumination. A blizzard caused the Great Melbourne tent to collapse in late April 1907, forcing the cancellation of shows in Edgerton and Stoughton. Fortunately, this caprice of nature caused no loss of life. When lightning struck the Ringling Bros. menagerie tent in River Falls in 1893, it killed seven people and seriously injured more than twenty others.

The larger exotic animals posed another kind of risk. During the nineteenth century, the Wintermute shows featured domestic animals such as Thomas's dogs, ponies, and goats. In nearby Evansville, however, George W. Hall and his family developed shows with elephants and large cats in addition to unusual domestic animal acts, such as "talking" pigs. Popcorn George's daughter Mable (sometimes spelled Mabel) was still a teenager when she performed with Big Charlie, an elephant billed as "Jumbo the Second." Unlike the original Jumbo, which P. T. Barnum had purchased from the Royal Zoological Gardens in England for $10,000 (equivalent to about $220,000 today), this Jumbo had a nasty temper. One day, after appearing for years in the ring with Mable, Big Charlie suddenly picked her up with his trunk, whirled her around, and threw her into a barn wall. It was either Big Charlie or another elephant that attacked her father, knocking Popcorn George unconscious and crushing his hip.

They might have fared much worse. When an elephant belonging to the Wallace Show misbehaved in Racine in 1898, its handler jabbed it behind the ear. The *New York Clipper*, an entertainment trade magazine, reported what happened next: "This infuriated the animal, and with a roar he rushed for Anderson, grabbing him with his trunk, and, lifting him as though he were a peanut, he dashed him three or four times against the ground, hammered him against the water trough, and then threw him on the ground, stood over him, buried his tusks in him and disemboweled him."

Notwithstanding such risks, the Wintermutes began early in the twentieth century to lease large animal acts from the Hall family circuses. Advertising for the Great Melbourne Big United Shows of 1907 features Jargo (also called Jericho) the Performing War Elephant and Wallace the Untamable Lion. Jargo is described as battle scarred yet gentle enough for children to ride, "A veritable moving mountain of flesh beneath whose mighty tread the very earth doth tremble, selected in part on account of his great intelligence and docility." That characterization, together with the claim that Jargo had cost them ten thousand dollars, was probably meant to recall Barnum's gentle giant.

Wild animals posed a threat not only to those who trained and performed with them but also, on occasion, to innocent bystanders. Suitably restrained or caged, a dangerous animal was sure to produce a pleasurable frisson in the circus-goer. Banking on this psychology, the Wintermutes boasted that Wallace, their "untamable" lion, had killed five trainers. A wild animal on the loose was another matter. One Sunday in 1901 a leopard escaped from Popcorn George's circus and remained at large until Thursday. During that time it was reported to have killed three head of cattle and seven sheep belonging to one farmer and two sheep belonging to another. A group of thirty armed men finally cornered the animal in a woods three miles southeast of Evansville. Though they shot the leopard at close range, it sprang upon two men in its death throes, injuring both seriously.

The circus animal run amok was a spectacular violation of civil order. Though rare, it symbolized threats of a less spectacular but more insidious nature. One of these was economic. Financially, circuses benefited the towns in which they were headquartered, particularly when circus entrepreneurs contributed their skills and resources to civic improvements. Popcorn George cultivated the good will of Evansville residents by donating generously to civic projects, shrewdly publicizing his largesse in each case. According to a Whitewater newspaper, Harry Wintermute served on the board of supervisors and the school board, both presumably in Hebron.

Communities along the circus route, in contrast, regarded the shows as a drain on their economy. Though circuses spent money locally, they also siphoned off quarters (each turn-of-the-century quarter worth about $6.70 today) that might otherwise have gone to local merchants. To compensate for the loss of income, communities imposed licensing fees and taxes. The Wintermutes realized that they could not afford to lose the good will of client communities by exposing them to financial loss. When forced to cancel the show in Stoughton, for example, they returned to settle accounts and, incidentally, to secure favorable publicity. The local newspaper reported that the brothers came to town and paid all their bills, "which [spoke] well for the company."

Besides the monetary threat there was the moral. Today we think of the circus as family entertainment. Before the Civil War, however, communities regarded circuses much as they regard exotic dance clubs today. Antebellum shows often appealed to the baser instincts of their largely male clientele with titillating or obscene performances. The equestriennes and women aerialists wore stockings and knee-length skirts—later, tights—in a day when decent women did not dress in that fashion.

Drunkenness and petty crime flourished in the vicinity of the big top. Clergymen consequently inveighed against circuses from the pulpit, and congregations disciplined members who failed to heed the warning. When the first circus came to Prairieville in 1843, the First Congregational Church summoned circus-going members to appear and confess their error publicly. The Church excommunicated one man who remained unrepentant. When the next circus visited in 1846, the same congregation charged a woman member with "attending during the present summer in the Village of Prairieville a certain low theatrical performance commonly known as a circus."

Communities objected not only to the content of the shows and the behavior of patrons but also to the unsavory character of camp followers. When a circus came to town, the local newspaper typically warned its readers to beware of grifters and petty criminals. In July 1880, for example, the *Milwaukee Sentinel* advised Racine residents "to keep their back doors locked and to watch their premises closely to-day, as there is a circus in town, and it is expected a lot of thieves and burglars are following it." When a circus departed, the newspaper duly reported the number of pockets picked, homes burglarized, and citizens duped by skin games, three-card monte, and shell games.

By the end of the nineteenth century most people regarded the circus more favorably due to changes in social mores and the circus itself. Those who still objected to shows under the big top could enjoy another component of the circus, the menagerie. Originally a separate enterprise, the traveling zoo merged with the circus in 1828. Unlike the rest of the show, the menagerie was exempt from state laws against lewd behavior. Far from being a source of temptation, it was promoted as an education in the wonders of God's creation. Circuses often charged separate admissions to the menagerie and big top show, allowing church members and even clergy to enjoy the circus without tarnishing their reputations.

Like today's Hollywood executives who calculate the difference between a PG-13 and an R rating in dollars and cents, circus entrepreneurs began to see the bottom-line advantage in producing shows for women and children as well as men, for churchgoers as well as church-abstainers. Circus proprietors wrote sobriety and decent behavior clauses into contracts with their employees. The larger shows, such as Barnum & Bailey and Ringling Bros., hired Pinkerton agents to police the show grounds. Most important, they publicized the probity of their shows and promised uplifting, educational entertainment.

The Wintermutes were among those who cultivated a reputation as a "Sunday School" show. In their advertising they promised entertainment "As pure in its entirety as the crystal springs. Not a spot upon its untarnished name." No generation or social class could afford to miss a show that was "so instructive to the gray haired sire and gilded youth, so intensely interesting to prince or peasant." "You will be better, wiser and happier," the brothers claimed, "for having visited the Big Show."

The Wintermutes promised not only to run a clean show themselves, but also to drive the moneychangers from their temple. "Our past reputation for presenting only strictly moral and refined entertainments," an 1892 courier announces, "is a sufficient guarantee for the future, and we invite the attendance of ladies and children, who may rest assured that they can visit OUR FIVE BIG UNITED SHOWS with safety and propriety. No thieves, gamblers, or fakirs of any description, will be tolerated with or about our Five Big Shows, and no 'games of chance' to cheat the unwary by unscrupulous mountebanks." The courier goes on to offer a one-thousand-dollar donation to any charity if a patron could prove that the Wintermutes had ever permitted dishonesty in connection with their show.

As far as we know, the brothers never had to make good on that offer, and they reaped the rewards of savvy marketing to their niche clientele, the small towns that were bypassed by the railroads and consequently by the larger circuses. Their efforts generally met with favorable reviews, though like all seasoned troupers they had to shrug off the occasional pan, as when a Richland Center newspaper dismissed a show as "rotten from start to finish." With their profits they were able to add 115 acres to their headquarters on the Bark River in the fall of 1900. In subsequent years they also wintered in nearby Whitewater or Fort Atkinson.

The first decade of the twentieth century was a period of transition for the Wintermutes. While the show was touring Iowa in 1905, Thomas developed appendicitis and died following an unsuccessful operation. Soon after, Halsey and his wife retired and took up full-time farming on the family property near Hebron. Harry had therefore to look outside the family for partners. He ran the show in 1906 and 1907 with Clarence H. Black, then became the sole owner until 1910, when he joined George W. Hall Jr., Popcorn George's son, in a venture called Vanderburg Bros. Trained Animal Show. The name was apparently meant to recall the legendary animal trainer Isaac A. Van Amburgh. Both of the George W. Halls had toured with the Great Van Amburgh Circus before striking out on their own, and both featured exotic animals in their shows.

By 1912 Harry Wintermute and George W. Hall Jr. were running separate shows under their family names. When Hall retired after that season, Harry formed a partnership with George's son Frank for the 1913 season. The name of the 1914 Wintermute and Hall Wagon Show reflected the merger of the two circus families. So it was called, with variations, through 1917; and so it might have remained for many years, but for personal tragedy. Harry's wife, Clara, had died in 1908, three years after their marriage, leaving him with an infant son, Ralph. When his son turned ten, Harry quit the circus to spend more time with the boy. But time had run out, for Ralph died in 1918, just as Harry was completing their new home in Hebron. Free of parental responsibilities but too heart-stricken to return to circus life, Harry remained on his farm, raising chickens and rabbits. Though he remarried in 1920, he did not start a second family. The man who identified himself in the 1910 federal census as a "show man" described himself a decade later as a "general farmer."

For friends and neighbors Harry occasionally put on marionette shows and performed the feats of legerdemain that had delighted small-town audiences. A devout Christian Scientist, he studied the Bible and read voraciously in religious history, often

Bark River Woods Historical Society
Harry Wintermute in retirement, performing his "philosophical fan" act

deploying his knowledge against religious intolerance. "At one time," according to his obituary in the *Whitewater Register*, "he was known as an agnostic but that was not so. He was a student of the Bible and finding contradictory statements therein he took delight in confounding any fundamentalist who would debate with him."

One Memorial Day, in the same town hall that currently displays his clown marionette and a photograph of his "philosophical fan" act, Harry delivered a lecture on "Religious Equality." Did Hebron's sleight-of-hand man see a connection between religious fundamentalism and blind faith in the laws that govern the physical universe? If so, he delighted in challenging people's complacent assumptions about this world and the next. Harry became ill during a church service in 1939 and died several days later of peritonitis, presumably without benefit of a doctor.

～～～～～

With Harry's retirement in 1918 the Wintermute name disappeared from circus posters. His nephew Thomas Clarence Wintermute might have carried on the family tradition, but the young wire walker and hurdler died in Georgia in 1918 while serving in the military. It was Halsey's daughter Zella who took up the standard, though she was not supposed to have a career in the circus. Her parents had tried to protect her from circus fever by leaving her with a grandmother when they went on tour. Their efforts came to naught when Frank Hall, Popcorn George's grandson, noticed the petite young woman with auburn hair when he delivered an elephant to the Wintermutes. He made Zella his wife in 1912, forging a marital bond between two families with a long history of business ties. Eight weeks later the newlyweds were touring with the circus of George W. Hall Jr., which featured Frank's large animal acts.

Zella, only twenty at the time, hated circus life at first, especially sleeping in a tent and eating under the stars in remote parts of the Midwest. The couple quarreled and might have dissolved their partnership but for marriage counseling from an unlikely source. The circus clown made the young bride his special project that season, improvising humorous songs as he drove the wagon behind Frank and Zella's. "Thank God for that clown, James Murphy," Zella said many years later. "He was always trying to lift my spirits with pranks and jokes."

Overcoming her shyness, Zella became a featured performer as the trainer of Jargo the Performing War Elephant. A herald from about 1915 describes her as "A Little Lady weighing scarcely 100 lbs., [who] yet controls the Largest of all

Big beasts as with a magic wand." In the illustration on the herald a towering bull elephant with prominent tusks dwarfs a miniscule "Mlle. Zella." She may have worked with another elephant as well, for a postcard photograph taken during the 1910s shows her with a medium-size elephant lacking ivory. Records in the Circus World Museum suggest that the smaller elephant was an Asiatic female named Pearl, which George Hall Jr. owned from 1904 to 1917. These may even have been the same animal, Jargo being a Pearl hyped for publicity.

Whatever the name of her charge, Zella's performances required extraordinary physical courage. Her nephew recalls one act in particular that caused the noisiest audience to hold its breath: Zella lay on a colorful blanket in the center ring as an elephant stepped over her, one foot at a time. Yet it was her moral courage that circus life tested to the utmost.

Much had changed since the early days of the American circus, especially for women performers. Due partly to the female physical culture movement of the 1880s, women no longer risked moral censure when dressed for physical exertion. A shrewd circus publicist could have it both ways, appealing simultaneously to prurient and hygienic interest. Thus a 1923 courier for the George W. Hall show contains this teaser, bracketed by drawings of equestriennes: "Most Beautiful Women in the World Whose Perfect Forms and Loveliness demonstrate the result of Continual Physical Exercise."

To be seen with Wintermute Bros. & Hall's Circus and Trained Wild Animal Shows.

Bark River Woods Historical Society

Zella Wintermute Hall with the elephant Pearl, about 1913

Other unpleasant features of circus life had not disappeared. Small towns still turned out their quota of rowdies who showed up spoiling for a fight, often the braver for drink. When these baited the circus people beyond endurance, a trouper might respond with the taunt "rube!"—the signal for the company to gather and confront the hecklers. One of Zella's friends recalls her telling of these imbroglios and speculates that they helped to steel her for some of the clients she encountered in her second career as a welfare caseworker.

But that was later. After one season with George Hall Jr., Frank and Zella became Harry Wintermute's partners for the 1913–1917 seasons. Shortly before the 1914 season the couple lost their firstborn, Lenora Jessie Hall, to pneumonia. Deeply affected by the loss, they postponed having another child for ten years. Following Harry's retirement they tried going it alone for a season, then joined the Campbell Brothers railroad circus (Frank's aunt Mable was the wife of William P. Campbell) until they could start their own wagon show in 1921. Zella gave birth to their daughter Bonnie Jean in July 1924, while the show was playing in Argus, Indiana. Frank hired a minstrel band to play outside the hospital, a fitting welcome for a child who would spend the first twelve years of her life traveling with her parents' circus.

At first Frank and Zella called their show the Hall Bros. Circus. Because Frank's brother ran a show under the same name, they changed theirs to the Vanderburg Bros. Circus in 1926, reviving the name that Harry Wintermute and George Hall Jr. had used sixteen years earlier. The late 1920s were good years for Frank and Zella. They replaced their wagons with red trucks in 1926, touring with as many as fifteen vehicles. They expanded their tent show from one ring to two and employed Zella's younger sister, Zetta, and her husband, Charles Wesley Beetow. Zetta and Charles's son remembers Zella as a "grand lady" during this period, especially when mounted on a beautiful white horse at the head of the circus parade or leading the grand entry into the big tent. She was not only a featured performer with the elephant Pearl—possibly the second she had worked with under that name—but also the troupe's bookkeeper.

When the economy collapsed in 1929, fewer people could afford the price of admission. The Vanderburg show did not venture out in 1930 or 1931. Back on the road in 1936, they faced the ultimate setback. That August Frank suffered a ruptured appendix in Hutchinson, Minnesota, and died of a blood clot in the local hospital. It was a somber day when his widow, then forty-four and the mother of a twelve-year-old, assembled the Vanderburg company to tell them the sad news, pay their wages, and bid them farewell. Zella soldiered on through the 1937 season, taking the aerialists Lew and Elsie Christensen as partners. After wintering in Missouri, they set out the following spring. Playing to tiny audiences, clearing barely enough to keep their trucks in gasoline, they finally reached the end of their sawdust trail in July 1938. It was also the end of a circus dynasty that had lasted for two generations on the Wintermute side of the family and three on the Hall.

In need of a job to support herself and her daughter, Zella took a position as a caseworker in the Walworth County Welfare Department and stuck with it for twenty-two years. Though she joined the Whitewater and Bark River Woods Historical Societies, she declined invitations to speak about her circus experiences. Shyness may account for her reticence, together with the sense that those summers under the big top were not "history" of the kind to be found in museums and libraries. "Oh, my show years were so long ago," Zella told an interviewer in 1977, when she was eighty-five; "but I've never been able to get the circus out of my blood. I dream all the time of being with the circus and Frank."

Zella has been with Frank and their daughter Lenora Jessie since she passed away in 1989 at the age of ninety-seven. In 1998 their other daughter, Bonnie Jean, joined the cluster of Halls and Wintermutes in the Hebron Cemetery, laid out on a hilltop overlooking the Bark River valley.

~~~~~~~

The Wintermutes and Halls could not have foreseen that the tools of their trade would share a room in the Hebron Town Hall with their neighbors' farm implements. They would nevertheless have seen the fitness in such an arrangement. Their play, too, was hard work, often pursued in defiance of physical hardship and personal tragedy. In its own way it bolstered the work ethic. "Stop the plow," urges one Great Melbourne courier; "—hang up the scythe, take a day off. You can make it up." When the soil resisted the plow and draft animals balked, when muscles ached from swinging a scythe, it was refreshing to enter an arena where the stuff of daily life—flesh and wood, leather and steel—seemed to take a holiday from the laws of nature. Was a day at the circus an expense or an investment, so calculated? Farmers who took the long view were inclined to agree with the courier: You could make it up.

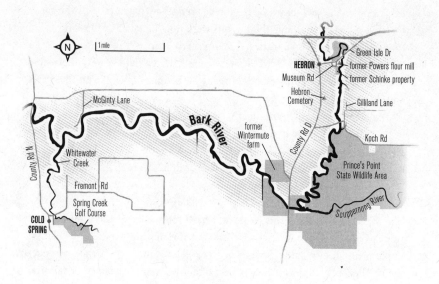

N

1 mile

McGinty Lane

Bark River

former
Wintermute
farm

HEBRON

Green Isle Dr

former Powers flour mill

Museum Rd

former Schinke property

Hebron
Cemetery

Gilliland Lane

County Rd D

Koch Rd

County Rd N

Whitewater
Creek

Fremont Rd

Spring Creek
Golf Course

COLD
SPRING

Prince's Point
State Wildlife Area

Scuppernong River

CHAPTER 13

Hebron to Cold Spring

On a warm, breezy Saturday morning in September we are back in Hebron, ready to resume our journey. I have parked our minivan at a wayside on County Road N near Cold Spring and have bicycled back to the put-in on Green Isle Drive. We carry our canoe down the fishermen's path to the pool formed by a large eddy in the Bark River. On our right, barely visible through the trees, is the flour and sawmill that Robert and Joyce Shipley converted to a home in the 1970s. In 2001, a decade after Mrs. Shipley sold it to Jim and Nancy Schneider, Puck and I had a chance to see the inside of the building.

Approaching the structure from Museum Road, we could easily detect the bones of Joseph Powers's old flour mill. A wooden awninglike structure overhangs the front porch, similar to those over mill loading docks. Like the typical mill dock, it is a favorite nesting site for birds. Nancy greeted us at the door, her infant daughter in her arms, and graciously showed us through the building, pointing out the original plank floor and the walls paneled with rough-sawn boards. A spiral metal and wood staircase leads from the foyer to the second floor.

Walking toward the rear of the house, we passed through a small room that was once a grain chute. Now it is outfitted with a fireplace. Doors on either side of the room lead to a spacious living room in the south wing, formerly the sawmill portion of the building. From the back of the house we looked through glass patio doors to see a terraced rock garden sloping down to the old millrace. Water still collects there, though it no longer flows from the millpond. Looking down the race, which is being rapidly reclaimed by the woods, we could see where it joins the river. On our way out we paused to study historic photos on display in the foyer.

We have reached the put-in and are ready to lower our boat into the water. "Now that was true Midwestern hospitality," Puck says, alluding to our tour in 2001. "Especially since we were just a couple of strangers who knocked on the door. And I appreciated their fire even more."

The fire figured in our second encounter with the Schneiders. One chilly, overcast November day we had paddled from Rome to Hebron, arriving after dark. Heavy winds had apparently struck the flooded woods between Cushman Pond and Hebron, requiring us to lift over or carry around at least fifteen downfalls. Hearing our commotion at the take-out, Jim came down to investigate. By then we had hauled most of our equipment to the road and no longer needed a helping hand. But he had something better to offer. While I went to get the minivan, Puck joined the Schneiders—Jim, Nancy, and their two children—at a campfire beside their home.

Today, as I step into the stern and shove off, I notice that I've left my usual muddy tracks in the bottom of the boat. This time at least I know what's in that sticky stuff. After last month's outing I didn't get around to sponging out the canoe until the next day. By then the mud had dried like smears on a laboratory slide. Using a whiskbroom to sweep the material onto a piece of paper, I examined it closely. It consisted of pumicelike silt, silica particles, and tiny shells. The latter, ranging from microscopic up to five-sixteenths of an inch, had either the clam shape of freshwater mussels or the spiral form of periwinkle snails.

We pass the tailrace from Joseph Powers's mills on the right and, shortly after, the site of the brickyard that supplied construction material for his home. Also on the right, extending about 250 yards downstream from the tailrace, is property that belonged to Otto Schinke and his wife during the 1940s. Schinke had his eye on a five-acre island in the river. Hoping to reclaim it for agriculture, he brought in a dredging machine. The dredge soon bit into something hard beneath the top layer of soil. Rock, perhaps? It proved to be compacted sawdust, swept into the Bark decades earlier by workmen in the sawmill and furniture factories. The debris had collected in a bend of the river, swelling like a cancerous tumor and forcing the river to carve another channel around it.

Besides sawdust, the dredge unearthed a walnut bedstead spindle not quite twenty inches long, made either in Powers's factory or in a small turning shop that Northwestern Manufacturing maintained in Hebron to produce spindles. An 1871 issue of the *Jefferson County Union* boasted that the turning shop's state-of-the-art lathe could manufacture two thousand spindles in the time it took conventional machines to make two hundred. In 1953 Mrs. Schinke donated the bedstead spindle to the Dwight Foster Historical Museum in Fort Atkinson. The relic was destined, however, for a more mysterious apotheosis. When the Hoard Historical Museum absorbed the Dwight Foster collection some years later, the spindle vanished altogether.

Below Hebron the river turns sharply south and maintains this course for about three miles until it joins the Scuppernong River. Then it veers west for a fourteen-mile run to the Rock River. On a map the stretch from Hebron to Fort Atkinson resembles a capital L tipped onto its back. Had Byron Kilbourn and Increase Lapham gotten their way, the Milwaukee and Rock River Canal would have taken the shortest route between the two communities, forming the hypotenuse of the triangle.

Between Hebron and Koch Road a high ridge parallels the river on the west. Situated at the crest of this glacial drumlin, on a pine-studded knoll off County Road D, is the Hebron Cemetery. Some of the community's early settlers are buried there, together with members of the Wintermute and Hall circus families.

The Koch Road bridge marks the transition from farmland to forested wetland. Some years ago, approaching the bridge on a sunny, windless afternoon in March, Puck and I noticed a tall column of black smoke on the left bank. It proved to be a barn on fire. Fire trucks arrived and blocked the approach to Gilliland Lane. Like the other onlookers who converged on the spot, however, they could do little more than bear witness to the fiery manifestation. The scene had a solemn, quasi-religious quality to it. In fifteen minutes the spectacle was over. A solitary blackened spar was all that remained standing. Then it too toppled into the charred rubble, and the sky was as sunny and serene as before.

Below the bridge the Bark River enters the Prince's Point State Wildlife Area, a remnant of the great Scuppernong Marsh. Known also by the homonym Princess Point, the area may have taken its name from an early settler who owned a farm near Whitewater. Prince was also a carpenter, and he made the window and door sashes for the building that Enoch Darling loaded on a scow and took to Jefferson. Today the State Wildlife Area embraces over 1,500 acres, some of it purchased from Kincaid Farms. As a place to view spring wildflowers it has few peers in southeastern Wisconsin. Visitors can expect to see, among other species, Dutchman's breeches, spring beauties, blue violets, anemones, wild ginger, prairie and nodding trilliums, toothwort, skunk cabbage, marsh marigolds, trout lilies, woodland phlox, and Virginia waterleaf.

At Prince's Point the Scuppernong River, flowing west from Palmyra, joins the Bark. Their confluence is usually flooded in the spring, creating a navigational nightmare. More than once we have paddled through stands of silver maple and willow in search of the river channel. Is that an opening in the treetops ahead? Does the water really flow that way, or is it merely the wind on the surface? When we can't answer those questions we just bushwhack a southerly course through the woods until we reach the earthen dike that marks the intersection of the two rivers.

There are actually two dikes. By constructing one on the east bank of the Bark and another on the north bank of the Scuppernong, the DNR created a delta-shaped wetland-within-a-wetland. Cattail marsh dominates the pond, which attracts a dazzling variety of birdlife—yellow-headed blackbirds, soras with their distinctive whinny and *ker-wee* calls, green and great blue herons, egrets, and waterfowl of all kinds. At the north end of the impoundment are dead trees that once supported a heron rookery. The birds left after their homesteading turned the green boughs to dry sticks.

The pond is also conducive to the propagation of carp. One year a foul odor assailed our nostrils as we approached the dike. Clambering out of the canoe and onto the bank, we discovered its source. Hundreds of dead carp were strewn along the shore, the casualties of either a winter kill or a dose of rotenone administered by the DNR.

Visiting the pond today, we find it relatively lifeless. A straggling flock of blackbirds tries to work up enthusiasm for the journey south. The only other sound is the metallic clashing of cattail leaves in the light breeze. Though the waterfowl season won't open until October, the ducks are getting in practice, swimming well out of shotgun range. From hunting with my father in other Wisconsin marshes, I know that today's mild weather would not be conducive to success. The birds are content to raft up in the middle of the larger bodies of water or bob for tasty plants in out-of-the-way potholes.

We return to the canoe and stroke down to the mouth of the Scuppernong River, observing a mink as it scuttles along a downed tree. In 1890 a hunter shot an otter in this vicinity that was large enough to make the newspaper; it measured five feet long and weighed twenty-five pounds. The man who bagged the otter was one link in the chain that connects today's recreational hunters with the Paleo-Indians who hunted for subsistence in the glacial lake basin. Soon the boat landing upstream from the County Road D bridge will be crowded with pickup trucks and SUVs, some of them towing trailers. Hunters without boats will hike into the marsh along the south bank of the Scuppernong. Others will infiltrate from the north, using access points along Koch Road. During the high season at Prince's Point, natural selection favors the paddler who bears no resemblance to a duck or a deer.

We glide past the parking lot, all but deserted today, and under the highway. The first bridge across the Bark was apparently located here. It has had many replacements over the years, some of them carried off by floods. The uncertainty of travel between the north and south banks strongly influenced the decision to divide the former Bark River Township into smaller townships on either side of the water. Since then Hebron and Cold Spring have been able to schedule town meetings and elections without regard for the river's whims.

A quarter mile downstream from the bridge, we notice signs that claim the river bottom for the Muskego Rod and Gun Club. Here the shoreline fringe of willow and box elder grows an annual crop of deer-hunting platforms, awaiting use later in the fall. Presuming on the club's hospitality, we disembark near one of the larger ones on the left bank and carry our lunch up to the platform.

"Not a bad field of fire," I remark as we settle into our sandwiches. A previous occupant has trimmed away any branches that might deflect a bullet or an arrow. "It certainly provides a different view of the river."

"Speaking of perspective," Puck says, "has yours changed, do you think, since we launched our canoe in April? One more outing and the voyage will be done."

"I've discovered that the story of the Bark River is the story of Wisconsin."

"That's a big claim for a small river. And I suppose that the story of the state is the story of the whole country."

"Why stop there? Look at it closely enough, and the Bark becomes—how does William Blake put it?—'a world in a grain of sand.'"

"Or a drop of water?"

"Exactly—though I have to admit that I'm ready to finish this drop and move on to another. Life is short and rivers are long. Not that I regret any of the time we've spent on the Bark, either this summer or in the past. It takes time to develop a sense of place."

"I hear that phrase all the time. I've even seen condo developments that promise a 'sense of place.' But what does it mean, really?"

"You've got to read an essay by Neil Evernden, who explains it better than I can. He compares our sense of place to an animal's territoriality. When an animal is in its territory it behaves as though its 'self' is as large as the territory. Its skin seems to expand to include its surroundings. It becomes not merely an animal, but an animal-in-place."

"How does Evernden know what an animal feels?"

"No one really knows, of course. But his model explains behavior that biologists have observed, particularly in fish. People aren't so different. When we're in a place that we know well, a place that looks and sounds and smells just right, we lose some of our usual detachment from the world. The invisible membrane between inner and outer becomes permeable. We truly inhabit our location rather than passing through it as voyeurs or tourists. Most of us are tourists, even in our own country. That's especially true of urban professionals—including college professors. We try to make a virtue of our rootlessness by calling it globalism."

Puck unscrews the cap of our water bottle and takes a sip. "Are you saying people should stay home rather than travel to foreign countries? Isn't it better to be rootless than provincial?"

"It depends on how you travel. It's hard not to get caught up in the checklist mode, like birders with their life lists. You read the travel guides, make a list of 'must-see' destinations, and then methodically tick off each item. When you return home, friends quiz you to see whether you touched all of the bases on their checklists."

"Sounds pretty dreary. What's the alternative?"

"To travel well, I think you have to be provincial. You have to bring a sense of your place to other places. Remember that time in Spain, when we were hiking from village to village in Las Alpujarras? Those mountain villages were on the checklists, but not the best part of the hike, that abandoned mill with the grinding stone still in place. If we hadn't spent so much time studying mills on the Bark River, making them part of our 'territory,' we would have walked right past it. During the hour we spent exploring the old ruin we felt right at home. At least we felt less like tourists and a bit more like the Spanish millers who once worked there."

"There was also that old hand grinding mill beside the trail up Mount Tai in China. Same principle, different technology."

"Without a sense of place you see neither the same in the different nor the different in the same. Your globalism lacks meaningful content. You may as well stay home and watch the Rick Steves video. That'll give you the generic tour of everything on the checklist."

"I have to admit that I actually enjoy his videos. He has an eye for the offbeat. Do you think that we could get him to do a piece on the Bark River?"

"It's not exactly a checklist destination."

"But suppose that he came, and suppose that he hauled his camera up to this platform. Where should he point it?"

"At the river itself, of course. That border of cattail marsh and box elders. That field of dead cornstalks across the river. The farm buildings on the crest of the hill. He'd have to zoom in for a close-up of the elephant."

"The elephant?"

"I'm being historical, not delusional. That farm was the winter headquarters of the Wintermute circus for several decades during the late nineteenth and early twentieth centuries. Paddling the Bark back then, you might have glanced uphill and seen not cows and draft horses, but trick ponies. Maybe even an elephant."

"Your historic elephant will be a problem for the camera."

"Granted. Yet it's still 'there,' in a way. Our sense of place differs in that respect from animal territoriality. It includes not only what we know with our five senses but also what we know intellectually about a place—its history, geology, plant and animal life, cultural achievements, and so forth."

"I get the picture—like those biology textbooks we used in high school. You start with the picture of a skeleton on glossy paper. Then you add the acetate overlays with the vital organs, muscle, skin, and hair. Voila! The whole person."

"Yes, though my textbook had no overlays for thought or emotion. You asked whether my perspective on the Bark has changed this summer. It has. I'm more 'here' when I'm here, partly because I've learned more about the river. For the same reason, I expect to be more 'there' when I'm elsewhere."

"We'll be here overnight, Professor, unless we get back on the water. You climb down first, and I'll hand you our stuff."

From here to Fort Atkinson, a distance of about a dozen miles by water, the Bark River descends only a few feet. Lacking any significant fall of water, the lower Bark attracted no pioneers looking for power to saw their lumber and grind their flour. Consequently, there are no historic settlements of the kind that grew up around the mills upstream. Farmers likewise kept their distance from the river in this area because it often overflows its banks into marshes and forested wetlands. In 1835 the federal surveyor described the valley as "Mostly Impassible Marsh." Unable to walk the section lines, he had to resort to trigonometry to locate the corners. From the river bottom he could see higher ground with "First rate Bur Oak openings & Timber Land." Farmers gravitated to the oak openings, and their fields now extend, treeless, to the horizon.

During the next hour and a half we see no bridges or other access to the river until we come upon a couple of recreational vehicles parked on the right bank, next to picnic tables. It appears to be a semipermanent camp, perhaps accessible from McGinty Lane. Nearby, drainpipes deliver a steady stream of water into the river, probably from reclaimed marsh. Twenty minutes later, and another mile downriver, we arrive at the steel truss bridge that straddles the mouth of Whitewater Creek.

"I wouldn't mind paddling the creek again," Puck says. "We could launch the boat in Whitewater and paddle all the way to Fort Atkinson."

"That sounds like a plan. But do you really want to do the section below Cold Spring again?"

One April morning several years previously, we had put in north of Whitewater at an undeveloped wayside off Fremont Road. It was not an auspicious launch, due to the trash in that urban stretch of Whitewater Creek. The city's storm sewers and sewage treatment plant discharge effluent into the creek, and the farms downstream are ditched and drained, adding fertilizer and pesticides to the brew. The creek has, nevertheless, some lovely reaches. We saw deer, cranes, muskrats, beaver, warblers, and—surprisingly—many owls. We encountered a fisherman who regularly catches catfish in the creek and occasionally a walleye, including one that measured—so he claimed—thirty-six inches.

Between Whitewater and the village of Cold Spring the creek channel was relatively free of obstacles. We carried around a farm bridge and a couple of fallen trees. Below Cold Spring, where the banks are more heavily wooded, a half-dozen portages slowed our progress. A couple of the carries took us through the rough of the Spring Creek Golf Course. There, in contrast to the golfers whose Titleists were strewn about like so many goose eggs, we had to play it where it lay. Considering that Whitewater Creek required four hours to run, we were glad that we hadn't planned to continue down the Bark to Fort Atkinson.

Our April adventure pales beside another in The Bark River chronicles, however. In September 1837 Charles Rockwell planned to raft lumber from the nearest sawmill, the one in Bark River Mills (now Hebron), to his claim at the mouth of the Bark. Anticipating a pleasant one-day junket, he and his two companions brought hunting and fishing gear. Due to a late start and the low water, they didn't reach the marshy section above Prince's Point until nightfall. There they encountered wild rice growing six to eight feet high, which further slowed their progress. Mosquitoes feasted on their blood, wolves howled nearby, and a thunderstorm soaked them to the skin. One of Rockwell's helpers was soon in excruciating pain from gunpowder that dissolved in his pocket and ran down onto his feet, already rubbed raw during the ordeal.

They reached the Scuppernong River at daybreak on the second day and Whitewater Creek early in the afternoon. Here Rockwell and his other companion left the disabled man with the raft and walked the rest of the way to Fort Atkinson to get help. Recounting the adventure years later, Rockwell managed a jaunty tone. Their travail had, after all, yielded a tangible result: "In due time the raft got to its destination and was used in the construction of a comfortable shanty for the young pioneers." Rockwell went on to build several of the first frame buildings in Fort Atkinson.

Had Rockwell waited another year, he might have gotten his lumber from Cold Spring. In 1838 Abram Brink built a dam on Whitewater Creek, just upstream from the Fremont Road bridge. Soon he had a sawmill, a gristmill, and a turning shop up and running. In 1846 he hired Milo Jones to plat the village, then known as Brink's Mill. Two years later, at the age of thirty-five, Brink died in an accident, and the village chose a natural feature near the mills as its namesake.

Cold Spring's best-known native son is George W. Peck, whose family came from New York State to the village in 1843, when the boy was three years old. The Peck home still stands, identified today by a historical marker. A few years later the Pecks moved upstream to Whitewater, where George attended school and learned the newspaper trade. Following the Civil War, during which he served in a cavalry unit, he returned to the newspaper business and after several failed ventures became the owner and editor of *Peck's Sun* ("It Shines for All" was its slogan) in La Crosse. Peck's ascent to fame and fortune began in 1878, when he moved the paper to Milwaukee. There the weekly *Sun* attained a national circulation of 100,000. It even reached English subscribers through a branch office in London.

PA SAID, "NOW HENNERY."

From *Peck's Bad Boy and His Pa*, 1900 edition, published by W. B. Conkey

Illustration by True Williams for Peck's Bad Boy and His Pa

The newspaper's appeal derived partly from the humorous sketches Peck contributed to each issue. He had experimented with the form in previous newspapers and collected the results in volumes such as *Adventures of One Terence McGrant* (1871) and *Peck's Fun* (1880). In the *Sun* pieces he hit upon just the right formula, a prankster named Hennery who never passed up an opportunity for a practical joke, often at the expense of his long-suffering father. Peck collected the first series of Hennery stories under the title *Peck's Bad Boy and His Pa* (1883) and went on to publish five more volumes of "bad boy" sketches.

Peck was writing within a recognized and immensely popular genre, the frontier or western humor story. Mark Twain was its best known and arguably most skilled practitioner during the Gilded Age. Others included James Whitcomb Riley, Artemus Ward, and Bill Nye—the last of these also a newspaperman with Wisconsin connections. These humorists honed their craft on the lecture circuit, typically creating a persona whose vernacular speech and facial expressions identified him as a country bumpkin or a rascal. The audience, in collusion with the performer, sometimes laughed *at* the persona. But it also laughed *with* the persona at the primness, pretentiousness, and hypocrisy of "respectable" people. Occasionally the performer, himself a respected literary man, was the target of his persona's wit, much as Edgar Bergen endured the gibes of his dummy, Charlie McCarthy.

The stage humorist's intricate triangulation of performer, persona, and audience was difficult to reproduce on the printed page, though Twain succeeded brilliantly in works such as "The Notorious Jumping Frog of Calaveras County" and *Adventures of Huckleberry Finn*. The literary western humor story preserved the "tall tale" exaggeration of the oral performance and its nonstandard English, rendered in "eye dialect." It also retained the antagonism between the populist persona and the object of his insults, who was generally well bred, well educated, well heeled, and well connected.

Peck, who was much in demand as a humorous public speaker, deployed his "bad boy" to good effect against the minor vanities in his father's character. Today's reader may detect a malicious streak in Hennery and may even rejoice in the woodshed sessions that regularly conclude the episodes. By convention, however, Hennery is good at heart, and his pranks are a necessary preparation for mature citizenship. "Of course all boys are not full of tricks," Peck concedes in the second chapter of *Peck's Bad Boy and His Pa*, "but the best of them are. That is, those who are the readiest to play innocent jokes, and who are continually looking for chances to make Rome howl, are the most apt to turn out to be first-class business men."

Peck certainly made Milwaukee howl, most of its residents in delight but a few in outrage, depending on their social class and political affiliation. The city's Democratic minority persuaded him to run for mayor, an office he occupied in 1890. That same year he ran for Wisconsin governor against William Dempster Hoard, the popular Republican incumbent from Fort Atkinson. He defeated Hoard by the largest margin accorded a successful candidate for the position until then. The campaign's chief issue was the Bennett Law, which Hoard had supported and signed into law in 1889. The bill required English-only education in state-recognized schools, private as well as public, which infuriated Milwaukee's large German population. Peck promised to repeal the law and delivered on the promise soon after taking office.

Peck served a second term as governor and remained active in Wisconsin politics for the rest of his life. It was his literary creations, however, that brought him national and international celebrity. Even after Peck's death in 1916, Hennery lived on in stage adaptations, comic books, board games, magic lantern shows, and movies. Jackie Coogan played the title role in the silent film *Peck's Bad Boy* in 1921. Succeeding him were Jackie Cooper in 1934 and Spanky MacFarland in 1938. These popular media suggest how well Peck's boyhood on Whitewater Creek prepared him to tap into the cultural mainstream.

From the mouth of the creek we paddle another mile to our take-out. Though few trees are able to get a firm footing in the marshy banks, several of the oaks are enormous. When prairie fires regularly swept through the area, fueled by marsh hay, they must have stood alone, shorn of competing vegetation. Today smaller trees and brush, especially the invasive buckthorn, obscure their mighty trunks.

Approaching the County Road N bridge, we see a half-dozen fishermen along the south bank, where a wayside provides easy access. Several have parked their vans practically at the water's edge so they can listen to the Badgers game on the radio and reach into the cooler for a beer. Seated on folding chairs, they study their bobbers for any signs of interest from the local population of bass, walleye, and panfish. Though shorthead redhorse and white suckers also abound in this widening of the river, they are little sought after.

As we drag our canoe ashore at the wayside, we notice something new.

"Do you remember seeing that historical marker before?" I ask Puck.

"No. What does it say?"

"It's about General Atkinson and the Black Hawk War," I answer, coming up to the sign. "What do you know about the subject?"

"Not much. Just what I've picked up on our visits to the Hoard Historical Museum in Fort Atkinson."

"That's all I know, too. We'd better look into it before we return for the last leg."

Look into it we did. In fact it became my obsession for several weeks, during which I ransacked the library for books about Wisconsin's major frontier Indian campaign. In the next chapter I offer my personal and perhaps quirky take on the war. The story begins with a couple of fishermen on the Bark River, just about where we pulled out our canoe.

CHAPTER 14

Black Hawk and the Bark

On the morning of July 7, 1832, two fishermen were working a
bend in the Bark River, angling for anything that would take their
bait. Provisions were running low, and they could not afford to
be particular. One was a regular soldier in the First Infantry, the other a
volunteer in the Illinois state militia. Horses belonging to the militia grazed
the lush shoulder-high grass nearby. At their backs, about 120 yards south of
the river, they could hear the familiar sounds of a camp awakening, making
breakfast, and preparing to move upriver.

Across the water they could hear nothing and see very little, for a
dense fog lay over the land. A vast marsh stretched along the north bank
of the river. Somewhere in its midst was supposed to be a fifteen- to
twenty-acre bench of firm ground, approachable only from the northeast.
On that "island," according to Indian informants, the Sac war leader
Black Hawk and his band were camped. Once the soldiers found a place
to cross the Bark with their horses and wagons, they expected to engage
the Indians, who had eluded them since April. Perhaps today would be the
day of reckoning.

Suddenly, gunshots broke the eerie silence, and two lead balls tore into the regular infantryman. Soldiers in the camp grabbed their weapons and rushed to the river, half expecting to see Indian ponies charging through the water and to hear the war-whoops of Black Hawk's warriors. But there was nothing further to see or hear. The fog remained unbroken, impenetrable to sight.

After a futile attempt to locate his mount, Lieutenant Meriwether Lewis Clark returned to camp and resumed the letter that he had been writing to his father, William Clark, the superintendent of Indian affairs who together with Meriwether Lewis had explored the Northwest for President Jefferson. "The Indians are near us," he wrote, "for they have just shot but not killed a man of Capt T Smith's company of the 1st. Infantry. we have had some firing near the creek, in a thick fog, and where the horses were grazing. my horse cannot be found & I fear the poor fellow is sacrificed well it will only make me add one to the few scalps I am going to take from Black Hawk, Napope &c."

A few minutes earlier, as Clark searched for his horse and other soldiers hastened to assist the wounded man, those responsible for the shooting had slipped into the river on the opposite side. Carefully holding their muskets above the water, they half-waded and half-swam back to the south bank, where they melted into the group of about eighty Indians camped beside the federal troops and militia at the site of an old Ho-Chunk camp known as Burnt Village. All were Ho-Chunk, ostensibly friendly Indians who were helping General Henry Atkinson pursue Black Hawk and his band of Sacs, Foxes, and Kickapoo. But they nurtured grievances against the Long Knives in general and Atkinson in particular, for reasons that will appear in due course.

Atkinson's troops would eventually defeat Black Hawk and kill more than four hundred men, women, and children who had cast their lot with the aging warrior. But in early July 1832 it appeared that the Army of the Frontier, consisting of about 3,200 mounted militia, 500 regular infantry, and several hundred mounted rangers and Indian allies, would lose a war that today might be considered merely a "police action." For a couple of weeks their most formidable adversary was not the occasional disgruntled Ho-Chunk or even Black Hawk, who seemed determined to avoid military engagement, but the Bark River.

~~~~~

To understand what brought Atkinson's army to the Bark and why his Indian allies were also his enemies, we need to back up a bit. Except for the Ho-Chunk (called Winnebago by some neighboring tribes), none of the Indian tribes who rallied to Black Hawk—the Sacs, Foxes, Potawatomi, and Kickapoo—had lived in southern Wisconsin, then part of the Michigan Territory, before 1600. All had moved there to evade more aggressive enemies. The Sacs, for example, were driven from the area around Montreal in the seventeenth century by tribes belonging to the Iroquois Confederacy. They moved first to the Saginaw Bay region of eastern Michigan, then to Green Bay, where they formed an alliance with the Fox tribe. Pressed by enemies in that region, they migrated farther south to the Wisconsin River and finally the Rock River, where the two tribes established neighboring villages on the north bank, near the Rock's confluence with the Mississippi.

At Saukenuk they planted extensive cornfields and fished the rapids of the Rock River. They also mined lead from deposits farther north, around the Apple River. Each winter they traveled to hunting grounds in the Skunk River valley, now part of southeastern Iowa. They traded with the British, making an annual trek up the Great Sauk Trail to Fort Malden, located on the Ontario side of the Detroit River, to receive gifts for fighting the Americans during the Revolutionary War.

Black Hawk was born in Saukenuk in about 1767 and spent his young manhood in this land of plenty, with its yearly rituals of planting, hunting, mining, and trading. In a memoir dictated in 1833 he recalled that his people were "the undisputed possessors of the valley of the Mississippi, from the Ouisconsin to the Portage des Sioux, near the mouth of the Missouri, being about seven hundred miles in length." Sac and Fox control of the Mississippi was not quite uncontested, for the Potawatomi and Ho-Chunk claimed some of the same territory east of the big river, and on their winter hunting grounds they regularly skirmished with the Sioux and Osage tribes. Black Hawk distinguished himself in these battles and became a war leader while still very young, though never a tribal chief.

Life might have continued indefinitely in this manner were it not for the Louisiana Purchase, which transferred local oversight of the Sac and Fox lands from the French to the Americans in 1803. President Jefferson authorized William Henry Harrison, the governor of the Indiana Territory (from which the Michigan and Illinois Territories were subsequently formed) to negotiate treaties with the Indian tribes that would remove them west of the Mississippi.

For the Sacs and Foxes the crucial treaty, the one most responsible for the Black Hawk War, was the Treaty of 1804. In St. Louis that year, Harrison received a delegation led by Quashquame, the chief of a band of Sacs and Foxes living on the Des Moines River. Though they met ostensibly to deal with an outbreak of violence between the tribes and American squatters, Harrison used the occasion to extract the cession of all Sac and Fox lands east of the Mississippi between the Wisconsin and Illinois Rivers plus a large tract west of the river, a total of more than fifty million acres.

The cession included Saukenuk, whose people protested that they had not authorized Quashquame to sell their land to the Americans. They received none of the $2,234.50 in trade goods that the United States paid for the land because Quashquame seems to have exchanged the goods for whiskey, which he consumed before leaving St. Louis. Nor, according to Black Hawk, did his band ever receive any of the one thousand dollar annuity in trade goods that was also promised. Jefferson nevertheless presented the dubious treaty to Congress, which duly ratified it.

Years passed before the Indians began to feel the repercussions of the treaty. Article 7 of the agreement allowed the Sacs and Foxes to remain on their land as long as it belonged to the United States—that is, until the federal government sold it to individuals. For several years after the War of 1812 it appeared the sale might never take place, for the British won control of the upper Mississippi valley. That war divided the Sacs and Foxes into two factions. The so-called British Band, led by Black Hawk and others, fought on the side of their British trading partners, apparently under some compulsion. Another band, the Peace Party led by Keokuk, supported the Americans.

When the British relinquished their American claims in the Treaty of Ghent in 1814, the Americans naturally chose to deal exclusively with Keokuk. Black Hawk regarded the younger chief as a coward for his policy of appeasing the Americans. He was perhaps also jealous of Keokuk's eloquence and influence. Shortly before his death in 1838 he identified Keokuk—rather unfairly, considering the roles others played—as the cause of all his woe. More a warrior than a politician, Black Hawk tended to base his judgments on personal loyalty rather than political reality.

Political realists such as Keokuk understood that the Sacs and Foxes occupied land that American settlers wanted. The tribes might delay, but could not halt, the tide of westward migration. Especially after Superintendent Clark took Keokuk and other Sac and Fox chiefs (but not Black Hawk) on a tour of Washington, New York, and other eastern cities, they understood the extent of the Americans' human and material resources.

During the early 1820s some white entrepreneurs obtained leases to land in the lead mining region. Others simply squatted illegally. Between 1822 and 1832 the population of the region soared from fifty to ten thousand. The squatters knew that the state and territorial governments were on their side, regardless of what federal Indian agents and military officers might do to resist their incursions. After 1828, when Andrew Jackson became president, they also had a sympathetic ear in Washington.

When the tribes fought back, the squatters were quick to call for help from local militia and federal troops. Thus a confrontation between miners and the Ho-Chunk in the lead mining region of the southwestern Michigan (later, Wisconsin) Territory ignited the Winnebago War of 1827. Though it was not much of a war, it involved two men who would figure in the Black Hawk War, Henry Atkinson and Henry Dodge—leaders, respectively, of the regular and the volunteer troops.

Following closely on the heels of the Lead Rush was the land grab. Much of the land east of Saukenuk, one historian has pointed out, lay uncultivated. Congress set aside 3.5 million acres in the Military Tract between the Illinois and Mississippi Rivers for veterans of the War of 1812. Many of the veterans sold their land at a low price to eastern speculators who anticipated a substantial increase in its value. Settlers looking for affordable land were therefore compelled to seek it at the western edge of the advancing frontier. They typically squatted illegally on public land, holding it by forming claim associations or by main force until it was offered for sale.

Squatters began to arrive at Saukenuk in 1827, prompting a series of altercations with the Indians. In July 1829 the US General Land Office announced the forthcoming sale of ceded tracts around the village, and that October the land passed to private ownership. The Indians felt the more betrayed because George Davenport, a trader with whom they had cordial relations, bought much of the land on which their village and cornfields stood.

What recourse did the people of Saukenuk have? None at all, under the terms of the 1804 treaty. Accepting the inevitable, Keokuk removed his band west of the Mississippi. For a while it appeared that Black Hawk would resist removal, but when confronted with military force in June 1831 he agreed to surrender all claim to his ancestral lands and submit to the authority of Keokuk. He appeared ready, at the age of sixty-four, to spend his last years in peaceful retirement.

But there were further provocations, including the Americans' prosecution of Sac and Fox warriors who killed a group of Menominee. As the Sacs and Foxes saw it, they were simply avenging a Menominee and Sioux ambush of Fox Indians that had gone unpunished by the Americans. Sensing an injustice, some of the younger braves turned to Black Hawk for leadership. One young Sac chief in particular, Neapope, seems to have planted

Black Hawk's Route

the idea of a Tecumseh-like Indian confederation that would be powerful enough to resist the Americans, possibly with assistance from the British. From Fort Malden, in fact, he brought assurances of British help.

Flattered by the young braves' attention and still rankling at Keokuk's ascendancy, Black Hawk was also susceptible to the influence of White Cloud, better known to history as the Prophet. This medicine man of mixed Ho-Chunk and Sac parentage lived in a Ho-Chunk village on the Rock River, downstream from Dixon's Ferry. To Neapope's worldly counsel White Cloud added the authority of the spirit world. Much as Tecumseh had relied earlier in the century on the advice of his brother, the Shawnee Prophet, Black Hawk relied on the counsel of the Prophet, and with much the same result.

On April 5, 1832, Black Hawk made his move, crossing the Mississippi seventy miles south of the Rock River with about a thousand followers. Though the band included four to five hundred warriors, it was not exactly a war party, for the braves brought their women and children with them. Neither was it simply a migration in search of better land on which to plant corn, though Black Hawk professed to be going to the Prophet's village for that purpose. Rather, he was trying to gauge the extent of anti-American sentiment in the region, hoping for the kind of military opportunity that the Prophet and Neapope dangled before his eyes.

Their route took them up the Rock River toward Milwaukee, where, according to Neapope, the British would deliver shiploads of guns, ammunition, and other supplies. If disaffected Ho-Chunk, Potawatomi, and Kickapoo rallied to his cause, Black Hawk believed, naively, that he could sweep white settlers from the region and regain Saukenuk. In order to proceed up the Rock valley to the Prophet's village, he had to pass within a mile of Fort Armstrong. To avoid a premature confrontation with US troops, Black Hawk remained on the south side of the Rock River.

By this time General Atkinson had arrived at Rock Island, officially under orders to restrain the Sioux and Menominee from retaliating for the slaughter of their people by the Sacs and Foxes. When Atkinson realized Black Hawk's intentions, he might have deployed his infantry to block the band's passage up the Rock River and resolved the matter then and there. His subordinate, Colonel Zachary Taylor, believed that he should have done so. But Atkinson decided his two hundred regulars were no match for an Indian force that he estimated at six to seven hundred.

He therefore appealed for reinforcements to John Reynolds, the governor of Illinois. These decisions shaped the subsequent course of the war. Having lost the opportunity to prevent Black Hawk's advance, Atkinson would spend the next three months trying to catch up with the Indian band, many of whom were mounted, with his infantry. By calling for militia, he in effect licensed a mob of mostly untrained, unruly, and poorly officered men to hunt Indians. Because the Illinois militia was mounted, it was able to close with the Indians. But militia troops were so far in advance of Atkinson's regulars as to be out of his control.

Governor Reynolds raised a force of 1,500 mounted and 150 unmounted volunteers and placed them under the command of General Samuel Whiteside. On May 8 these joined 340 regulars commanded by Colonel Taylor and started up the Rock River in pursuit of the Indian band. By this time Black Hawk realized he would receive no significant help from any of his potential allies. The Ho-Chunk and Potawatomi in northern Illinois refused even to let Black Hawk's band raise a crop of corn near their villages because they feared retribution from the Long Knives. To avoid starvation, the band had but one option, namely, to return to their land west of the Mississippi. Black Hawk's defiance might have ended bloodlessly at this point, had the militia allowed him to surrender. But his attempt to surrender to Major Isaiah Stillman on May 14 ended, incredibly, in a rout of Stillman's battalion.

The name Stillman's Run has attached itself to both the shameful episode and the creek—formerly Old Man's Creek—where it took place. Stillman's men captured three envoys whom Black Hawk sent out under a white flag, then chased down and killed two others who were observing from a distance. Hastily improvising a response to the killings, Black Hawk charged the militia with about forty of his warriors and was astonished to see the much larger force turn tail and retreat. Stillman's battalion ran all the way back to Dixon's Ferry, twenty-five miles away, reporting as many as fifty casualties inflicted by a thousand Indians. When Whiteside's army arrived on the scene the next day, they found only eleven bodies. The forty missing soldiers had deserted, and those who regrouped at Dixon's had lost their taste for Indian fighting. When their term of service expired a couple of weeks later, most decided that it was time to return to spring planting.

The pursuit of Black Hawk had to wait while Governor Reynolds went through the time-consuming process of mustering out one army, levying another, and reorganizing the new volunteers. Not until mid-June would the second militia be ready to assist Atkinson's regulars. To protect the state between levies, Reynolds organized a brigade of 250 men. In the meantime some tribes took heart from Black Hawk's victory at Stillman's Run. A week after the debacle, a party of twenty to forty Potawatomi, assisted by three Sacs, killed sixteen men, women, and children at Indian Creek in Illinois.

The Potawatomi chose this moment to settle an old score with William Davis, a settler who had built a milldam on Indian Creek downstream from their village, preventing spawning fish from reaching the village. Davis had beaten a Potawatomi whom he caught tampering with the dam. On May 20 news of an Indian uprising reached Davis and several families, including the Halls and Pettigrews, who were staying with him. The other families prepared to seek safety in the fort at Ottawa, twelve miles away, but Davis persuaded them to remain. They were engaged in work about the farm and dam on the afternoon of the twenty-first, when the Indians descended on the Davis settlement.

Later, people were shocked when they saw what the attackers had done to their victims. Besides scalping them, de rigueur for both Indians and whites in frontier warfare, they removed the hearts from several and otherwise mutilated the bodies in ways no one was later willing to put into words. They hung the women upside down—"like butchered pigs," according to one account—and clubbed Davis's head to a bloody pulp.

Three of the Hall children survived to tell what happened that afternoon. John, who was twenty-three, escaped by running down the creek. He eventually reached Ottawa, where he organized a relief party. His sisters Sylvia, nineteen, and Rachel, fifteen, were spared, apparently because two leaders of the war party wanted them as wives. The Indians had previously offered to purchase them, Indian-fashion, from their father.

The Hall sisters endured a nine-day captivity during which the attackers took them to Black Hawk's camp near the present site of Janesville, Wisconsin. Along the way, they observed their captors stretching the new scalps, one of which they recognized as their mother's, on small hoops. At Black Hawk's camp they were entrusted to the Sac leader's wife and another Indian woman, who prepared them for a ritual that they feared would be their torture and execution. The women painted their faces red on one side and black on the other, then seated the girls beside a pole at the center of a clearing. Surrounding the sisters were fifteen to twenty spears bearing the scalps and hearts taken in the attack. For the next half hour the braves danced around them with spears in their hands.

Yet the Indians did them no physical harm. They seemed, in fact, to be adopting them into the tribe. Over the next few days the group moved steadily north, making a new camp each evening. At the end of May they camped near the junction of the Bark and Rock Rivers at a site that General Atkinson would not reach for another five weeks. From the Bark River they ranged north and east to the lakes around Oconomowoc and Horicon marsh, where the sisters witnessed Indians engaged in maple sugaring. On the seventh day an old Ho-Chunk chief, blind in one eye, appeared in the camp. He proved to be White Crow, who at the behest of the Indian agent Henry Gratiot negotiated a ransom for the girls' release.

The two Indian women shed tears at the loss of their adoptive daughters. There were a few tense moments when a warrior refused to let Rachel go. He cut off two locks of her hair as a pledge to reclaim her within a few days. When they left the Sac band, White Crow's party therefore traveled as quickly and deviously as possible to their rendezvous with Gratiot at Fort Blue Mounds, eighteen miles west of the present site of Madison. Near Portage they eluded a Sac party, apparently intent on fulfilling the warrior's pledge.

Negotiating the sisters' release at Blue Mounds required lengthy discussion and considerable speechmaking among White Crow, Gratiot, and Colonel Dodge. The episode sheds light on the white settlers' relationship with the Rock River Ho-Chunk and consequently on the shooting of the soldier beside the Bark River. For the record, Dodge praised the Ho-Chunk for their kind treatment of the girls. But he also accused them of being sympathetic to the Sacs and took three Ho-Chunk chiefs as hostages to assure the good conduct of the rest of the party. He further compelled White Crow, as a sign of good faith, to pinpoint the location of Black Hawk's band at the junction of the Rock and Bark Rivers. Negotiations for the Hall sisters further strained the already tense relationship between the Long Knives and the Rock River Ho-Chunk.

After a lengthy progress through the territory, Sylvia and Rachel Hall eventually went to live with their brother John, not far from the scene of their parents' murder. Both married within a year and raised families. Rachel is said to have suffered from "nervousness," which a contemporary psychiatrist might diagnose as post-traumatic stress disorder. Considering the horrors that they had witnessed and their age at the time, they must have suffered terrible nightmares, with only the mind-numbing drudgery of frontier life and perhaps the consolations of religion as therapy.

In 1834, at the request of General Atkinson, Rachel provided an account of the massacre and captivity. Sylvia did the same for John Wakefield, a militia veteran whose history of the Black Hawk War appeared in 1834. In 1867 the two sisters again committed their memories to paper. In contrast to the richly detailed Indian captivity narratives that came out of Puritan New England, the sisters' story has all the literary flair of a court deposition.

Newspaper accounts of the Indian Creek massacre and the sisters' captivity nevertheless served much the same cultural function as the narratives of the Puritan Mary Rowlandson and others on the New England frontier. Their ordeal was insufficient to rally the veterans of Stillman's Run, whose courage was broken beyond repair. But the outrages committed against American womanhood at Indian Creek, together with prurient fantasies of outrages that might have been committed, gave Black Hawk's pursuers another reason to prevent the band from returning unscathed to the Mississippi. Following the Battle of Wisconsin Heights on July 21, in which the militia finally succeeded in shedding Sac blood, Wakefield reflected, "We felt a little satisfaction for our toils, and thought that we had no doubt destroyed a number of the very same monsters that had so lately been imbruing their hands with the blood of our fair sex—the helpless mother and unoffending infant."

While Governor Reynolds was still organizing his second army, Colonel Dodge's volunteers from the lead mining region skirmished with Kickapoo warriors at the Pecatonica River on June 16. That same day Captain Adam Snyder's company of interim militia engaged a small band of Sacs at Kellogg's Grove, twenty miles to the south. Though both engagements counted as American victories, the new militia lost five men and many of their horses in a second battle with the Sacs at Kellogg's Grove on June 25.

A private in Captain Jacob Early's independent scouting company later described what the company found the morning after that battle: "I remember just how those men looked as we rode up the little hill where their camp was. The red light of the morning sun was streaming upon them as they lay heads toward us on the ground. And every man had a round red spot on the top of his head about as big as a dollar, where the redskins had taken his scalp. It was frightful, but it was grotesque; and the red sunlight seemed to paint everything all over."

Though these words lack the austere eloquence of the Gettysburg Address, likewise about blood-soaked ground, they have been attributed to the same man. Abraham Lincoln was twenty-three and working as a clerk in a store in New Salem, Illinois, when Governor Reynolds called for volunteers. The young frontiersman planned to run for the state legislature in August and understood the value of wartime service on his résumé. Enlistment also provided him with a chance to test his political appeal, for militia officers were elected rather than appointed to positions of leadership. When three-fourths of his company chose him as their captain the victory gave him more pleasure, he claimed later, than any subsequent run for office, including the office of the presidency.

Lincoln's service in the Black Hawk War generated a substantial body of legend and folklore, much of it concerning his wrestling matches, humorous quips, and storytelling. As an officer he relied more on cajolery than force, and his undisciplined subordinates occasionally got him into trouble with his superiors. He was twice compelled to wear a wooden sword, a sign of humiliation, for the misbehavior of his men. When Reynolds discharged the first militia on May 27, Lincoln enlisted as a private (the rank he held for the rest of his service) in the interim brigade, which mustered out on June 15. The following day he enlisted in Captain Early's company.

When General Atkinson finally began to move up the Rock River on June 28, he deployed Early's scouts, among others, to look for Black Hawk's trail. They expected to find the main body of Sacs where White Crow had said they would be, in the swampy triangle east of the Rock River and north of the Bark. Seven miles below the mouth of the Bark, on Lake Koshkonong, they came upon the site of a large camp with Indian graves, scalps, and evidence the Hall sisters had been detained there.

Atkinson remained at this site for three nights, sending scouts in all directions before proceeding to the Bark River on July 6. Unable to cross the river at its mouth, he turned upstream in search of a ford. Four miles up the Bark they encountered Whitewater Creek, which blocked their progress. They camped west of the creek until they could decide what to do next. Wakefield described the Bark River at Burnt Village as "almost impassable, as it was a perfect swamp on each bank, and very deep in the middle of the channel."

It was here that the regular soldier was shot the next morning, apparently proof the enemy was tantalizingly close. Atkinson's forces suffered another casualty the same morning when a jumpy sentinel in a nearby militia camp shot his company commander, Captain Charles Dunn, as the officer was making his appointed rounds. Though Captain Dunn recovered from the wound, he had to be evacuated to Dixon's Ferry.

After the shootings Atkinson's army broke camp and continued up the Bark. They made shift to span Whitewater Creek by cutting marsh hay with scythes and laying it across the water. Though all managed to cross in this fashion, Wakefield recalled that "many a horse mired down, and threw his rider into the water, where he and his gun were literally buried in mud and water." After proceeding some miles up the Bark, they had to abandon their quest for a suitable fording place.

Preventing any approach to the river was a wide margin of *terre tremblant*, or "shaking ground," soil that appeared firm but was actually afloat. Thomas Ford, who took part in the 1831 confrontation with Black Hawk at Saukenuk and later became governor of Illinois, described the terrain in near-fantastical terms in his account of the war. "In some places," he claimed, "the weight of the earth forces a stream of water upwards, which carrying with it and depositing large quantities of sand, forms a mound. The mound, increasing in weight as it enlarges, increases the pressure upon the water below, presenting the novel sight of a fountain in the prairie pouring its stream down the side of a mound, then to be absorbed by the sand and returned to the waters beneath."

Wakefield was nonetheless cheerful about the prospects of victory on the evening of the seventh, when he saw the militia and regulars camped together for the first time: "Our forces looked like they were able to whip all the Indians in the north western territories." Against an Indian force that Atkinson estimated rather generously at 700 to 800, the general massed an army of about 3,500 troops.

But they had yet to cross the Bark River. Unable to find a ford, Atkinson's troops retraced their steps to Burnt Village on July 8 and camped in the same place where they had spent the night of the sixth. By this time President Jackson, exasperated at the dilatory pace of the campaign, had notified Atkinson that General Winfield Scott was on the way to relieve him of command. Eager to show that he was making headway against Black Hawk, Atkinson reported to Scott on the ninth that his men were building a bridge across the Bark at that very moment. The bridge was composed of brush, sod, and more of the marsh hay that they had deployed successfully against Whitewater Creek.

Captain Early's scouts, possibly including Private Lincoln, crossed the Bark and scoured the area that was reputed to be Black Hawk's marshy redoubt. There they found evidence of the enemy but no enemy. Other scouting parties confirmed the Sac band had moved farther north. The Bark had served effectively as Black Hawk's rear guard. Other factors conspired against Atkinson. His troops had consumed or wasted their supplies, and he needed to send for more. Dysentery afflicted some of the soldiers, including General Hugh Brady. Brady, who had boasted that he could "whip the Sauks out of the country in one week" with just two companies, had to be evacuated to Detroit. A more serious food- and waterborne illness, cholera, had not yet reached the Army of the Frontier. But it had disabled the force that was sent to relieve it, General Scott's Army of the Northwest.

On July 10, the same day that Scott arrived in Chicago with a boatload of stricken troops, Atkinson discharged most of the militia. With no immediate prospect of engaging Black Hawk, he led the remnant of his army down the Bark and built a stockade west of its confluence with the Rock River.

The work detail that raised Fort Koshkonong did not include Private Abraham Lincoln. He mustered out at Burnt Village on July 10 and set off with a companion for Peoria. Their horses had been stolen the previous night, probably by fellow soldiers, so they started out on foot. At Peoria they bought a canoe and paddled down the Illinois River to Havana, then hiked east across the prairie to New Salem. A month later the young Indian fighter failed in his first try at elective office. In 1834, however, he would win a seat in the Illinois General Assembly and would hold one political office or another for the rest of his life.

Atkinson was in the meantime trying to salvage his campaign—indeed, his military career—at Fort Koshkonong. He sent Colonel Dodge's rangers and the volunteer brigades led by Generals Milton Alexander and James Henry to Fort Winnebago, located about fifty miles away on the portage between the Fox and the Wisconsin Rivers, for supplies. At the fort they were told that Black Hawk had continued up the Rock River and was probably camped near the rapids at present-day Hustisford. Construing Atkinson's orders strictly, Alexander took the most direct route back to Fort Koshkonong when he set off with supplies on July 15.

Dodge and Henry risked the general's displeasure by detouring east to Rock Rapids. On the eighteenth, ten miles from the rapids, two couriers and a Ho-Chunk scout carrying a message from Dodge to Atkinson discovered a fresh trail made by the main body of Black Hawk's band. The Sacs had left the Rock River valley and were heading southwest toward the Wisconsin River. Evidence of starvation marked the trail: holes in the ground where roots had been dug and the exposed whiteness of trees that had been stripped of edible bark.

Dodge and Henry sent news of their lucky find to Atkinson, who, lacking a better plan, was already on his way to join them at Rock Rapids. Again the general had marched his regulars and Alexander's volunteers up the Bark River, White Crow serving as his guide, and again he had come to grief along the soggy south bank. On July 19 his army spent a miserable night in a rainstorm ten miles up the river in the Scuppernong Marsh. Many of the volunteers lost their horses in a stampede that was thought to be the work of their perfidious Ho-Chunk scouts.

All the more welcome, therefore, was the startling news from Dodge and Henry. Atkinson sent a message urging them to "press on with all haste and never lose sight of the object till the enemy is overtaken, defeated & if possible captured." Then he returned to his command post at Fort Koshkonong, regrouped, and set off for Blue Mounds, where he expected to catch up with the militia units.

Fifteen weeks had elapsed between Black Hawk's crossing of the Mississippi and Dodge and Henry's discovery that he was leading his band back to the river. The next two weeks saw the tragic dénouement of the Black Hawk War, which resembled a large-scale hunt rather than a war. Beating the bushes in the rear were the militia troops led by Dodge and Henry, soon reinforced by Atkinson's combined army of regulars and volunteers. Other hunters lay in wait along the Mississippi River, some near the mouth of the Wisconsin River, others about thirty-five miles upstream at the mouth of the Bad Axe River. The scene was set for slaughter, and no one seems to have considered allowing Black Hawk's band to surrender and return peaceably to their assigned lands across the river. President Jackson himself ordered that the band be "chastized" in such a way as to deter other Indians from hostile behavior.

Dodge and Henry first glimpsed the Sacs as they fled through the Four Lakes region, where Madison is located today. To delay the militia's pursuit, Neapope and twenty warriors fought a rearguard action. They would show themselves on one flank long enough to force their pursuers to stop and form for battle, then disappear, only to reappear on another flank. About a mile from the Wisconsin River, on an elevated expanse of rolling hills south of an abandoned Sac village (today's Sauk City), Black Hawk and fifty warriors joined Neapope in harassing Dodge and Henry's troops. Both sides drew blood in the Battle of Wisconsin Heights on July 21. The militia suffered one fatality and the Sacs anywhere from five to sixty-eight, depending on whose figures you accept.

The volunteers were ecstatic over what they regarded as a major victory. In subsequent years partisans of Dodge and Henry disputed whether the Wisconsin colonel or the Illinois general deserved credit for the victory. Considered from the standpoint of military objective rather than body count, the battle was hardly an unqualified triumph, for Black Hawk had managed to delay the militia while his band crossed the Wisconsin River. To his surprise, the militia did not press their advantage. Instead, they took a day to celebrate and then returned to Fort Blue Mounds for supplies. That is where Atkinson caught up with them on July 26.

Once across the river, the Sacs proceeded downstream to present-day Gotham, where they improvised elm-bark canoes for a small party to float down the Wisconsin to the Mississippi. Most of these were killed when they encountered Fort Crawford regulars and their Menominee and Ho-Chunk allies near the mouth of the river.

The main body turned up the Pine River along a trail known to the Prophet and another Ho-Chunk guide. This arduous trek took them through the Ocooch Mountains in the Driftless Region, so called because the great ice sheets left it untouched, hence mostly free of glacial debris or "drift." To the Illinois flatlanders who pursued the Sac band, the steep hills along the route seemed veritable "Alps or Pyrinies mountains," though none exceeds 1,400 feet in elevation. There was little forage for Black Hawk's horses, and as their mounts died off his followers subsisted on the meat. Leaving a trail of dead horses and people behind them, they angled west and slightly north through places known today as Richland Center and Soldiers Grove.

Even President Jackson, had he seen the band that arrived at the Mississippi on August 1, might have considered them sufficiently chastised. For a month they had subsisted on bark and roots with the occasional morsel of horseflesh. Many were walking skeletons. They had been compelled to leave the bodies of family members behind, lacking time to bury or mourn them properly. Now, with Atkinson in hot pursuit, they wanted only to return to their cornfields. Their guides had chosen to cross the Mississippi where the Bad Axe River entered from the east and the Upper Iowa River from the west. There a group of wooded islands provided cover and a natural bridge for part of the crossing.

Shortly after reaching the water's edge they saw a steamship heading their way. It was the *Warrior*, carrying twenty-one regulars and volunteers and a crew of twenty. What happened during the next fifteen to twenty minutes is uncertain. Black Hawk claimed that he recognized the captain and showed a white flag, as at Stillman's Run. Communicating through a Ho-Chunk aboard the steamship, he identified himself as Black Hawk and his band as Sacs, then offered to board the boat and give himself up, probably in return for the safe passage of his people across the river. After a pause of about fifteen minutes, the steamboat fired a load of grapeshot at the band, a response that Black Hawk attributed to a misunderstanding or mistranslation of his words. Indian witnesses corroborated this version of the encounter.

The steamboat captain and one of the military officers aboard the *Warrior* likewise testified that the band displayed a white flag. But they claimed that the Indians identified themselves as Ho-Chunk and motioned for the captain to bring the boat in to shore. Suspecting a ruse, the whites directed the Indians to send two representatives out to the *Warrior*. When they declined, the soldiers opened fire. Whatever actually happened, that cannon blast and the ensuing volley of rifle fire signaled the beginning of the last act in a bloody drama.

Toward nightfall the *Warrior* ran short of wood for its boiler and had to return to Prairie du Chien at the mouth of the Wisconsin River to refuel. Though some of the Sacs succeeded in crossing the Mississippi during the night, most were still on the east bank when Atkinson caught up with them on the morning of August 2. As Indian agent Joseph Street later reported, "The Inds. were pushed litterally into the Mississippi, the current of which was at one time perceptibly tinged with the blood of the Indians who were shot on its margin & in the stream."

Early in the afternoon the *Warrior* returned from Prairie du Chien and raked the islands with grapeshot. Some of the band who tried to swim across were shot in the water or drowned. Many of those who made it to the west bank were killed a week later by Sioux warriors.

By the end of the day, according to Atkinson's estimate, the soldiers had killed about 150 Indian men, the exact number being impossible to calculate because many of the bodies washed downstream. Just five regulars and volunteers were killed, a tally that crept up to ten as others died of their wounds. What happened at the mouth of the Bad Axe was, in the words of one officer, "more a massacre than a battle" because the braves fought only when they had to.

Apparently no one counted the dead women and children. According to one veteran there were few such casualties. Another, Wakefield, conceded that the sight of dead noncombatants was "enough to make the heart of the most hardened being on earth to ache." But he claimed it was difficult to distinguish between warriors and their families when all took cover together. Another soldier made much the same point, adding that the Indian women goaded their men on to battle and even took up arms themselves. In a treaty council with the Sacs and Foxes a few weeks later, General Winfield Scott expressed regret at the killing of women and children who had the misfortune to belong to Black Hawk's band.

The principal leaders of the renegade band—Black Hawk, the Prophet, and Neapope—took no part in the final battle. After failing to negotiate with the *Warrior* on August 1, Black Hawk took a small party northeast to seek refuge among the Ojibwe. He was on his way the following morning when he learned what had happened to the main band on the Mississippi.

On August 27 a group of Ho-Chunk delivered him and the Prophet to Street at Prairie du Chien. Though the Ho-Chunk professed to have captured Black Hawk at the Dells of the Wisconsin River and the Prophet on the Black River, they treated the Sac leaders as honored guests rather than prisoners. They showed their respect in the way they choreographed the surrender. Ho-Chunk women dressed Black Hawk in white deerskin clothing, and in formal speeches the men urged the Americans not to mistreat the captives.

From Prairie du Chien a steamboat conveyed the prisoners to Jefferson Barracks near St. Louis. Their escort was Lieutenant Jefferson Davis, later the president of the Confederacy, and another officer. When their boat came to Rock Island on September 5, Black Hawk requested an interview with General Scott, who had belatedly reached Fort Armstrong. For Scott's ears only, he indicated, he had "important disclosures" regarding Ho-Chunk participation in the war. However, the steamboat captain, fearing contamination by an outbreak of cholera at the fort, refused to allow Scott on board. Scott instead prompted Atkinson to question Black Hawk about the Ho-Chunk in St. Louis, but by that time the Sac leader had decided to remain silent on the subject.

What might Black Hawk have told Scott if they had met face to face? Ho-Chunk participation in the war had been equivocal at best. The Prophet, half Ho-Chunk, had enticed Black Hawk across the Mississippi with the promise of land on which to grow corn and perhaps also of Ho-Chunk allies against the Americans. The tribe had provided guides for the Sac band and supplied them with food. They had on occasion decoyed troops away from the band, stampeded their horses, and even killed Americans when they could do so by stealth.

On the other side of the ledger, the Ho-Chunk had assisted in the slaughter of the Sacs at the Mississippi River and subsequently helped to hunt down straggling bands that survived the Battle of the Bad Axe. On the Bark River, for example, at the same place where Ho-Chunk had shot the infantryman in July, five Ho-Chunk came upon a party of four Sacs— three braves and a girl of about twelve. They killed the men and took the girl prisoner. It was the Ho-Chunk who had secured the release of the Hall sisters and the surrender of Black Hawk and the Prophet.

Perhaps in his interview with Scott, Black Hawk would have taken the same tack as Neapope, whom Keokuk's band turned in at Fort Armstrong on August 20. Like several other Sac chiefs and warriors, Neapope blamed his people's misfortunes on the Prophet and a Ho-Chunk chief who wore a black silk handkerchief over a blind eye. The one-eyed chief was none other than White Crow, whom Juliette Kinzie, the wife of the Indian agent at Portage, described in her memoir *Wau-Bun* as "the friend of the whites during the Sauk war."

Certainly he behaved like a friend in the presence of white people. But on two occasions, according to the testimony of Sac chiefs, White Crow prevented the peaceful resolution of the conflict. When the Sac band reached the Prophet's village in April, they received a letter from Atkinson urging them to turn back. By then some of the Sacs were inclined to obey. White Crow not only encouraged them to persevere but also, acting as interpreter between Black Hawk and agent Gratiot, framed a defiant response to Atkinson. Again in early July, when their food was running out, the band was ready to surrender at the Bark River, but White Crow urged them not to.

Even without confidential information from Black Hawk, therefore, General Scott had reason to suspect White Crow of being a double agent. He confided as much to Secretary of War Lewis Cass, though he doubted that he could hold the Ho-Chunk chief accountable. Both Scott and Atkinson scolded the Ho-Chunk, particularly those in the Rock River band, for assisting the Sacs, but they had little success in prosecuting individuals. The Ho-Chunk voluntarily surrendered nine members of the tribe who were suspected of attacking whites, including a father and son who were thought to have shot the soldier at Burnt Village. These subsequently escaped from the guard-house at Fort Winnebago. At a council called by Scott, White Crow not only recalled his service on behalf of the Hall sisters but also took the opportunity to remind the general that he had yet to be compensated for his services.

Ultimately, however, the Ho-Chunk paid a high price for their imperfect devotion to the campaign. In the aftermath of the Winnebago War of 1827 they had been forced to cede land in the lead mining region. Following the Black Hawk War they had to forfeit a portion of their lands in reparation for the Prophet's involvement and sell all land southeast of the Wisconsin and Fox Rivers to the United States.

Ho-Chunk associated with the Prairie du Chien agency, north of the Wisconsin River, were at first exempt from removal because agent Street made a strong case for their loyalty. In 1837, however, a tribal delegation was compelled to cede all remaining lands in the Wisconsin Territory under circumstances that recall the 1804 treaty with the Sacs and Foxes. The Ho-Chunk had sent a delegation to Washington to plead for their lands. Though the delegates lacked tribal authorization to sell any land, they were not allowed to leave until they did so.

When held to the terms of this dubious treaty, the Ho-Chunk responded like the Sacs and Foxes by passively resisting removal. General Atkinson, whose career seems to have been fatefully entwined with the tribe, returned in 1837 to places familiar from five and ten years earlier. Though he succeeded in rounding up many Ho-Chunk and escorting them to reservations west of the Mississippi, they soon drifted back to their old lands. Unlike the Menominee, who were staunch American allies in the war against Black Hawk, the Ho-Chunk never secured a reservation in Wisconsin. They lived as fugitives in the state until 1875, when they qualified for residence as homesteaders. Today they number just over five thousand people in Wisconsin and are among the more successful operators of gaming casinos. In Sauk County, named for the tribe's sometime ally, the Ho-Chunk Casino is the county's largest employer.

The Potawatomi shared a similar fate. For their role in the Black Hawk War they had to forfeit all of their Wisconsin lands in 1833. The Sacs and Foxes predictably paid the highest price in land as well as lives. The tribes had to cede about six million acres of prime farming land along the west bank of the Mississippi. Though they were paid an annuity for the so-called Black Hawk Purchase, much of the money went to traders to pay off debts. As the tribes continued to sell land to settle their accounts with traders, they were pushed farther west to reservations in Kansas and finally Oklahoma, where most of the Sacs and Foxes have lived since 1869.

Black Hawk suffered personal humiliation when the United States returned him to the custody of his old rival Keokuk. Even before his death in 1838, however, he began a second life as a cultural symbol. In April 1833, following a winter at Jefferson Barracks, where George Catlin painted Black Hawk's most famous portrait, he was taken along with his son, Neapope, the Prophet, and other prisoners to meet President Jackson. After another six weeks' confinement at Fort Monroe in Virginia, where they posed for additional portraits, the prisoners resumed their tour of eastern cities, occasionally in tandem with Jackson's contemporary progress through the northeast.

WHS Museum 1942.40   WHS Museum 1942.484

Portraits of Black Hawk (left) and the Prophet (right) by Robert Sully, 1833

It was a de facto Wild West show, anticipating Buffalo Bill's enterprise by a half century, and newspapers were quick to turn a despised enemy into a marketable commodity, the noble savage. In the fall of 1834 Black Hawk could be seen with the Prophet and several Sac braves on a "Museum Boat" in St. Louis, where they performed a war dance in return for donations.

Today, one of the more bizarre reinventions of Black Hawk can be found in New Orleans, where he figures as a "saint" in Spiritual (formerly, Spiritualist) Churches. It was apparently Mother Leafy Anderson, a black woman from Chicago, who introduced New Orleans congregations to the Sac warrior's story in the 1920s. Today members of Spiritual churches place statues and pictures of Black Hawk on their altars and make pilgrimages to a large statue in his likeness on Rock Island. They venerate Black Hawk as a "spirit guide" who facilitates communication with the deceased. In the metaphor of a church hymn, he occupies a position "on the wall" between the living and the dead:

> He'll fight your battles
> He's on the wall
> He's on the wall
> He's a mighty good watchman
> On the wall!
> He's a mighty good warrior
> On the wall!

Considering that Spiritual Churches are composed mostly of black women, we cannot overlook an irony in the choice of Black Hawk as a spirit guide. Sac women supported Black Hawk's decision to cross the Mississippi in April 1832 partly because they believed a rumor that Americans were planning to breed them with black slaves after castrating Indian men.

The race issue came up during Black Hawk's eastern tour when people asked him how the United States should resolve its conflict over slavery. His solution, as spelled out in his autobiography, is almost as preposterous as the rumor of miscegenation. Let the free states remove their black men to the slave states, he proposed; then buy black women from slaveholders as soon as they reach the age of puberty and sell them for a fixed period of servitude in the free states. Segregated by sex, the black race could not reproduce and would eventually die out in the United States. During the interim, Black Hawk magnanimously offered to absorb superfluous black women into Sac villages, where they could help Indian women to tend the cornfields.

Black Hawk's solution to the slavery problem doubtless derived from the Indian practice of absorbing enemy captives into the tribe. In Florida the Seminoles had extended the practice to runaway slaves, producing a mixed race known as "black Seminoles." In New Orleans Spiritual Churches, assimilation proceeds the other way, with black people seeking to appropriate spiritual and moral values that they associate with Indians and especially with Black Hawk. His power, determination, and defiant pride appeal to people who share his marginal relation to mainstream culture. As the hymn continues,

> He's a mighty good leader
> On the wall
> He's a mighty good watchman
> On the wall
> He's a mighty good battler
> On the wall
> He's a mighty good warrior
> On the wall . . . on the wall.

Mainstream American culture has likewise found ways to appropriate Black Hawk. No sooner do we dispose of the living representatives of a native culture than we try to recuperate their values in a more sanitized form. Thus "Black Hawk" remains a phrase to conjure with in the region where he once threatened the conjurers' ancestors. Though the city located at the site of Fort Koshkonong was named, by Congressional fiat, for the general who defeated Black Hawk, the Sac leader's name has proven far more popular for the city's streets, residential developments, businesses, and sports teams. The name remains potent because Black Hawk is still "on the wall," mediating between fear and desire, between identification with the dominant culture and alienation from it.

The Black Hawk War likewise metamorphosed into something larger than itself because it shaped several remarkable careers. Colonel Zachary Taylor and Captain (later Private) Abraham Lincoln would ascend to the presidency of the United States. Secretary of War Lewis Cass and General

Winfield Scott ran unsuccessfully for that office. Lieutenant Jefferson Davis became the president of the Confederacy, and Lieutenant Albert Sidney Johnston, aide-de-camp to General Atkinson, became one of Davis's most trusted generals. General Joseph Duncan and Captain Thomas Carlin succeeded Reynolds as governors of Illinois. Colonel Henry Dodge became the first territorial governor of Wisconsin.

For many lesser lights, too, service in the Black Hawk War was a political steppingstone. Because military rank was elective in the volunteer units, popularity and political savvy rather than military skill or experience often determined leadership and, indirectly, strategy. Even Frank E. Stevens, whose history of the war generally touts the valor of the militia, expresses misgivings about this practice. "While it was the boast of the army of volunteers that it contained the leading spirits of the state [of Illinois]," he reflects, "we are forced to the conclusion that it had been much better for the state and the reputation of the army if there had been in it and commanding [it] fewer judges of the Supreme Court, members of Congress and candidates for various other offices, and more of such men as Henry and Dodge."

For the war to serve as a political credential, it had to be represented as a noble cause. Governor Reynolds was among the most active in burnishing the image of the Black Hawk War—and also in securing federal compensation for himself and other veterans. John Wakefield's *History* is a sustained encomium to the volunteers who rescued Illinois from "those merciless savages."

More recently, Denton J. Snider, a St. Louis writer better known for his promotion of Hegelian philosophy, published in 1910 a 357-page epic poem on the subject of Lincoln's participation in the war. Composed in tetrameter couplets, *Lincoln in the Black Hawk War* is by turns Homeric, Miltonic (imagine Black Hawk as Satan), and Arthurian (picture Lincoln with an Excalibur-like sword) in style. Denton adds a dash of international intrigue by including a Spanish Jesuit in his cast of characters. Padre Francesco Molinar, hoping to reestablish Spain in the New World, goads Black Hawk into resisting the Americans. Like so much of this "epos of the Northwest," Molinar is a creature of fantasy, meant to raise the stakes of the Black Hawk War and thereby ennoble Lincoln.

Honest Abe himself, though proud of his militia captaincy, tended to play down his war record. In 1848, poking fun at the Democrats' attempts to represent Lewis Cass as a hero in the War of 1812, Lincoln famously asked the Speaker of the House, "[D]id you know I am a military hero? Yes, sir; in the days of the Black Hawk War I fought, bled, and came away. If General Cass went ahead of me in picking huckleberries, I guess I surpassed him in charges upon the wild onions. If he saw any live, fighting Indians it was more than I did; but I had a good many bloody struggles with the mosquitoes, and although I never fainted from the loss of blood, I can truly say I was often very hungry."

Historians have generally taken their cue from Lincoln in minimizing the heroism of white soldiers and civilians during the campaign against Black Hawk. During the revisionist 1960s and 1970s, the massacre of the Sacs and Foxes at the mouth of the Bad Axe, like the massacre of the Sioux at Wounded Knee, came to epitomize the genocidal corollary of Manifest Destiny. It was a commonplace of the 1960s that the frontier Indian wars were a rehearsal for the Vietnam War, so it was perhaps inevitable that Black Hawk's band would be represented as long-suffering Viet Cong and the Americans as avaricious buffoons. Cecil Eby's *"That Disgraceful Affair," the Black Hawk War*, published in 1973, typifies that era in its tone and interpretation.

As someone who survived a good many bloody struggles with the mosquitoes in Vietnam, I find the analogy between the two wars tantalizing but finally elusive in its implications. Was Vietnam an inevitable outcome of the nation's frontier Indian policy? Retribution for the sins of the fathers? The average soldier was unlikely to ask such questions, much less try to answer them.

Take, for example, the infantryman who was fatally wounded at Burnt Village. David W. Dobbs was a thirty-one-year-old from Virginia, a lowly private who had enlisted a year and a half before his death. He was most likely pondering his choice of bait and how best to present it when those lead balls abruptly rearranged his priorities. He was thinking about fish and how it would taste for breakfast. Indian policy concerned him only insofar as it affected his personal safety. Who were those Ho-Chunk anyway, he may have wondered, and how far could you trust them?

Picturing that soldier enveloped in Bark River fog, I recall those mornings when the rising sun found me in a guard tower on the perimeter of Chu Lai in the Quang Tin Province of South Vietnam. There, with the Annamese Cordillera as a dramatic backdrop, I watched the olive-drab deuce-and-a-half trucks pull up to the main gate of our base and discharge their contents. Dozens of women dressed in conical reed hats, blouses of myriad pastel colors, silky black pants, and beach sandals chattered in their birdlike language as they climbed down and lined up at the gate. The MPs checked their identification cards as they passed through, single file.

During the day these "mama-sans" swept our hooches, shined our boots, and laundered our fatigues. We knew them by their first names and joked with them in a pidgin of mangled English, Vietnamese, and French. On special holidays they wore traditional *ao dai* dresses and brought their children with them for the GIs to fuss over and spoil with candy and soda. We were winning the battle for hearts and minds, or so it seemed.

Nearly as predictable as the mama-sans' arrival each morning, however, was the arrival of rockets and mortars each night, forcing us to take cover in mosquito-infested bunkers. Beyond the concertina wire there were people whose hearts and minds we had not won, who wanted us out of there or worse. We knew what had happened months earlier in My Lai, a village twenty miles to the southeast. None of us condoned the murder of more than three hundred Vietnamese civilians, to which Eby compares the massacre of Black Hawk's band at the Bad Axe. But when the rockets came in we understood why some of those soldiers behaved as they did.

The Ho-Chunk who lived along the Bark and Rock Rivers shared not only racial and cultural ties with the Sacs and Foxes but also, in some cases, family ties. Rather than return to their lands beyond the Mississippi, some Sacs and Foxes simply joined their relatives in Ho-Chunk villages. The Ho-Chunk had good reason to hate the Americans, who had used Red Bird's uprising in 1827—the so-called Winnebago War—as a pretext for seizing their land in the lead mining region.

Though Juliette Kinzie and other whites reported warm personal friendships with the Ho-Chunk, their cooperation was mostly a matter of policy. It was useless to contend against superior force, and they had come to depend on annuities from their "father" in Washington. Black Hawk's march up the Rock River therefore placed the resident tribes in an intolerable position. Their hearts tended one way, their minds another. Like the

Vietnamese villagers who could please neither American soldiers nor Viet Cong cadres, the Ho-Chunk found themselves in a no-man's land between the two camps.

General Scott told the Ho-Chunk that their removal would do them good because it would elevate them to the status of farmers. "It is schools and agriculture," he maintained, "which give the Whites their superiority over the Red man." Governor Reynolds, who was present at that council, later told the Illinois General Assembly that Indians who accepted removal in the proper spirit would "discard their wandering and savage habits, for the arts and enjoyments of civilized life." John Wakefield, another believer in the civilizing effect of agriculture, implied that Black Hawk's band deserved to be slaughtered at the Bad Axe because they were "wretched wanderers, that have no home in the world, but are like the wild beasts more than men—wandering from forest to forest, and not making any improvement in the natural mind."

Like many native people the Sacs, Foxes, and Ho-Chunk migrated seasonally between winter hunting grounds and the fields where they planted maize, squash, and beans each summer. It was eviction from their ancestral lands that made them true wanderers. Black Hawk, though he was in many respects a flawed leader and a naïve thinker, understood that he and his people lost more than a piece of prime real estate when they lost Saukenuk. They lost a home and a civilization. Passing the village site on his journey down river to Jefferson Barracks, he mused bitterly, "I surveyed the country that had cost us so much trouble, anxiety, and blood, and that now caused me to be a prisoner of war. I reflected upon the ingratitude of the whites, when I saw their fine houses, rich harvests, and every thing desirable around them; and recollected that all this land had been ours, for which me and my people had never received a dollar, and that the whites were not satisfied until they took our village and our grave-yards from us, and removed us across the Mississippi."

~~~~~~~

Near Saukenuk was Rock Island, where Black Hawk was denied a meeting with General Scott. There the Sac leader must have glanced at the cave where a great white spirit was supposed to have dwelled until it was driven away by the Americans who built Fort Armstrong. Many of his people had seen the spirit, which had wings that were ten times the size of a swan's.

What sort of spirit dwells at Burnt Village on the Bark River? Here the soil soaked up the blood of an American soldier and three Sac braves. Here a local tribe, caught between deadly enemies, lost everything in a high-stakes game of diplomacy and deception. Nearby a pair of traumatized sisters spent the night among people whose intentions they understood no better than their language. Insofar as the spirit of this place takes its character from the Black Hawk War, it is the spirit of greed for mineral wealth and cheap land, notwithstanding efforts to represent the war as a noble cause. If the spirit of Burnt Village has wings, they are neither as white as those of the Rock Island cave spirit nor as grand.

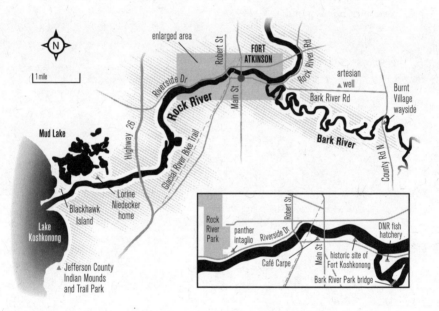

enlarged area

Robert St

FORT
ATKINSON

Rock River Rd

artesian
▲ well

Burnt
Village
wayside

Riverside Dr

Rock River

Main St

Bark River Rd

Highway 26

Glacial River Bike Trail

Bark River

County Rd N

Mud Lake

Lorine
Niedecker
home

Blackhawk
Island

Lake
Koshkonong

▲ Jefferson County
Indian Mounds
and Trail Park

1 mile

Rock
River
Park

panther
intaglio

Riverside Dr

Robert St

Main St

DNR fish
hatchery

Café Carpe

historic site of
Fort Koshkonong

Bark River Park bridge

Cold Spring to
Lake Koshkonong

W e return to the Burnt Village wayside on a crisp mid-October morning, not all that different from the April morning on which we began our voyage down the Bark River. The trees are showing color, but the temperature is about the same, in the upper forties. Flights of ducks form and re-form on the blue horizon, like handfuls of buckshot tossed into the air. In contrast to our April spirit of anticipation, though, we feel a tinge of regret. Just a few miles more, and our adventure will be over. To prolong it a bit, we've parked our minivan at the western tip of Blackhawk Island on the Rock River, about seven miles downstream from the mouth of the Bark. Our route will take us through the city of Fort Atkinson to the shore of Lake Koshkonong.

Paddling under the County Road N bridge, we notice the gourd-shaped mud nests of cliff swallows, lit from below by reflected sunlight. Plastered to the girders, they resemble a miniature pueblo abandoned by an ancient race of cliff dwellers. Unlike their human counterparts, these natives will return in the spring and repair their nests with some of the mud that bedeviled General Atkinson's mighty Army of the Frontier.

Participants in the Black Hawk War often referred to the Bark, mistakenly, as the Whitewater or Clearwater River. Because Black Hawk mentions in his autobiography that his starving people had to eat bark stripped from trees in the Four Lakes (Madison) area, some trace the river's name to this episode. But the Bark already had a name before Black Hawk crossed it. The Ho-Chunk called it "the place where they peel the bark." From trees along the lower reaches of the river the Indians harvested material for their lodges and food storage boxes. Taking their cue from the native people, some whites called the river the Peel Bark, others simply the Bark.

The Ho-Chunk presumably favored birch trees when harvesting bark. We see few of these today. Silver maples dominate the wooded areas in the flood plain, with a scattering of willow and ash trees. Stockings of light gray silt extend a couple of feet up their trunks, marking the spring high-water line. The leaves are in their autumn glory, mostly yellow with a rosy tinge. Some have fallen into the river and collect in the eddies.

The river meanders considerably between Burnt Village and the Rock River, with extensive marshes on the north bank. Recounting a duck-hunting trip on this section in 1856, a writer complained that the Bark "crosses itself at every turn, and runs into itself every half mile. Many a time in making such tortuous windings, its waters get turned around and run upstream by mistake." This sounds like hyperbole until you actually paddle it.

A couple of small feeder streams enter from the left, one about twenty minutes downstream from Burnt Village, the other a half hour later, just upstream from a grassy bank marked by a fire-scorched tree. Here we come upon a four-point buck lying in the grass, ready to bolt if we get too close. The fall rut hasn't quite arrived, and the young bachelor seems disposed to linger in bed. We are already past him before he can make up his mind to run.

On this lazy Indian summer day the river has a sound track—in fact, two melodies in counterpoint. A bullfrog strums the bass in a pocket of cattail marsh while somewhere out of sight a musician is picking out tunes on a guitar. They seem to come from the only visible house, set in a grove of trees on the right bank.

Farther downstream on the left is a concrete boat launch framed by huge boulders. Beside it, atop a bluff, is a structure that appears to be a boathouse. Perhaps this was the access used by the only other craft we encounter on the river, an outboard with an electric trolling motor. The two fishermen are casting to rocks along the shore, trying to get the attention of the walleyes, largemouths, and crappies known to be in this stretch. Some of the walleyes are raised as fry in a DNR fish hatchery at the mouth of the river.

Downstream we encounter more fishermen, working from shore. On a bridge accessible from Bark River Park, we notice several teenage boys with fishing tackle.

"Any luck?"

"Nothing worth keeping. Just a couple of dogfish."

Their response recalls one of the less plausible derivations of the river's name. According to people who fished in Bark Lake, the river's source, that body of water was named after its large population of dogfish, the local name for bowfin (*Amia calva*). There certainly were, and still are, dogfish in Bark Lake and the other lakes and millponds strung along the river. But as far as I know they haven't kept anyone awake at night with their barking.

The channel under the Bark River Park bridge ends in a row of wooden stakes, perhaps the remains of a fish trap or barrier. Here the river forms an oxbow with a shallow shortcut. We stick to the main channel, looping northeast toward Bark River Road. Where the oxbow nearly touches the road is a favorite fishing spot, located not far from an artesian well. Today, for a change, no fishermen have claimed the bank next to the road, so we pull over for lunch.

"Does it get any better than this?" Puck asks, pulling our sandwiches out of the waterproof bag. "Icy well water to drink, the trees in their fall colors, geese and ducks flying overhead."

"We could nominate this stretch of highway for 'Rustic Road' status if the township hadn't beaten us to it. In 1998 it became the first Rustic Road in Jefferson County. It's my favorite part of the bike shuttle. Yet this road has also been a crime scene."

"What sort of crime?"

"You could call it a crime of passion. Murder. One night a few months before Bark River Road became officially rustic, a young couple parked their car east of here, beside the spring. He was an unemployed carpenter, she a divorced waitress. Though they'd lived together and even produced a child, they accused each other of having other lovers. That night—"

"I vaguely recall reading about it. What were their names again?"

"Daniel Brown and Barbara Heine. Anyway, that night their jealous quarrel escalated until he pulled out a .45 caliber pistol. She ran screaming into the woods, and he fired after her. Someone found her body early the next morning. Divers retrieved his pistol from the river."

"So much for rusticity. Do you remember *Wisconsin Death Trip*, that macabre little collection of nineteenth-century photos and news items that someone published in the 1970s? The story of Heine's murder would fit right in, except for when it happened."

"And where. That book was about Black River Falls. But the Bark would easily supply enough material for a *Death Trip II*. Murders, suicides, accidental drownings—the river has seen it all, especially between Cold Spring and Fort Atkinson. In 1857, for example, a couple of men from Cold Spring argued over a boat that one of them used to cross the Bark on his way to work. The argument ended with one beating the other to death."

"Over a boat?"

"Depressing, isn't it? And depression can kill. During the winter of 1890, closer to Fort Atkinson, a man left his home one morning in a fit of despondency. The following May a couple of spear fishermen found his body in a backwater of the Bark. After wading into the river he must have changed his mind about suicide and tried to regain the shore. But it was too late. The mucky bottom wouldn't let go."

We finish our lunch in silence. Brightly colored leaves tack back and forth on the surface of the river, reminding me of the passage in Book Six of the *Aeneid* where Virgil compares the souls of the dead to leaves struck down by the first frost. They gather beside the river Styx, waiting for Charon to ferry them across.

Before a bridge was built near the mouth of the Bark, living people likewise had to cross the river by boat. The journey could be perilous in high water. In May 1889 two men tried to row a neighbor's three children across the Bark. Two of the children drowned when the overloaded boat sank. After reporting the bare facts of the tragedy, the *Milwaukee Sentinel* added, "Bark river, which joins the Rock here, has swallowed up more human lives twice over than Rock river, in this vicinity, although the latter stream runs through the city and the former only skirts the eastern edge. The Bark is a treacherous stream, narrow between banks, but very deep. The shallow places are quagmires and the opposite banks are nearly perpendicular and of a greasy blue clay. Expert swimmers have mired and drowned in it, and novices practically leave all hope behind on entering its placid waters."

Back in the canoe, we leave our somber mood behind as we approach the bridge on Rock River Road. Located on the right bank, just upstream from the bridge, is a DNR fish hatchery that has supplied many of the walleyes in Rock River and Lake Koshkonong since 1993. Initially, DNR biologists tried to hatch the fry in river water, but found it too laden with sediment. A private group, the Rock River–Koshkonong Association, helped to pay for the three-hundred-foot well that currently supplies clear water at a constant temperature. Unlike most hatcheries, which keep the newly hatched fry for a period in holding tanks, this one releases them directly into the Bark, where they find abundant natural food.

Gliding under the bridge, we enter the Rock River. Water from the Bark hugs the left bank, and so do we, taking advantage of the current. The Rock approaches Fort Atkinson from the northeast, flows from east to west through the city, and then resumes its southwesterly course to the Mississippi.

On the south bank, about two hundred yards below the Bark, General Atkinson had his men construct a fort in July 1832. They dug a trench to form the perimeter, then inserted oak logs vertically into the excavation to create an eight-foot stockade. Atkinson had scarcely completed Fort Koshkonong when he left to pursue Black Hawk near Blue Mounds. The fort was abandoned at the close of the war. When Dwight Foster and other early settlers arrived a few years later, they salvaged the stockade pickets for firewood and material to build log cabins and rafts. Today a historical marker on Milwaukee Avenue shows the location of the fort.

Foster and his brother Alvin worked for the Rock River Land and Claim Company. Alvin was the millwright for Bark River Mills (present-day Hebron). The company sent Dwight to the stockade site to occupy another of their claims. In the fall of 1836 he built a cabin near the old fort. Later he built a tavern, and together with his wife, Almira, enjoyed a reputation for frontier hospitality. "Uncle Dwight," as he was called, also operated a ferry across the Rock River, so the settlement might well have been called Foster's Crossing. But in 1841 the US Congress named the community in honor of the general.

Besides the stockade pickets and traces of a military trail, Fort Atkinson's early settlers found another relic of the Black Hawk War. In a mound of sand and gravel outside the stockade, near its southwest corner, lay a grave surrounded by a miniature stockade of pickets and bearing an inscription on a barrelhead. Historians believe that it held the body of Private Dobbs, the infantryman who was badly wounded beside the Bark River on July 7, 1832. Local legend garbled the story, moving the scene of the shooting from the Bark to the Rock River, near the stockade. The name on the barrelhead was remembered variously as Lieutenant Daniel (or Peter, or John) Dobbs. Eventually an unsentimental villager acquired the gravesite and mined it for the sand and gravel. He dug up a skull and bones, along with remnants of a uniform, and gave the skull to a local clergyman. Thereafter Dobbs's remains disappeared from the historical record.

We pass under the Main Street bridge, where sculptured Indians peer into the river, holding electric flambeaux aloft to light it after dark. Downstream from the bridge is the floating patio of a restaurant. Puck asks the nearest diners to pass us a menu. They go along with the joke, extending one in our direction, but by then we are out of reach and abreast of a familiar landmark.

Café Carpe, perched on a bluff above the river, is a magnet for people who enjoy live music in a variety of genres—folk, blues, jazz, bluegrass, and the catchall "alternative." The second part of the café's name is pronounced like the fish, though the eye-pun on *carpe diem* is intentional. Puck and I have reserved seats at this evening's show to celebrate the conclusion of our adventure. After a meal served up by Bill Camplin and his wife, Kitty Welch, we'll stay for the performance in an eclectically furnished little room behind the restaurant. Besides working the grill and delivering famously droll introductions to the musicians, Bill composes, performs, and records his own bluesy songs.

"Shall we stop for a beer?" I ask Puck. A brew stop is one of the pleasures of urban paddling in Milwaukee, where we've docked our canoe beside luxury yachts at the Milwaukee Ale House. The Carpe's back porch is a delightful place from which to view the river.

"Let's save it for later," she responds. "Besides, there's no good place to land."

"Did you know that Impresario Camplin has done stints on the city council and planning commission? That places him in a long line of Fort Atkinson entrepreneurs and artists who were also public servants, going back to the city's first mayor, Milo Jones."

"Jones—the name is familiar."

"It should be. He was a partner in the Rock River Land and Claim Company. Besides his work as a territorial surveyor, he built Fort Atkinson's first hotel and ran a dairy farm, among other enterprises. He served as the first president of both the Jefferson County Agricultural Society and the County Dairymen's Association."

"So Wisconsin was the Dairy Territory before it became the Dairy State?"

"No, unfortunately. Most farmers kept a cow for milk and planted a few vegetables for their own table. Otherwise they devoted themselves and their land to wheat growing until monocropping took its toll on the soil. Those who knew no other way to farm had to pack up and move farther west. Jones, who had been a dairy farmer in Vermont, was one of the few who made dairying a priority."

"Therefore the inevitable choice for Dairymen's Association president."

"Either Jones or the man who founded the association and served as its first secretary. Let me give you a brief résumé: He came to Wisconsin from New York State. Served in the Civil War. Didn't really prosper until he started his own newspaper. Known for his wit and way with words. Parlayed his influence as editor and publisher into a term as state governor. Is often remembered in connection with the Bennett Law. Whom does that describe?"

"George W. Peck, of course."

"Of course—and also the man whom Peck defeated in the election of 1889, William Dempster Hoard. German immigrants were a significant voting block then, and their religious leaders, both Catholic and Lutheran, urged them to cast their ballot against the incumbent, Hoard, for signing the Bennett Bill into law."

"I thought the Bennett Law was about teaching the standard school subjects—reading, writing, arithmetic, history—in English. Who could object to that?"

"No one, as Governor Hoard saw it. He didn't care what language the students spoke at home and in church, but he believed that they would be handicapped in the marketplace—handicapped for life—unless they mastered the language of the country. Because the law applied to private as well as public schools, German religious leaders regarded it as state interference in their affairs.

"During the years 1888 to 1891, when the Bennett Law went from bill to law and finally to repealed law, state newspapers never lacked material for their op-ed and correspondence sections. Ironically, repeal of the law made little difference because the German private schools had come around to English instruction on their own. But it was a fascinating cultural episode and brought notoriety to a couple of good men from the Bark River valley."

"You said that Hoard was the secretary of the County Dairymen's Association? Did I miss the connection between the Bennett Law and dairying?"

"There is none. Farmers could use any language they wanted in the barn, including some that Hoard wouldn't print in his newspaper. Like Peck, he was much more than the sum of his political fortunes. As an advocate for dairy farming he accomplished more than he did as governor."

"What was there to advocate? After King Wheat was deposed, farmers had little choice but to try something else."

"They needed a nudge in the right direction. Also information. Hoard began to publish the *Jefferson County Union* at a fortuitous moment. It was 1870, and as he watched the wheat harvest decline he recalled New York State's successful transition from wheat growing to dairying. Using the newspaper as his bully pulpit, he cajoled and occasionally harangued local farmers into following the New York model.

"Mostly, though, he gave them practical 'how to' advice, drawing on his extensive reading in eastern trade journals. He moved the *Jefferson County Union* from Lake Mills to Fort Atkinson and added a dairyman's supplement to the paper. The supplement became a separate publication, *Hoard's Dairyman*, in 1885."

"Hoard's career certainly testifies to the power of the press," Puck reflects. Since Café Carpe we have paddled past a new condo development on the left bank and under a railroad right-of-way that now serves as the Glacial River Bike Trail.

"It does, and he found other ways to get his message out. Besides starting the Dairymen's Association he negotiated shipping contracts for state dairy products and lectured widely. He served on the University of Wisconsin board of regents and helped establish university programs in agriculture. In 1899, at the age of sixty-three, he bought a large dairy farm and shaped it into a model of the principles he'd promulgated in print and on the platform."

"Principles? For example?"

"'Thou shalt breed specifically for quality milk production' was Hoard's first commandment. He had little patience with farmers who tried to save money by crossing thoroughbreds with mixed bloods or raising cows that could be sold for beef when their milking days were over. He demonstrated that such economies were costly in the long run. Hoard also pushed for disease-free herds and sanitary processing of dairy products. He promoted alfalfa as a nutritious forage crop and silos as the best way to store feed for the winter months."

"Those aren't changes a farmer could make overnight. Did Hoard live long enough to see his principles adopted?"

"He did. When Hoard took up the cause of dairying, Wisconsin products were a joke. Easterners derided the butter as 'Wisconsin grease,' suitable only for lubricating wagon axles. Three decades later the state's butter and cheese had become the country's gold standard. Hoard pressed for legislation to defend that standard against filled cheese and oleomargarine colored to look like butter."

"Filled cheese?"

"Adulterated cheese. Made with skim milk and vegetable oil or animal fat in place of the natural butterfat."

"Next you'll be calling him our Dairy Godfather."

"He certainly deserves the title if anyone does, though he would doubtless have deflected it with one of his witticisms. The state honored him anyway, with a statue on the School of Agriculture campus in Madison."

Since entering the Rock River we have passed under the Main Street bridge and the Glacial River Bike Trail. Now we pass under the Robert Street bridge. Across the river, on the north bank, we can see cars and trucks moving along Riverside Drive. We ferry over to that side and scan the elevated bank for an ancient artifact described in Lapham's *Antiquities of Wisconsin*. Finally we catch sight of a historical marker atop a pole. Pulling into shore, we secure our boat and climb the hill.

There it is, practically on the shoulder of Riverside Drive, in the 1200 block of a residential neighborhood: the world's sole surviving Indian intaglio. It is a sort of "negative effigy mound" created by excavating a depression in the earth. Lapham found only eleven intaglios in Wisconsin, and none survives except this 125-foot specimen. At first it looks like a rumpled earthen bed covered with a grassy blanket. As the two deeper depressions and the tapering tail come into sharper focus, we can make out a shape that is usually described as pantherlike, though it could well be a water spirit.

Especially in the case of lower-world effigies, the mound builders sometimes excavated intaglios and left them open for a period before capping them with a mound in the same form. Hence this effigy, part of a cluster of mounds that were effaced after Lapham's 1850 survey, may have been a work in progress. The local chapter of Daughters of the American Revolution saved the intaglio by leasing the land in 1919. Even so, development nipped off a bit of its tail.

We scramble down the bank to our canoe and push off, hugging the right bank. We are looking for Rock River Park and its replica of Fort Koshkonong. The park entrance comes into view a few minutes downstream from the intaglio, but large trees screen the fort from sight. No matter—we had seen it on a previous trip by car. Constructed in the 1960s, it was the site of an annual Black Hawk Pageant during the 1970s. It has begun to show its age, and many of the log pickets in the stockade no longer stand at attention. Yet the replica has lasted far longer than the original fort.

Downstream from the park a bridge marks the place where a small creek enters the river. Several fishermen are trying their luck beside the bridge. Much of the river's south bank is a game refuge, ideally situated for birds that share the anglers' hankering for fish. We observe a couple of soaring ospreys and a squadron of three pelicans. Great blue herons are everywhere. A young heron perches on a limb overlooking the water, its parents circling overhead. In contrast to these signs of natural health is the junk that litters the shoreline. Trapped in the viscous mud like prehistoric beasts in a tar pit are industrial barrels, numerous tires, and a large plastic garbage cart.

Where the Highway 26 bridge crosses the Rock River we notice a heavily used boat landing on the south bank, followed by a string of houses. Then the shore seems to revert to game refuge. Across the river is the land mass known as Blackhawk Island, though it has only a tenuous connection to the Sac warrior— his band camped nearby during their flight from Atkinson's army—and is not really an island. It might qualify as a peninsula, bounded on the south by the river, on the west by Lake Koshkonong, and on the north by Mud Lake and an extensive wetland.

Few Indian bands used the island for camps or burials because it is prone to flooding. Early settlers considered it useless for farming. Later arrivals, though, were attracted by its easy access to Lake Koshkonong for hunting and fishing. From the 1870s until it burned down in 1970, an exclusive sportsmen's resort, the Blackhawk Club, occupied the western tip of the peninsula. During the nineteenth century, when Lake Koshkonong enjoyed a national reputation as a place to shoot canvasback ducks, the club attracted out-of-state hunters, including the Civil War general Philip Sheridan. Its Wisconsin contingent included George W. Peck and members of some of the state's most prominent families: the Pabsts, Does, Uihleins, Cases, Spooners, Sawyers, Plankintons, and Quarleses.

We continue to hug the right bank, searching for a particular one-story cottage. At last we see it and move in for a closer look. The poet Lorine Niedecker and her husband built the modest structure in the 1960s. Barely visible behind it is the cabin with vertical log siding that Niedecker's father built for her in the mid-1940s. There she wrote some of her most enduring poetry.

Niedecker spent most of her life on Blackhawk Island. She died from a cerebral hemorrhage in 1970. Were she still alive and watching us from shore, I know exactly how our canoe would look to her:

> One boat
>
> two—
>   pointed toward
>   my shore
>
> thru birdstart
>   wingdrip
>   weed-drift
>
> of the soft
>   and serious—
>   Water

Niedecker's "life by water" (to quote from the title of this poem) began in 1903. Her father, Henry, had married Theresa Kunz a couple of years earlier. Theresa's parents owned much of Blackhawk Island and operated a resort hotel, the Fountain House Inn. As a wedding gift the Kunzes gave Henry and Theresa several large parcels of land and the inn, which the young couple ran for nine years.

Theresa, usually called Daisy or BP (short for Bean Pole, a nickname reflecting her tall stature), lost her hearing when she gave birth to their only child. When Daisy's failing health forced the couple to sell the hotel in 1910, Henry took a partner and went into the carp-fishing business, modifying a pleasure launch he had formerly used to take guests on tours of Lake Koshkonong.

Henry also divided the Kunz property into lots, selling some and building rental cabins on the others. In this way he was able to provide for the family until the late 1930s, when the fishing business failed and he had to sell most

Image courtesy of Hoard Historical Museum,
Fort Atkinson, Wisconsin

Lorine Niedecker with her parents, about 1912

of the remaining property. The Niedeckers' marriage deteriorated along with their financial security. As Daisy became depressed and withdrew into her silent world, Henry sought sexual and emotional solace in a neighbor woman.

Despite her parents' misfortunes, Lorine spent a mostly happy childhood on Blackhawk Island, observing its natural phenomena and enjoying the company of her Kunz grandparents and other relatives and neighbors. When she was old enough to attend elementary school, the Niedeckers moved to Fort Atkinson. They returned to the island when she was in high school, arranging for their daughter to board with other families during the week. After graduation Niedecker attended Beloit College for two years, leaving in 1924 when her father was no longer able to afford the tuition.

Beginning in 1928 she held a series of jobs away from home: as a library assistant at the Dwight Foster Public Library in Fort Atkinson, as a writer and research editor with the Federal Writers' Project in Madison (1938–1942), and briefly as a radio scriptwriter, also in Madison. After returning to Blackhawk Island she worked for a half-dozen years as a stenographer and proofreader for *Hoard's Dairyman* until her failing eyesight became a handicap. During the years 1957 to 1963 she was a cleaning woman at the Fort Atkinson Memorial Hospital.

Niedecker was married twice—in 1928 to Frank Hartwig, a former employee of her father; and in 1963 to Al Millen, an industrial painter at Ladish Drop Forge in Milwaukee. Her most significant romantic relation-ship, however, was with a very different kind of man. In 1931, shortly after her first marriage dissolved, she happened upon an issue of *Poetry* magazine devoted to the work of a group who called themselves Objectivists. These second-generation modernists emphasized the poem's status as an independent verbal object rather than a system of purely referential signs. They also disparaged the traditional notion of poetry as a medium of self-expression.

An aspiring poet herself—she had published a couple of poems in 1928—Niedecker wrote to the guest editor of the Objectivist issue, Louis Zukovsky, enclosing samples of her own work. Thus began a lifelong correspondence and a friendship that drew her to New York City several times between 1933 and 1939. She and Zukovsky became lovers, then platonic confidants. Though they went their separate ways domestically, he remained for her an important con-nection to the world of urban, avant-garde poetry.

Their relationship inevitably recalls that of the nineteenth-century poet Emily Dickinson and her "preceptor," Thomas Wentworth Higginson, and requires the same kind of tact when gauging the influence of the more assertive and well-connected mentor. Like Dickinson, Niedecker brought her own voice to the encounter, one shaped by the surrealists and the imagism of Ezra Pound and H. D. (Hilda Doolittle). Notwithstanding frequent expressions of self-effacement and deference to her mentor, she maintained her literary inde-pendence throughout the relationship. As Niedecker submitted poems to little magazines besides *Poetry*, her literary network grew to include writers and editors around the world.

In her early poems Niedecker blended surrealism with folk materials, particularly the nursery rhymes and Mother Goose stories she had learned from her grandfather, Gottfried Kunz, and her mother. Her research for the 1942 *Wisconsin: A Guide to the Badger State*, funded by the Federal Writers' Project, surfaced in poems about Black Hawk and Increase Lapham. During the same period she wrote a poem about Thure Kumlein, the Swedish naturalist whose granddaughter she had joined on an outing to his cabin site beside Lake Koshkonong. Following auto excursions to Lake Superior and Door County in the late 1960s, she wrote poetic sequences about those places.

As an artist who preferred abstraction and "objectivism" to self-disclosure, Niedecker avoided autobiography in her writings. Some of her poems and prose sketches deal nonetheless with the challenges of finding and holding a job as age and failing eyesight take their toll. Others allude to loneliness and the sense of having little to show for years of literary labor. Like many grown children she mythologized her parents and thereby herself as the product of their union. "Paean to Place," written shortly after her sixty-fifth birthday, includes verbal snapshots from the family album:

> he seined for carp to be sold
> that their daughter
>
> might go high
> on land
>   to learn
> Saw his wife turn
> deaf
> and away
> She
>   who knew boats
>   and ropes
> no longer played

Here, years after Daisy's death, the poet expresses regret that her mother's infirmity drained her life of joy, including the pleasures of sound:

> I mourn her not hearing canvasbacks
> their blast-off rise
>   from the water
>   Not hearing sora
> rails's sweet
>
> spoon-tapped waterglass-
> descending scale-
>   tear-drop-tittle
>   Did she giggle
> as a girl?

What sets Niedecker apart from urban modernists such as Zukovsky, what makes hers a poetry for all times and places, is, paradoxically, her attention to local phenomena. Like William Faulkner, whose novel *As I Lay Dying* she adapted as a radio script in 1952, she listened carefully to the speech of the people and the cries of the animals (the "spoon-tapped waterglass" call of the sora rail, for example) that shared her postage stamp of American soil. Then she transformed her prosaic materials into the most exacting art.

If George W. Peck is Wisconsin's most popular author, Niedecker is arguably its finest poet, though most state residents have yet to discover her work. The English poet Basil Bunting was rather too optimistic when, shortly after her death, he wrote, "I have no doubt at all that in 10 years time Wisconsin will know that she was its most considerable literary figure."

One of Niedecker's first poems, published in her high school yearbook, was a piece that she characterized as "an ode to Lake Koshkonong." It would be only a slight exaggeration to say that her *Collected Works* could be described in the same way. Together with the Rock River watershed and Blackhawk Island, the lake was her equivalent of Faulkner's Yoknapatawpha County.

Niedecker was a poet of place and, as she says in the epigraph of "Paean to Place," "the place was water." Water is a source not only of sustenance and life in her poems, but also of death and destruction. Her writings chronicle the annual floods that occasionally brought the river into her home, leaving a trail of debris to be cleaned up. Even as she fought

against the water, she understood how it schooled her in detachment from
material possessions:

> O my floating life
> Do not save love
>   for things
>   Throw *things*
>   to the flood
>
>   ruined
>   by the flood
>   Leave the new unbought—
>   all one in the end—
> water

As we drift past the place where Niedecker lived her "floating life," I
recall a line from one of Ezra Pound's *Pisan Cantos*: "What thou lovest
well remains." Niedecker learned how to find stability in the midst of flux.
Fortunately for us, what she loved best remains in the poems. The rest she
gave back to the river.

~~~~~~~~

Evidence of the river's destructiveness lines the shore of Blackhawk Island.
Some of the older homes appear to be abandoned. The foundation of one has
collapsed, rendering the house unusable. Yet there are also signs of renewal—
the construction of new homes and new foundations under existing homes.
We can feel Lake Koshkonong before we see it, in the form of a refreshing
breeze. Lorine Niedecker walked almost daily to the western tip of Blackhawk
Island, where today a trailer park occupies land that once belonged to the
Blackhawk Club. Just upstream from the park is a public access with a couple
of docks. Parked near the docks are several vehicles, including our minivan.
But we aren't quite ready to take out. Instead, we paddle out for an unob-
structed view of the lake.

When Increase Lapham visited Lake Koshkonong in July 1850, he found
it overgrown with wild rice, lending it the appearance of a meadow. Lucien
B. Caswell, whose family settled on the lake's south shore in 1837, recalled
that as fall approached the rice grew "from five to seven feet high above the

Dwight Foster Public Library

The Niedecker cabin during a flood, between 1979 and 2004

water, and so thick all over that it was difficult to push a canoe through it." In September Indians came from far and wide to harvest the crop. According to Eli May, who came to Fort Atkinson in 1839 and built a large frame house on the stockade site, it was not unusual to see three to four hundred Indians paddling down the Rock River to the lake.

Between the retreat of the Wisconsin Glacier and the Indian removals of the early nineteenth century the Koshkonong–Rock River basin provided rice, fish, mussels, and wild game to people from a succession of cultures—Woodland, Mississippian, and possibly Oneota. The last of these displaced or evolved from its predecessors around 1000 AD and is distinguished by its corn-based agriculture. Corn allowed the Oneota to live most of the year in stable village clusters beside lakes and rivers, moving to other hunting grounds during the winter, when ice glazed the water and game was scarce near the villages. Unlike the mound builders, they buried their dead beneath the floors of their houses or in flat underground cemeteries near their villages. From the Oneota descended the Ho-Chunk and related Indians of the historic period.

Lapham's maps show extensive Indian earthworks along the Rock River between its junction with the Bark and its exit from Lake Koshkonong. There were about five hundred mounds around Lake Koshkonong alone. Though farming and development obliterated most of them, Hugh Highsmith, a Fort Atkinson businessman and the author of *The Mounds of Koshkonong and Rock River*, saved eleven effigy mounds from the bulldozer by purchasing a five-acre parcel of oak woods and donating it to the county. Visitors can view this group in Jefferson County Indian Mounds and Trail Park, located next to a golf course on the south shore of Lake Koshkonong.

Except for such protected corners, the mound builders would hardly recognize Lake Koshkonong today, even if it were not encircled by homes and cottages. Soon after Lapham's visit, settlers built a dam at Indianford, drowning the wild rice beds. The dam was meant to hold the lake at a predictable level so that mills downstream could tap its water for power. In 1877 the owner raised the height of the structure, prompting a protest from lakeside farmers whose lands were flooded. They threatened to tear it down. Though larger, Koshkonong still resembled the lake that had attracted Indians and early settlers. Its waters were clear and shallow, surrounded by marsh and thick with aquatic plants. An account of the lake published in 1879 described it in florid prose as "an 'inland sea' of exquisite beauty, where one may pass the sultry days of August in an atmosphere as pure as kissed the cheeks of Eve in Paradise."

In 1917 the dam owner raised the structure another two feet, prompting landowners to complain to the Wisconsin Railroad Commission. According to one estimate, the higher water caused $5 million worth of damage to surrounding property, equivalent to about $85 million today. The Railroad Commission ordered a six-inch reduction of the water level, which did little to stem Koshkonong's deterioration. Its waters became deeper, turbid, and almost devoid of aquatic plant life. In 1971 the DNR estimated that the lake was 858 acres larger than it had been in 1916, due to the dam and shoreline erosion. When heavy winds drove down the six-mile stretch of shallow water, there was little vegetation to buffer the shore against waves.

What had happened to the plant life? It was a casualty not only of the higher water but also of a newcomer to the lake community: the common carp. *Cyprinus carpio* came to Lake Koshkonong by a circuitous route. The species evolved in the Caspian Sea and migrated to the Black and Aral Seas, then east as far as mainland Asia and west as far as the Danube River. It became a valued food fish in Asia and Europe. During the 1830s Americans on the east coast imported carp for private ponds and released a few into public waterways.

In an effort to augment the depleted native fishery, the US Fish Commission imported adult brood stock from Germany in 1877 in exchange for Great Lakes whitefish, California salmon, and brook trout. A couple of years later the commission began to release carp fingerlings (about three inches long) throughout the United States. Immigrants from Europe, Germany in particular, were familiar with the species and eager to have it introduced into nearby streams and lakes. Often the carp were simply dumped from railroad cars into waterways spanned by bridges.

Carp may have entered Lake Koshkonong this way, too, but they apparently also had help from the Blackhawk Club. According to one account the club manager requested a shipment of carp for stocking, and when the fish-filled milk cans arrived he loaded them onto a wagon, hauled them to the shore, and released their contents into the lake. That simple act had far-reaching consequences. Once the carp-genie was out of the bottle, it would not go back in.

The carp thrived in the lake. Prior to the 1870s Koshkonong and the upstream reach of the Rock River enjoyed a reputation as an especially fertile fishery. Aaron Rankin mentions perch, bass, pickerel, red horse, suckers, sturgeon, and catfish as the species most sought after in the 1830s. When settlers constructed a dam at Johnson's Rapids (now Watertown) in 1837, spawning fish could travel no farther upstream. "The first year after the dam was built," Timothy Johnson's daughter recalled, "the fish came up here in such swarms they seemed to fill the river full. We had them in every form, fried, boiled, baked, and roasted. Also smoked and salted."

After the carp were introduced, native fish lost spawning beds on Lake Koshkonong as well as upstream. Carp feed by rooting in the lake bottom, stirring up sediment that ruins the spawning beds. They ingest the eggs of other species and destroy vegetation that the other fish use for cover. The loss of aquatic plants, particularly the wild celery beds, also made the lake less attractive to ducks and therefore to duck hunters, leading to the demise of the Blackhawk Club. After 1895 the US Fish Commission ceased distribution of carp, leaving to states the problem of dealing with the havoc wrought by the invader.

Lake Koshkonong could not be drained completely, nor could it be poisoned without damage to native fish species. The prolific carp would have to be netted. Fortunately for commercial fishermen such as Henry Niedecker, there was a demand for carp in New York and other cities on the eastern seaboard. The Chicago and Northwestern Railroad linked Fort Atkinson to that market. Some fishermen outfitted their boats with an engine on each side to haul in nets full to bursting with carp and buffalo, a rough fish belonging to the sucker family. Soon after the catch was brought in, it could be shipped to New York in refrigerated cars.

In 1903 the *New York Times* reported that an Ohio entrepreneur had contracted with the state of Wisconsin to remove carp from Lake Koshkonong and other waters in the southern counties. He planned to deliver twenty tons of carp daily to New York City, barreled in ice. If he failed to rid the selected lakes of carp, he would be subject to a heavy fine. Whether he had to pay the fine is unknown. Clearly he failed to rid the lake of carp, and commercial fishermen are still netting Koshkonong carp and shipping them to both coasts. Jewish consumers use them for gefilte fish on holidays. Asian Americans prefer to buy whole live fish in markets and restaurants, so the carp usually travel by tank truck to those destinations. Midwesterners, though they consume some smoked carp, have not acquired a taste for the fish in other forms.

Neither sport fishermen nor duck hunters are entirely happy with commercial seining on Lake Koshkonong. Fishermen dislike interference with their pastime in the spring and summer, and hunters suspect that the nets do as much damage to aquatic plants as the carp. Both parties want fewer carp, however, and seining is an effective way to reduce the population. In February 1954 the *Jefferson County Union* reported the netting of 50,000 pounds of carp in one day on the Bark River, bringing the seasonal total to 400,000 pounds. Larger catches were routine on Lake Koshkonong. In 1973 a single haul with a seine net brought in 750,000 pounds. In 1980 one haul netted 1.25 million pounds of the fish.

Today commercial netting is one component of the DNR's three-part strategy for managing the Rock-Koshkonong fishery. The others are releasing walleye fry at the Bark River hatchery and transplanting stunted panfish from nearby lakes to Lake Koshkonong, where they thrive and grow. Though residents and sportsmen cannot evict carp from Koshkonong for once and for all, they have found ways to live with their obnoxious neighbor.

The equilibrium may be short lived, however. The *Cyprinus carpio* disaster should have deterred anyone from releasing more carp in North American waters. Unfortunately, catfish farmers in the South introduced four new carp species in the 1970s, this time from China. They used the silver, bighead, grass, and black carp to keep their ponds clear of algae, snails, and parasites. When the Mississippi River flooded in the 1980s, the carp escaped into the river. Since then the silver, bighead, and grass species have been spreading upstream throughout the Mississippi watershed. Bighead carp caught in the lower Wisconsin River and near the mouth of the St. Croix River in 2011 suggest that the fish are poised to invade Wisconsin's inland streams and lakes.

Because silver carp have a habit of leaping out of the water when agitated by the vibration of motorboat propellers, they pose a physical threat to boaters and water skiers. Taking advantage of this trait, one enterprising guide leads bow-hunting excursions on the Illinois River. The archers skewer the carp in midair as though they were pheasants or grouse. Asian carp pose a more substantial threat to native fish than to people, however. They are prolific (females carry up to two million eggs) and voracious, eating 40 percent or more of their body weight per day in phyto- and zooplankton. Because the fish may exceed a hundred pounds as adults, they can quickly deplete the food supply on which native fish depend.

Illinois, whose inland waterways have already been infiltrated by Asian carp, is attempting to control the invaders with commercial netting. As with the common carp, there is demand for the fish in Asian markets on both coasts and in Chicago. One Illinois processor is even planning to export the fish to China and other overseas markets.

But the supply will outpace the demand, and fisheries biologists fear the invaders have entered the Great Lakes by way of the Illinois River and the Chicago Sanitary and Ship Canal. The canal's chief line of defense, an electrical fence, is by no means impermeable. Water samples taken between the fence and Lake Michigan frequently test positive for Asian carp DNA. In 2010 a netting crew caught a twenty-pound bighead carp in Lake Calumet, which is connected directly to Lake Michigan. Wisconsin has joined four other Great Lakes states in lawsuits (so far unsuccessful) to force closure of the locks leading to the canal. The plaintiffs seek ultimately to restore the historical separation of the Mississippi and Great Lakes watersheds. The financial stakes are high on both sides, as the case pits Chicago shipping against Great Lakes commercial and sport fishing. The environmental stakes are much higher, to judge from Lake Koshkonong's history.

Asian carp are by no means the only aquatic invaders in southeastern Wisconsin. In 2003 the DNR caught a twenty-four-inch giant snakehead while conducting a fish survey in the Rock River. Mistaking the Asian transplant for the native bowfin, the crew released it into the river. A popular aquarium fish when small, the snakehead had probably outgrown its tank.

Unlike carp and snakeheads, which were deliberately introduced into US waters, zebra mussels arrived in the 1980s as larvae in the ballast water of ocean freighters. From the Great Lakes they hitchhiked into inland lakes and rivers, including the Bark, by attaching themselves to the hulls of pleasure craft. Zebra mussel colonies monopolize oxygen and plankton and clog the intake pipes of water treatment plants. Following the same route into the Great Lakes, quagga mussels have done even more damage, virtually wiping out commercial fishing in parts of Lake Michigan.

The list of invasive species seems endless and growing. In North America as a whole it includes about fifty thousand species. Among the more troublesome in southeastern Wisconsin, besides the fish and mussels already mentioned, are plants such as purple loosestrife, common and shiny buckthorn, honeysuckle, and Eurasian milfoil; birds such as the mute swan; mammals such as feral hogs; and insects such as the emerald ash-borer and the Asian gypsy moth. All of the earthworm species in northern Wisconsin arrived from Europe and Asia after the glacier killed off native worms, if there were any natives that far north. Long regarded as the gardener's friend, they consume the leaf litter in which native plant species germinate, clearing the ground for fellow invaders such as garlic mustard.

State and federal agencies spend millions of dollars annually to control invasive species—$45 million on purple loosestrife alone—and volunteer organizations contribute countless hours to the same campaign. After all, what else can we do?

We might, some people contend, change the way we think about invasive species. Representing one school of thought, a professor at the University of Massachusetts claims that the language we use to discuss the subject betrays our xenophobia. We are, she argues, applying to nonhuman species a rhetoric that was once used against human immigrants. This may seem to carry political correctness to a zany extreme. Yet the sociopolitical argument has some support, in practice if not in theory, from environmental historians and scientists.

According to historians such as William Cronon and Charles C. Mann, much of North America was already a man-made environment when European explorers and settlers arrived. Using fire as their primary tool, native people had reshaped the land to favor game animals such as deer, buffalo, and elk and make them easier to hunt. The oak openings of southeastern Wisconsin, regarded by early settlers as vestiges of the Garden of Eden, were the product of annual burning, a form of cultivation. After crossing the Bering Strait during the Ice Age, humans transformed the terrain to a degree unmatched by other invasive species. They made it literally a landscape.

So what did the land look like before it was "scaped"? Botanists who reconstruct prehistoric patterns of vegetation, usually by studying the pollen in soil core samples, conclude that North America has always been a work in progress. There is no single, stable moment in the evolutionary continuum that we might call the "American wilderness" or the "virgin land." Consequently, there is no benchmark to which we might return, even if that were possible.

Restoration ecology typically proceeds on the assumption that native species will return when the aliens have been evicted. But in some cases, nothing replaces the invaders. A biologist who studied prairie and oak savanna in Canada discovered that invasive grasses did not drive out the native species. They merely occupied a niche left vacant when the natives succumbed to climate change. The exotics actually helped the prairie to resist erosion and the encroachment of woody plants. By analogy, it would be futile to try to restore the woolly mammoth to the Bark River valley even if a breeding pair could be found. The climatic conditions that favored mammoths during the Pleistocene have disappeared along with the animals.

Aldo Leopold, the father of restoration ecology, stated its key criterion succinctly: "A thing is right when it tends to preserve the integrity, stability, and beauty of the biotic community. It is wrong when it tends otherwise." This pragmatic proposition makes no distinction between natives and exotics. Either can be "right," scientifically as well as ethically. Considering the inevitability of environmental change and the impossibility of eradicating all exotics, some ecologists argue that we should abandon the distinction between native and nonnative species. We should manage the ecosystem for a functional, balanced, and aesthetically pleasing mixture of species, regardless of origin. A naturalized citizen such as the ring-necked pheasant may contribute more to a particular biotic community than, say, the native Canada goose.

Planet Earth has evolved a dazzling array of organisms, as though bent on filling even the least hospitable crevices with life. Humankind began that way, as an experiment that played a specific role in a particular corner of the world.

We might easily have become a footnote to evolution, our passing marked only by fossil remains. Instead, we became the planet's dominant invasive species. We have succeeded so well, according to some criteria, that today we hold the power of life and death over many of our fellow creatures. The world that we live in tomorrow will be to some extent our own invention. It is a staggering responsibility. We can make the earth a place of integrity, stability, and beauty (Leopold's ideal) or just another dead cinder circling the sun.

~~~~~

Defending the western tip of Blackhawk Island is a rampart of concrete slabs recycled from some highway or parking lot. Without this unsightly riprap the trailer park would probably have succumbed to erosion. Two boys are leaping from slab to slab, their lean figures spotlighted by the setting sun. They pause long enough to wave at us, and we wave back. From their point of view we must look much as we did in April, suspended on the liquid membrane of Bark Lake.

Much as, but not the same. As the Greek philosopher said, you can't step twice into the same river. Water from the brushy little creek we paddled in the spring has long since freshened the Gulf of Mexico. More than once, in fact, it has doubtless evaporated, fallen as rain, and swelled another river's stately progress or frantic dash to the sea. It may even be circulating in our veins, though we haven't knowingly drunk a drop of it.

"Ready to call it a day?" Puck asks.

"And a season," I respond, taking aim at our parked minivan and stroking forward. Something about the scene—its lucid tranquility, perhaps—reminds me of an experience I've had before.

Till then I'd been skeptical when people told me about moments of sudden illumination, transient states in which everything seemed as simple and transparent as crystal. So I was more embarrassed than uplifted when I had such a visitation myself. One moment I was walking along, thinking of nothing in particular. The next moment I knew, just knew, what my final conscious thoughts would be.

My life will not flash before my eyes, like a video in manic fast-forward. Nor will a figure in white greet me on the threshold of a mysteriously lighted chamber. There will be no Hollywood stagecraft whatsoever. Instead, I will be enveloped, bathed, in a swarming, amorphous cloud of sensations and images. Some I will recognize, abstractly, as pleasant; others as painful. But

I will feel neither pleasure nor pain. None of my accomplishments, modest as they are, will matter. Whatever good I have done will elicit no pride, the evil no regret.

The cloud will consist mostly of faces and places. Among the faces will be those of the people closest to me—Puck, my children, my parents, my sister and brother, longtime friends. The places will include spectacular landscapes viewed just once or twice: glaciers in Alaska, mountaintops in Tibet and China, vineyards in Italy, rolling green pastures in England, sand dunes in Morocco, ancient ruins in Mexico, cloud forests in Costa Rica, walled cities in Spain, coastal estuaries in Portugal.

Conspicuous in the cloud, surging to the fore and fading away, then surging back again, will be the places that I have known in all seasons, in all kinds of weather, at all hours of the day. Among these, winding sinuously through my last mortal moment like a silver thread in a tapestry, will surely be the Bark River.

Puck has noticed my silence. As we lift our paddles from the water and glide into shore she asks, "Okay, Mr. Muse, what are you thinking about now?"

"Supper! Aren't you hungry? The sooner we load our stuff in the van and pick up the bike, the sooner we'll get to the Carpe."

Notes

ABBREVIATIONS

DNR DSFS	DNR Bureau of Watershed Management, Dam Safety and Floodplain Section
JCU	*Jefferson County Union*
MJ	*Milwaukee Journal*
MJS	*Milwaukee Journal Sentinel*
MS	*Milwaukee Sentinel*
WCMRC	Waukesha County Museum Research Center
WF	*Waukesha Freeman*
WSJ	*Wisconsin State Journal*

Currency inflation is calculated with Lawrence H. Officer and Samuel H. Williamson's "Purchasing Power of Money in the United States from 1774 to Present," MeasuringWorth, 2011 (www.measuringworth.com/ppowerus).

CHAPTER 1

2 *opening figure*: Don Behm, "Tiny Richfield Lots Fetch High Bids," *MJS* 14 Oct. 2007.

2 *I respond*: Public Land Survey Plat Map 1836, T9 R19E.

3 *clearly legible*: David M. Mickelson, "Wisconsin's Glacial Landscapes," *Wisconsin Land and Life*, ed. Robert C. Ostergren and Thomas R. Vale (Madison: U of Wisconsin P, 1997), p. 37.

3 *moraines, and kettles*: David M. Mickelson and Kent M. Syverson, *Quaternary Geology of Ozaukee and Waukesha Counties, Wisconsin*, Bulletin 91 (Madison: U of Wisconsin–Extension, 1997), p. 4.

4 *toward the southwest*: Barbara A. Nelson and Margaret S. Holzbog, *Richfield Remembers the Past* (Richfield, WI: Richfield History Committee, 1996), p. 3.

4 *dumped in the pit*: Loren H. Osman, "Serenity of Amy Belle Shaken by Quarry Plan," *MJ* 28 Dec. 1975. The information in the next paragraph is from the following articles by Osman in the *MJ*: "Tighter Rules Urged for Pits in Richfield," 7 Dec. 1976; "New Rules on Gravel Pits OK'd," 14 Dec. 1976; "Scaled Down Plans for Gravel Pit Close to Approval," 8 Mar. 1979; and "Plans for Gravel Pit Approved," 15 Mar. 1979.

5 *plant growth*: Mickelson, "Wisconsin's Glacial Landscapes," pp. 46–47.

5 *and Bavaria*: Population Schedule for Richfield Township, Washington County, Wisconsin, Federal Census of 1860.

6 *near the lake*: Jo Sandin, "Bark Lake Residents Win a Sewer Dispute," *MJ* 17 May 1988.

6 *slender madtom*: This paragraph draws on the following articles in the *MJ*: "Bark Lake Area Forms Sanitary District," 11 May 1984; Anne Spitza, "Rare Fish in River May Endanger New Treatment Plant," 24 Apr. 1985; Spitza, "Fish Put Sewer Plans in Jeopardy," 2 May 1985; Michael Krenn, "Bark Lake May Join City System," 21 Apr. 1986; and Krenn, "Bark Lake to Seek Sewer District Link," 28 July 1986.

6 *isolated communities*: William Breyfogle, "Homeowners Want to Disband Sewerage District," 28 Sept.; and "Richfield Considers Sewer Ideas," 13 Oct.; both in 1989 issues of the *MJ*.

7 *yellow fever*: Lee E. Lawrence, "The Wisconsin Ice Trade," *Wisconsin Magazine of History* 48 (Summer 1965): 257.

8 *servants in India*: Gavin Weightman, *The Frozen Water Trade: A True Story* (New York: Hyperion, 2003), pp. 173, 195.

8 *by blacksmiths*: Weightman, p. 106; and Richard O. Cummings, *The American Ice Harvests: A Historical Study in Technology, 1800–1918* (Berkeley: U of California P, 1949), pp. 19, 195–96.

8 *railroad boxcar*: Joseph C. Jones Jr., *America's Icemen: An Illustrative History of the United States Natural Ice Industry, 1665–1925* (Humble, TX: Jobeco Books, 1984), pp. 78, 93.

8 *market dictated*: For the Walden Pond ice harvest see Cummings, pp. 46, 51–52; and Weightman, pp. 167–70.

8 *Washington Counties*: Jones, p. 119; and Lawrence, p. 260.

9 *battles took place*: Account of ice war from Lawrence, p. 264; and Weightman, p. 233.

9 *ice per year*: Lawrence, p. 258.

10 *around the country*: Lawrence, p. 258.

10 *tons of ice*: Jones, p. 119.

10 *horse-drawn wagons*: This paragraph is indebted to Jones, pp. 79, 141.

10 *weed-cutting scows*: Lauretta Wieland, "The Pewaukee Ice Industry: A Tale of a Remarkable Industry, with Maps and Pictures," ca. 1981, typescript in Humanities Reading Room, Milwaukee Public Library, p. 3.

10 *remove the snow*: Jones, pp. 21–23, 62.

12 *each chamber*: Wieland, p. 5.

12 *in Milwaukee*: Wieland, p. 2.

12 *around the operation*: Lawrence, p. 260.

12 *the ice cutters*: "Our County Mirror," *WF* 22 Jan. 1891.

12 *Milwaukee or Chicago*: Wieland, p. 5.

13 *in 1903*: Lawrence, p. 265.

13 *State Archaeologist*: Site WT-0221, Office of the State Archaeologist, Madison, Wisconsin.

CHAPTER 2

18 *of the Bark*: Scott Williams, "Gravel Pit Operators Seek Approval for Expansion," *MJS* 19 July 2002.

26 *west of the village*: "Notes on Merton from Old Settlers' Meeting, Feb. 22, 1871," *Waukesha Plain Dealer* 28 Feb. 1871; and *Hartland: A Chronicle, 1838–1976* (Hartland: Hartland History Group, 1976), p. 3.

26 *Sylvanus Warren*: *Hartland: A Chronicle*, p. 3. According to Theron W. Haight's *Memoirs of Waukesha County* (Madison, WI: Western Historical, 1907), p. 675, Warren arrived in 1836.

26 *and Michigan*: *Hartland: A Chronicle*, p. 3.

26 *in the state*: Haight, *Memoirs*, p. 296. I have not been able to locate another Warren post office that was active in 1848.

26 *came to pass*: The resident was the wife of Henry Shears, who together with George Trowbridge built a gristmill in 1847. See S. G. Lapham, "Waukesha County Scenes and Landmarks Recall Memories of the Early Residents," *Milwaukee Morning Sentinel* 18 Feb. 1917; and "The Early History of Merton," typescript of a paper presented by William H. Kuntz on 3 Nov. 1951, in the WCMRC.

26 *commercial nucleus*: Anonymous memoir in typescript entitled "Merton" at the WCMRC; and "Notes on Merton."

26 *to the village*: According to "Merton Builds a New Dam," *MS* 10 Apr. 1967, the feed company owned the dam and used it to generate power until about 1962. The feed company owners, Benjamin and Ethel Serres, petitioned the State Public Service Commission to transfer ownership to the village of Merton in 1963 (*MS* 2 Mar. 1963).

27 *buried their dead*: "Old Immigrant Trail Winds Around Kuntz Property Across Bark River," *WF* 14 June 1954.

27 *Christian faith*: *The Antiquities of Wisconsin, as Surveyed and Described* (1855; Madison: U of Wisconsin P, 2001), p. 39.

28 *Indian antiquities*: *Milwaukee Advertiser* 24 Nov. 1836, quoted in Robert P. Nurre's introduction to Lapham's *Antiquities*, p. xia.

28 *study them*: Robert A. Birmingham and Leslie E. Eisenberg, *Indian Mounds of Wisconsin* (Madison: U of Wisconsin P, 2000), p. 3.

29 *Waukesha mound*: *Wisconsin State Register* 23 Jan. 1886, issue 49.

29 *native Indian*: "My First Trip West—1836," *"It Seems Like Only Yesterday . . .": Stories from Fort Atkinson's Early Days 1836–1914* (Fort Atkinson: Fort Atkinson Historical Society, 2001), pp. 41, 45.

29 *ancient structures*: *Antiquities*, p. 29.

29 *contemporary Indians*: *Antiquities*, p. 92.

30 *ritual cannibalism*: Birmingham and Eisenberg, pp. 143–45, 161; and Birmingham and Lynne G. Goldstein, *Aztalan: Mysteries of an Ancient Indian Town* (Madison: Wisconsin Historical Society Press, 2005), pp. 100–101.

30 *have descended*: Birmingham and Eisenberg, pp. 141, 165.

30 *as ancestors*: Birmingham and Eisenberg, pp. 58, 185.

30 *kind of effigy*: *Antiquities*, p. 38 and Pl. XXXI, No. 1; also in Charles E. Brown, "A Record of Wisconsin Antiquities," *Wisconsin Archaeologist* 5:3–4 (Apr.–Oct. 1906): 402.

30 *linear mounds*: *Antiquities*, p. 38 and Pl. XXX. Full description in Brown, p. 401.

31 *water spirits*: Birmingham and Eisenberg, pp. 90, 122.

31 *mischievous behavior*: Birmingham and Eisenberg, pp. 107–108, 118; Fig. 5.3.

31 *North America*: Birmingham and Eisenberg, p. 174.

32 *water spirit clan*: Birmingham and Eisenberg, p. 116.

32 *seventeenth century*: Mentioned, for example, in Carl Quickert, ed., *Washington County Wisconsin: Past and Present* (Chicago: S. J. Clarke, 1912), 1:59–61; discredited in Barbara A. Nelson and Margaret S. Holzbog, *Richfield Remembers the Past* (Richfield, WI: Richfield History Committee, 1996), p. 159.

32 *his honor*: "Lapham Peak Trip Offers Panoramic View of Countryside," *WF* 10 June 1954. Lapham had used the Government Hill site for weather observations.

CHAPTER 3

35 *drop a foot*: "Vandalism Could Have Hindered Firefighting," *MJS* 22 July 2003.

37 *far behind*: Don Behm, "Environmentalists Push to Close Gaps in Kettle Moraine Forest Corridor," *MJS* 28 Sept. 1998.

37 *Ice Age Trail*: "Report of the Kettle Moraine Task Force," *Wisconsin Academy Review* 42.3 (Summer 1996): 44f.

38 *west of here*: Amy Rabideau Silvers, "Wisconsin Statesman Proved Visionary," *MJS* 15 Jan. 2002.

40 *with skaters*: SaraBelle Van Buren, "One of the Early Landmarks," typescript in the WCMRC, p. 8. An excerpt from the memoir appears in *Hartland: A Chronicle, 1838–1976* (Hartland: Hartland History Group, 1976), pp. 56–58.

41 *other side*: From Nellie Mary Warren Reed, "History of Hartland from the Time of the Coming of the First White Settlers to the Present Time," typescript dated 1934 in the WCMRC, pp. 17–18. In the typescript the last quatrain begins, "But higher . . . ," apparently a typographic error.

42 *Watertown Railroad*: *Hartland: A Chronicle*, p. 56. Elsewhere this source indicates that the mill was built in 1842 (p. 4).

42 *the weir*: Van Buren, p. 7.

42 *as Hersheyville*: Theron W. Haight, *Memoirs of Waukesha County* (Madison, WI: Western Historical, 1907), p. 275; and *Hartland: A Chronicle*, p. 4.

42 *in 1891*: Van Buren, p. 2.

42 *in operation*: The following interview is based on Van Buren's memoir, "One of the Early Landmarks."

45 *this article*: W. J. C. Ralph, "Oldest of All" in column "Pen-Pictures," unidentified newspaper 10 Mar. 1939 (WCMRC).

45 *beautify the river*: "Bark River Plan Seen," *MJ* 21 May 1982.

46 *150 to 13*: "13 Take a Cool Dip; Make That Fool Dip," *MJ* 2 Jan. 1983.

CHAPTER 4

47 *as Kilbourntown*: Third and Chestnut is now Old World Third Street and West Juneau Avenue.

48 *spot selected*: James S. Buck, *Pioneer History of Milwaukee*, rev. ed. (Milwaukee: Swain and Tate, 1890), 1:221–22.

48 *John Hustis*: West Water Street is now Plankinton Avenue.

49 *each year*: Russell Bourne, *Floating West: The Erie and Other American Canals* (New York: Norton, 1992), p. 162.

49 *Green Bay*: Robert C. Nesbit, *Wisconsin: A History*, rev. and updated William F. Thompson (Madison: U of Wisconsin P, 1989), p. 93.

49 *and speculators*: Nesbit, p. 138.

49 *45,000 residents*: Goodwin Berquist and Paul C. Bowers, Jr., *Byron Kilbourn and the Development of Milwaukee* (Milwaukee: Milwaukee County Historical Society, 2001), p. 91.

49 *the Menomonee*: Nesbit, p. 101.

51 *feasible financially*: Richard C. Barnum, *The Politics of Public Aid: The Effort to Obtain Municipal Financial Aid from the City of Milwaukee for the Milwaukee and Mississippi Railroad* (University of Wisconsin–Milwaukee master's thesis, 1968), p. 1.

51 *doubling the cost*: Alvin F. Harlow, *Old Towpaths: The Story of the American Canal Era* (New York: Appleton, 1926), p. 83.

52 *was reduced*: Harlow, pp. 109–110.

52 *their children*: Michael P. Conzen, "The European Settling and Transformation of the Upper Mississippi Valley Lead Mining Region," *Wisconsin Land and Life*, ed. Robert C. Ostergren and Thomas R. Vale (Madison: U of Wisconsin P, 1997), p. 167.

52 *shipping costs*: Barnum, p. 3.

52 *the Mississippi*: Harlow, p. 5.

52 *possible routes*: Increase Lapham reprinted the *Advertiser* articles in *A Documentary History of the Milwaukee and Rock River Canal* (Milwaukee: Advertiser, 1840), which is the source cited or quoted in the following paragraphs.

53 *projected canal*: Lapham, p. 19. According to Moses M. Strong these mines had been shipping lead down the Pecatonica since 1830. See his *History of the Territory of Wisconsin, from 1836 to 1848* (Madison: State of Wisconsin, 1885), p. 596.

53 *to New York*: Lapham, p. 20.

53 *cost of shipment*: Lapham, p. 20.

53 *and Mukwonago*: Lapham, p. 12.

53 *the East*: Lapham, pp. 20–21.

53 *Birmingham of Wisconsin*: Lapham, p. 13.

53 *building materials*: Lapham, pp. 10, 15.

54 *construction costs*: In an 1836 sketch of the canal route now in the WCMRC, Lapham projected a towpath along the south shores of Nagawicka, Upper Nemahbin, Lower Nashotah, and Oconomowoc Lakes.

54 *of locomotion*: Bourne, pp. 136, 162.

54 *tightly together*: Bourne, pp. 20–21.

55 *620-foot summit*: Bourne, p. 22.

55 *traverse it*: Lapham, p. 7.

55 *providential arrangement*: Lapham, p. 12.

55 *Illinois River*: Lapham, pp. 11–12.

55 *of Watertown*: Lapham, pp. 8, 15.

55 *Prairie du Chien*: Lapham, pp. 15–16.

55 *Sugar Rivers*: Lapham, p. 18.

55 *Rock Rivers*: Described in Strong, pp. 608–9.

56 *and New Jersey*: Harlow, p. 389.

56 *Ohio's wave*: Quoted in Harlow, pp. 28–29.

56 *Revolutionary War*: Bourne, p. 13.

56 *the south*: Harlow, pp. 11, 122.

57 *for Badgers*: Lapham, p. 10.

57 *native resources*: Lapham, p. 16.

57 *mines of Peru*: Quoted in Berquist and Bowers, p. 94.

57 *million today*: Lapham, pp. 35–37; 98; 144.

58 *by 1835*: Bourne, pp. 116, 127.

58 *internal improvements*: Berquist and Bowers, p. 94.

58 *Miami Canal*: Letter of 31 May 1838 quoted in Lapham, p. 59.

58 *eventually approved*: Berquist and Bowers, p. 99.

59 *Rock River region*: Strong, p. 601.

59 *that body*: Lapham, p. 47.

59 *than settlers*: Nesbit, p. 144.

59 *160 acres*: William R. Smith, *History of Wisconsin* (Madison: Beriah Brown, 1854),
    part 2, p. 357.

60 *your nod*: MS 31 July 1838.

60 *in 1844*: Barnum, p. 15.

60 *the Pacific*: Quoted in Lapham, p. 95 (spelling and punctuation *sic*).

60 *for construction*: Alice E. Smith, *History of Wisconsin* (Madison: State Historical Society,
    1973), 1:452.

61 *with stone*: Strong, pp. 620–21.

61 *repudiating resolutions*: Strong, p. 628.

61 *the overcharge*: John G. Gregory, *History of Milwaukee, Wisconsin* (Chicago and Milwaukee:
    Clarke, 1931), 1:296.

61 *in 1839*: Barnum, p. 9.

63 *a tannery*: For the names of the factories and the value of their products in 1847–1848 see
    Gregory, pp. 296–97.

63 *to Lake Michigan*: Kathleen Wolski and William Wawrzyn, "River on the Rebound,"
    Wisconsin Natural Resources Magazine Apr. 2005, p. 2.

63 *Kilbourn Canal*: Adapted from "Low Bridge, Everybody Down," a traditional song about
    the Erie Canal.

CHAPTER 5

66 *built up*: Jamaal Abdul-Alim, "Records Seized from Mill Place Developer," 7 July 1997;
    Kris Radish, "'Nightmare' in Mill Place," 27 July 1997; and Vikki Ortiz, "Plan to Install
    Sidewalk Angers Some in Subdivision," 1 July 1999; all in the *MJS*.

66 *other fill*: Sam Martino, "Knowledge of Contents Denied," *MJ* 20 July 1993.

66 *drinking-water standard*: State of Wisconsin v. Chrysler Outboard Corporation,
    case no. 96-1158, 19 June 1998, p. 3.

66 *higher concentrations*: "State Plans to Probe Cancer Link," 23 Apr.; and "Tests Find 1 Private
    Well Unsafe," 19 May; both by Sam Martino in 1993 issues of the *MJ*.

67 *Supreme Court*: Sam Martino, "State Supreme Court to Decide Application of Waste
    Discharge Law," *MJS* 1 Oct. 1997.

67 *1978 law*: State of Wisconsin v. Chrysler Outboard Corporation, pp. 40–41.

67 *be unearthed*: MJS 20 June 1998.

67 *$3.2 million*: Sam Martino, "Site Near Piggly Wiggly Pollution-Free," 11 Sept. 1997; and
    Lisa Sink, "DaimlerChrysler, State Settle Lawsuit," 27 Apr. 1999; both in the *MJS*.

67 *cleanup technology*: DaimlerChrysler PR Newswire, 5 Feb. 1999.

68 *Hartland Marsh*: Information in this and the next paragraph is from the following articles in the *MJS*: Vikki Ortiz, "Nature Center Advocated for Hartland Marsh," 13 July 1999; Ortiz, "180-Acre Ice Age Wetland Project Planned for Hartland Marsh," 18 Nov. 1999; Ortiz, "Groups Join Together for Wetlands," 24 Jan. 2000; Dave Sheeley, "A Wetland for the Ages," 30 Dec. 2001; and Darryl Enriquez, "Grant Would Help Expand, Preserve Marsh," 6 Oct. 2006.

68 *June 16, 2010*: Jill Ricks, "Hartland Marsh Reborn," *Lake Country Reporter* 21 June 2010.

70 *North Lakes*: Public Land Survey 1836, Plat Map, T7N R18E. The trail crossed the Bark in the middle of the NW quarter of Sec. 9.

70 *fragile ecosystems*: Rick Barrett, "Dredging Sought for Lake Nagawicka," *MJS* 14 Oct. 2000.

70 *Nashotah residents*: Dave Sheeley, "Many Back Dredging," 3 Sept. 2003; and Mike Johnson, "Study Group Suggests Dredging Lake," 24 Nov. 2006; both in the *MJS*.

71 *polluting the river*: "Nagawicka Residents' Petition Opens Hartland Polution [*sic*] Fight," *WF* 12 Sept. 1952.

71 *for analysis*: "Specimens from Nagawicka Lake Sent to State for Pollution Tests," *WF* 20 June 1955.

71 *treatment plant*: "Specimens"; and Mark Lisheron, "Sewage Treatment Plant Rescues Waterway," *MJS* 12 Sept. 1995.

71 *into the river*: "Nagawicka Residents' Petition" and "Specimens."

71 *Genesee Street*: John R. Stallard, "Waste Stench Hits Delafield," *MJ* 8 May 1966.

71 *sampled it himself*: "Sewer Plant Urged," *MJ* 14 May 1966.

71 *could connect*: Stallard, "Waste Stench."

71 *sewage plant*: Aqua-Tech, "Survey of the Bark River for the Determination of Water Quality" (1970), DNR regional office, Milwaukee.

71 *were inadequate*: "Rock River Pollution is Heavy," *Oshkosh Daily Northwestern* 5 Mar. 1971.

72 *Hartland operation*: "Hartland Praised on Sewage Plant," *MJ* 6 Sept. 1974.

72 *new treatment plant*: Lisheron, "Sewage Treatment Plant."

72 *remaining cost*: Lisheron, "Sewage Treatment Plant."

72 *waste per day*: Dave Sheeley, "Sewage Treatment Plant to Be Expanded," *MJS* 3 Oct. 2001.

72 *species in Wisconsin*: Adam Cort, "Conservancy Buys Bog," *Lake Country Reporter* 10 Feb. 1997.

73 *owned the land*: Site WK-0415, Potawatomi West Camp, Office of the State Archaeologist, Madison, Wisconsin.

74 *scythe in it*: Jerry Keenan, *The Great Sioux Uprising* (Cambridge, MA: Da Capo, 2003), pp. 32–33.

74 *point out*: According to Douglas Hennig, there were nine thousand Indians in Wisconsin in 1862. See "Waukesha County, Wisconsin: A Military History," *From Farmland to Freeways*, ed. Ellen D. Langill and Jean Penn Loerke (Waukesha: Waukesha County Historical Society, 1984), p. 366.

74 *the conflict*: Keenan, pp. 81–82. The information in the following sentence is from "Indian Affairs," *Superior Chronicle* 14 Feb. 1863.

74 *the warpath*: The information in this and the next sentence is from "The Indian Massacres," *New York Times* 20 Aug. 1862. According to Keenan, Little Crow led eight hundred warriors in his second attack on Fort Ridgely (p. 47).

75 *panic button*: Robert W. Brown identifies Bernard Steutgen as the perpetrator of the hoax in his memoir "Indian Scare Is Still Remembered," *Merton Review* 25 Feb. 1915; see also Harriet N. Pettibone, "Paul Revere, Reversed," *MS* 19 Mar. 1922. For Waukesha as a refuge see *History of Waukesha County* (Chicago: Western Historical, 1880), p. 424.

CHAPTER 6

78 *his sons*: "Sprucin' Up the Bark," *WF* 24 May 1999.

79 *Paraclete Potter*: *The History of Waukesha County, Wisconsin* (Chicago: Western Historical, 1880), p. 733.

79 *seemed euphonious*: Theron Wilber Haight, *Three Wisconsin Cushings* (Madison: Wisconsin History Commission, 1910), p. 19.

81 *its waters*: Haight, pp. 8–17. According to an anonymous typescript entitled "Early Days of Wisconsin" in the WCMRC, the Cushings were Millerites, a religious sect that believed the world would end in 1842. Consequently, they baptized their sons in the Bark River in the spring of 1842, even before the ice had left the lakes (p. 3).

81 *of the land*: Kent Masterson Brown, *Cushing of Gettysburg: The Story of a Union Artillery Commander* (Lexington: U P of Kentucky, 1993), pp. 12–13.

81 *Margaret Zerwekh*: Dirk Johnson, "Winning a Battle to Honor a Civil War Hero," *New York Times* 11 June 2010.

82 *its construction*: Mike Johnson, "Walkway to Open in Patriotic Salute," *MJS* 23 Sept. 2006.

82 *Wisconsin Glacier*: Site WK-0419, Office of the State Archaeologist, Madison, Wisconsin. Nelson C. Hawks mentions that chunks of float copper were found in the gravel deposit used to repair his father's dam; see "Recollections of Early Days of Delafield," typescript in the WCMRC, p. 18.

82 *from Castleman*: Haight, pp. 15–16, 18; Brown, p. 14.

87 *early settlers*: J. D. McDonald, for example, in a memoir published in the *Waukesha Plain Dealer* 1 Feb. 1875 (transcription in the WCMRC).

87 *great energy*: "Fire at Delafield," *MS* 26 Dec. 1853.

87 *Wisconsin Territory*: Margaret Zerwekh tells the story of Hawks's early travels and business ventures in "Nelson Page Hawks: New York and Wisconsin," *Hawkes Talks* [*sic*] Apr. 1993, pp. 7–10.

87 *Second Streets*: The Fountain House was torn down in 1876. See "Local Miscellany," *MS* 26 Feb. 1876.

88 *her himself*: Alden's granddaughter, Caroline V. Brewster, traces the family back to John Alden and Priscilla Mullens in a typescript in the Albert Alden Papers, University of Wisconsin–Milwaukee Area Research Center.

88 *Milton B. Cushing*: Located in the NW quarter of Sec. 19, T7N R18E (Waukesha County, Wisconsin, Deed Book K, p. 564).

88 *water rights*: True copy in the Albert Alden Papers.

89 *banks WSW*: Public Land Survey Interior Field Notes 1836, T7N R18E between Secs. 17 and 18 (North). Thirty links is slightly less than twenty feet; "WSW" indicates the west-south-westerly direction of flow.

89 *two lakes*: Quoted in Increase Lapham, *A Documentary History of the Milwaukee and Rock River Canal* (Milwaukee: Milwaukee and Rock River Canal Co., 1840), p. 97.

89 *waterpower downstream*: Leonard S. Smith records a twenty-one-foot descent in *The Water Powers of Wisconsin* (Madison: State of Wisconsin, 1908), p. 313. A map dated 10 Aug. 1916,

entered as evidence in the case of Apfelbacher v. the State of Wisconsin, Waukesha County Circuit Court, Aug. 1916, shows a drop of twenty feet (Box 463, WCMRC). A twenty-two-foot drop appears on the USGS 7.5 minute series quadrangle map for Oconomowoc East (revised 1971, 1976).

89 *Broken & Hilly*: Public Land Survey Exterior Field Notes 1836, T7N R17E, Secs. 24 and 25, East boundary (North).

89 *millponds overflowed*: The DNR outlines the history of dam regulation in Wisconsin in its *Water Regulation Handbook* (Madison: WDNR, 1992), pp. 5–15.

90 *was situated*: Albert Alden's son, also named Albert Alden, entered the articles of agreement, dated 3 Oct. 1846, as evidence for the defense in the case of Apfelbacher v. the State of Wisconsin. Hawks declared the contract satisfied in a release dated 3 Nov. 1849 (Waukesha County, Wisconsin, Deed Book 5, p. 437). The defense also entered an undated receipt signed by Alden to demonstrate Hawks's ownership of the mill property.

90 *feet of lumber*: Seventh Federal Census, 1850; Waukesha County Products of Industry, p. 575.

90 *the 1850s*: Jerry Apps, *Mills of Wisconsin and the Midwest* (Madison: Tamarack Press, 1980), pp. 23–24.

90 *the norm*: N. C. Hawks, p. 40.

90 *state-of-the-art turbine*: Among the Hawks papers (Miscellany, 1839–1852) in the Wisconsin Historical Society Archives is a patent dated 27 Nov. 1852 from Zebulon Parker of Ohio, granting Hawks the right to use the Parker turbine.

91 *around the mill*: N. C. Hawks, p. 41.

91 *wheat production*: Robert C. Nesbit, *Wisconsin: A History*, rev. and updated William F. Thompson (Madison: U of Wisconsin P, 1989), pp. 273, 281.

91 *industrial output*: Apps, p. 39.

92 *millers' wives*: N. C. Hawks, p. 7.

92 *a cent from*: N. C. Hawks, p. 43. He tells the story of the fire on pp. 15, 25, 38–39.

93 *of the river*: Testimony of Albert Alden and William R. Notbohm, the sons of the senior Albert Alden and the senior William Notbohm, in the case of Apfelbacher v. the State of Wisconsin.

93 *in the process*: United States v. Nelson P. Hawks, February Term 1848, Waukesha County District Court records, WCMRC, Box 58.

93 *intent to ravish*: United States v. Nelson P. Hawks, February Term 1848, Waukesha County District Court Docket, vol. 1, p. 12. Other information in this paragraph is taken from the case of Ophelia Jones v. Nelson P. Hawks, WCMRC, Box 16.

94 *real value*: N. C. Hawks, p. 35.

94 *the flour*: Apps, p. 59.

95 *new machinery*: Walter F. Peterson and C. Edward Weber, *An Industrial Heritage: Allis-Chalmers Corporation* (Milwaukee: Milwaukee County Historical Society, 1978), p. 39.

95 *the Dakotas*: Apfelbacher's testimony in Apfelbacher v. the State of Wisconsin.

97 *old mill*: Dave Sheeley, "Delafield Residents Seek to Preserve Dam, Habitat," *MJS* 22 Dec. 2004; and Caley Meals, "Delafield Resident Sells 152-Year-Old Equipment to Pennsylvania Community," *WF* 11 Dec. 2006.

97 *October 2004*: Sarah Murray, "Margaret Zerwekh Writes a New Chapter for the Bark River," *Wisconsin Rivers* (publication of Wisconsin Rivers Alliance) 14 July 2006.

97 *without the pond*: Sheeley, "Delafield Residents."

97 *with abandonment*: Dave Sheeley, "Dispute Flows Over Dam," *MJS* 26 Mar. 2005; and Caley Meals, "Controversial Government Tool Under Fire," *WF* 4 Mar. 2006.

97 *to $850,000*: Murray, "Margaret Zerwekh." The DNR cited an independent estimate of $672,000 to $854,466 in its 2008 report "Environmental Analysis and Decision on the Need for an Environmental Impact Statement," p. 16.

97 *proved unsuccessful*: From the following articles by Mike Johnson in the *MJS*: "Injunction Sought to Preserve Millpond in Delafield," 28 Sept. 2005; and "Bark River Dam May Be Abandoned," 27 Apr. 2006.

97 *downtown Delafield*: Amy Rinard, "Dam Fails Jeopardizing Homes," *MJS* 11 June 2008; Kelly Smith, "Officials 'Confident' Nagawicka Lake Will Not Overflow," *Lake Country Living* 12 June 2008; and Mike Johnson, "DNR Set to Remove Delafield Dam," *MJS* 13 June 2008.

98 *through the water*: Meg Kissinger, "More Rain Stalls Flood Recovery," *MJS* 15 June 2008.

98 *North Lake*: The information in this paragraph is from "Environmental Analysis," p. 5; a DNR press release, 2 July 2008; Common Council meeting minutes, City of Delafield, 18 Aug. 2008, p. 2; and Lori Holly, "Court Rips DNR in Dam Suit," *MJS* 8 Mar. 1998.

98 *abandonment permit*: The information in this paragraph is from two articles by Kelly Smith in the *Lake Country Reporter*: "Council Splits on Dam Loan," 8 Apr. 2009; and "Judge Says Zerwekh Dam Can be Removed," 22 Apr. 2009.

99 *have suffered*: The information in this and the preceeding paragraph is from articles by Kelly Smith in the *Lake Country Reporter*: "Neighbors Continue to Fight Dam Removal," 24 May 2009; "Delafield Approves Dam Permit," 6 July 2011; "Hearing Set for Dam Lawsuit," 13 July 2011; "Dam Neighbors Win Court Round," 21 Sept. 2011; and "Jury Rejects Delafield Land Claims," 28 Feb. 2012.

99 *and wrong*: "The Land Ethic," *A Sand County Almanac* (1949; New York: Ballantine, 1970).

CHAPTER 7

102 *Venice Park*: Plat and advertisement courtesy of Jim Babcock, curator of the Hawks Inn Historical Society, Delafield.

102 *for a lot*: "Among Our Neighbors," *WF* 22 July 1909.

103 *five years*: "Connect Many Lakes," *MS* 17 July 1892. A photo of the Fowler–La Belle lock appears in *Early Oconomowoc Heritage Trail Guidebook* (Oconomowoc: John S. Rockwell Chapter 721, Daughters of the American Revolution, 1975), p. 18.

103 *Nagawicka Lakes*: "Connect Many Lakes."

103 *January 1895*: Incorporation Papers of Defunct Domestic Corporations, series 356, box 646, file O-190, Wisconsin Historical Society Archives. The company forfeited its rights and privileges in 1907 for failure to submit annual reports.

103 *Fourth of July*: The information in this paragraph is from "Lakes of Oconomowoc," *MS* 12 July 1892; "Canal at Oconomowoc," *MS* 26 Sept. 1894; "New Wisconsin Corporations," *MS* 29 Jan. 1895; and "Connecting Several Lakes," *MJ* 30 Jan. 1895.

103 *power launches*: A sentiment expressed, for example, in "Leave It As Nature Designed," *MS* 16 Apr. 1893.

103 *the project*: "New Wisconsin Corporations."

104 *the bill*: "City and County Bills," *MS* 8 Mar. 1895. Armour's name does not appear in the incorporation documents for this company or the Oconomowoc Waterways Company.

104 *summer resort*: "Will Last a Month Yet," *WF* 14 Mar. 1895.

105 *idle hour*: "The Waukesha County Canal," *MS* 10 Mar. 1895. The information in the next sentence is also from the *MS*: "Canal Project Is Dead," 14 Mar. 1895.

105 *any progress*: "May Buy Water Power," *MS* 13 Mar. 1898. The idea was briefly resurrected in 1897; see "To Connect the Lakes," *MS* 5 Sept. 1897.

105 *legal stealth*: The information in this paragraph is from "Canal Project a Sure Thing," *MJ* 29 July 1899; and "Likely to Be Built," *MS* 27 Mar. 1899.

105 *Waterways Company*: The company submitted papers of incorporation on July 1, 1899, and they were recorded officially on Sept. 5 (Incorporation Papers: Domestic Corporations 1848-1945, series 356, box 655, file O-612, Wisconsin Historical Society Archives).

106 *for pleasure*: "Will Connect Lakes," 12 Aug. 1899.

106 *each passenger*: Oconomowoc Waterways Company papers of incorporation, p. 4. These were the maximum tolls permitted under Wisconsin Statutes Chap. 288, Sec. 2, Art. 9.

106 *exited the lake*: A photo of the Danforth (Armour) lock and keeper's cottage appears in Mary A. Kane, *Oconomowoc*, Postcard History Series (Charleston, SC: Arcadia, 2006), p. 107.

107 *a reason*: "Rural Mail Delivery," *MS*, 15 Oct. 1899.

107 *against holdouts*: Wisconsin Statutes Chap. 288, Sec. 2, Art. 3.

108 *his end*: This account of Zuta's murder draws on Barbara and David Barquist's *Oconomowoc: Barons to Bootleggers* (Oconomowoc: David and Barbara Barquist, 1999), pp. 310–19; and two articles in the *Chicago Tribune*: "Gang Kills at Hotel Dance," 2 Aug. 1930; and Philip Kinsley, "Inquiry Clears Up Issues in Lingle Murder," 3 Aug. 1930.

109 *in 1977*: Milo Bergo, "Amphicar Is His Bridge to Home," *MJ* 2 Aug. 1977. The information in the rest of this paragraph is from "Island Lots Sold," *WF* 29 Nov. 1952; and Nelson C. Hawks, "Recollections of Early Days of Delafield," typescript in WCMRC, p. 10.

109 *least 1907*: The *WF* reported on 11 Apr. 1907 the sale of the island and plans to build a bridge.

109 *obstructed navigation*: "Commission to Hold Hearing at Oconomowoc," *WF* 16 June 1921.

110 *and women*: "Modern Adams and Eves Thrust Out Owner from His Island of Paradise," *WSJ* 15 Mar. 1923.

110 *feet of it*: The *WF* is the source for information in this paragraph: "Breese Brings Suit to Stop Roadway," 9 July 1924; and "Supreme Court Affirms Lower Court Decision," 12 May 1925.

110 *or Milwaukee*: "Klan Reprisals Hinted in 4-Year Lake Battle," *MJ* 30 June 1925.

110 *black family*: "Klan Reprisals."

111 *tennis courts*: "Negro Scouts View Island," *MJ* 19 July 1925.

111 *within bounds*: "Lake Residents Form to Repel Invaders," *MJ* 3 Aug. 1925.

111 *the road*: "Sugar Island Still Rumbles," 29 May 1926; and "Sugar Island Again on Map," 4 Mar. 1927, both in the *MJ*, are the sources for this and the next sentence.

111 *lake water*: "Favor Roadway to Sugar Island," *MJ* 30 Mar. 1927.

111 *city dwellers*: "Sugar Island May Again Be 'Plaintiff' in Suit," *WF* 2 Apr. 1927.

111 *his promise*: "Nemahbin Island Bridge Is Denied," *MJ* 4 Apr. 1931.

CHAPTER 8

114 *molten metal*: Eli May describes an unsuccessful attempt in "Reminiscences of Early Days," *"It Seems Like Only Yesterday . . .": Stories from Fort Atkinson's Early Days 1836–1914* (Fort Atkinson: Fort Atkinson Historical Society, 2001), p. 61.

114 *of exhaustion*: Quoted in Lawrence Martin, *The Physical Geography of Wisconsin* (Madison: U of Wisconsin P, 1965), p. 276.

114 *its product*: Marlin Johnson, "Natural Features and Land Use," *From Farmland to Freeways: A History of Waukesha County, Wisconsin*, ed. Ellen D. Langill and Jean Penn Loerke

(Waukesha: Waukesha County Historical Society, 1984), p. 8. According to Lee Clayton, there was marl exploration in the 1930s. He mentions an abandoned pit north of Eagle in *Pleistocene Geology of Waukesha County*, Bulletin 99 (Madison: Wisconsin Geological and Natural History Survey, 2001), p. 25.

115 *one child*: Sites WK-0178 and WK-0174, Office of the State Archaeologist, Madison, Wisconsin. See also Charles E. Brown, "A Record of Wisconsin Antiquities," *Wisconsin Archaeologist* 5:3–4 (Apr.–Oct. 1906): 401.

115 *portaging boats*: PSC letters of 14 July 1931 and 8 Oct. 1931 (DNR DSFS, Madison office, file 67.33).

116 *southeastern Wisconsin*: "Wilderness on the Doorstoop," *MJ* 26 Aug. 1962.

116 *of the lake*: Brown, p. 401.

121 *and 2002*: Don M. Fago, *The Distribution and Relative Abundance of Fishes in Wisconsin* (Madison: Department of Natural Resources, 1984), pp. 357–58.

121 *alkaline-rich water*: John T. Curtis, *The Vegetation of Wisconsin: An Ordination of Plant Communities* (Madison: U of Wisconsin P, 1959), pp. 361–62.

122 *with eggs*: "Rebuilding a Riverbed, For the Love of a Tiny Mussel," *New York Times* 26 Apr. 2004. What follows in this paragraph is from "Plans for Sawmill Replica on River Pits History Against Habitat," *MJS* 18 May 1997.

122 *dismantled it*: Jacqueline Seibel, "Gift Allows Wade House to Reconstruct Dam, Sawmill," *MJS* 25 July 1999.

122 *each other*: David Paul Nord, "The Greenbush Mill Project: A Report Prepared for the State Historical Society of Wisconsin," 27 Dec. 1978, p. 142 (typescript at Wisconsin Historical Society, Madison). Nord, a historian, also wrote a visitors guide to the Wade House.

123 *water star-grass*: Don Behm, "Probe Turns Up Illegal Detergents," *MJ* 12 Aug. 1990.

124 *for polluted*: For a current listing of Impaired Waters, see http://dnr.wi.gov/org/water/wm/ wqs/303d/index.htm.

124 *we passed*: "Letters from a Pedestrian," *MS* 8 June 1860, Issue 124 (spelling *sic*).

CHAPTER 9

128 *natural springs*: DNR, *Lower Rock River Water Quality Management Plan*, 2001, LR13, p. 2.

129 *near Janesville*: Lee Clayton, *Pleistocene Geology of Waukesha County*, Bulletin 99 (Madison: Wisconsin Geological and Natural History Survey, 2001), pp. 21–23.

129 *or ditching*: "Mastodon Bones Located in State," *MJ* 3 Aug. 1961; and "Farm Boy Plows Up the Tusk of 25,000 Year Old Mastodon," *MJ* 10 June 1949.

129 *Michigan Lobe*: Don Alan Hall, "Great Lakes People Lived 2,000 Years with Glacier," *Mammoth Trumpet* 13.2 (1998).

129 *for the hay*: Hannah Swart, *Koshkonong Country: A History of Jefferson County, Wisconsin* (Fort Atkinson, WI: W. D. Hoard, 1975), p. 96.

130 *reclaim them*: See "A Century of Wetland Exploitation" on the USGS webpage: www.npwrc .usgs.gov/resource/wetlands/uswetlan/century.htm#swamp.

130 *one at that*: "Farm and Dairy," *MS* 12 Feb. 1884.

130 *still living*: International Crane Foundation website, www.savingcranes.org. The Leopold quotation that follows is from *A Sand County Almanac* (1949; New York: Ballantine, 1970), p. 103.

130 *in the state*: Curt Meine, *Aldo Leopold: His Life and Work* (Madison: U of Wisconsin P, 1988), p. 330.

130 *western states*: Tom Vanden Brook, "Cranes in the Crosshairs," *MJS* 11 Apr. 1999.

131 *this marsh*: Quoted in Marlin Johnson, "Natural Features and Land Use," *From Farmland to Freeways: A History of Waukesha County, Wisconsin*, ed. Ellen D. Langill and Jean Penn Loerke (Waukesha, WI: Waukesha County Historical Society, 1984), p. 26.

131 *other owners*: The information in this paragraph is from Johnson, p. 26; and "Out of the Muck: Jefferson County Farmer Calls it Quits," *MJS* 23 Apr. 2000.

132 *of the case*: Public Land Survey Interior Field Notes 1836, T6N R17E, between Secs. 6 and 7 (West). Spelling and punctuation *sic*.

132 *meandered reach*: Luna B. Leopold and W. B. Langbein, "River Meanders," *Scientific American* 214 (June 1966): 60–70.

133 *be played*: Henry Fountain, "After 9,000 Years, Oldest Playable Flute Is Heard Again," *New York Times* 28 Sept. 1999.

133 *the purchase*: "Land Conservancy," *MJS* 8 Feb. 1995.

133 *of wetland*: Public Land Survey Interior Field Notes 1836, T6N R16E between Secs. 1 and 2 (North).

133 *same effect*: PSC memo of 2 Nov. 1959 (DNR DSFS, Madison office, file 28.08).

135 *of the dam*: Janneyne L. Gnacinski and Louise B. Longley, *Sullivan, Town 6 North: A History of the Town of Sullivan, Jefferson County, Wisconsin* (Waukesha, WI: Freeman, 1970), pp. 89–92. According to Swart, William Warren built a sawmill in 1845 that Heath subsequently converted to a flour mill (p. 100).

135 *other businesses*: *Daily Sentinel and Gazette*, 5 Nov. 1847, issue 176.

135 *there daily*: Gnacinski and Longley, p. 127.

136 *Edward Hainke*: "Memories of Heath's Mill," *Sullivan News* 6 July 1916, quoted in Gnacinski and Longley (pp. 89, 91).

136 *in 1966*: Gnacinski and Longley, p. 161.

136 *of the river*: Leopold and Langbein, pp. 60–70.

137 *with trilliums*: DNR, *Lower Rock River Water Quality Management Plan*, 2001, LR13, p. 6.

137 *onto wagons*: Gnacinski and Longley, p. 43.

CHAPTER 10

141 *of the village*: Janneyne L. Gnacinski and Louise B. Longley, *Sullivan, Town 6 North: A History of the Town of Sullivan, Jefferson County, Wisconsin* (Waukesha, WI: Freeman, 1970), pp. 95–103.

141 *Improvement Association*: *MJ* 18 June 1966. The information in the next sentence and the next paragraph is from the DNR DSFS, Fitchburg office, file 28.08.

142 *public waterways*: Letter to Carl Reich, 24 Apr. 1969 (DNR DSFS, Madison office, file 28.08).

142 *lay preacher*: Gnacinski and Longley, pp. 44, 105–7.

143 *Notbohm Sr.*: Gnacinski and Longley, p. 106.

143 *and 1950s*: Gnacinski and Longley, p. 107.

143 *part of it away*: Letter from PSC to R. Winfield Scott, 21 May 1969 (DNR DSFS, Madison office, file 28.11). Information in the rest of this paragraph is from two letters in the same file, one dated 28 Aug. 1969, the other a letter of 24 July 1972 from the Bureau of Water and Shoreline Management to the Town of Sullivan, recommending removal of the dam.

144 *rapid current*: Public Land Survey Exterior Field Notes 1836, T6N R15E, Sec. 24, East boundary (North).

144 *the DNR*: DNR, *Lower Rock River Water Quality Management Plan*, 2001, LR13, p. 1.

145 *in Bark River*: "The Life and Times of Dorothy Cushman Rosewall," typescript memoir by Dorothy C. Rosewall and Jean E. Rosewall provided by Bill and Joanne Cushman, p. 11.

146 *Cyrus Curtis*: Gnacinski and Longley, p. 10; and Hannah Swart, *Koshkonong Country: A History of Jefferson County, Wisconsin* (hereafter, *KC*) (Fort Atkinson, WI: W. D. Hoard, 1975), p. 100.

146 *of Rome*: Gnacinski and Longley, p. 10.

146 *a sawmill*: *Koshkonong Country Revisited: An Anthology*, ed. Hannah Swart (Fort Atkinson, WI: Fort Atkinson Historical Society, 1981), 1:88.

146 *the mortises*: Mark Curtis memoir in *The History of Jefferson County, Wisconsin* (Chicago: Western Historical, 1879), p. 547.

146 *Rockford, Illinois*: Swart, *KC*, p. 77.

146 *became available*: The *JCU* of 12 July 1901 mentions Cushman sending the rollers to Milwaukee for sharpening.

146 *Berkshire hogs*: Swart, *KC*, p. 77. The *JCU* of 21 Apr. 1871 singled out Cushman's production of two thousand pounds of maple sugar as unusual.

146 *Cushman home*: History of Jefferson County, p. 549; and *JCU* 19 Jan. 1900.

147 *family historian*: Rosewall and Rosewall, p. 10. The rest of this paragraph is based on pp. 11–12.

147 *the family*: Rosewall and Rosewall, p. 11.

147 *beside the river*: Rosewall and Rosewall, p. 10.

147 *the millpond*: Interview with Bill and Joanne Cushman, 27 Mar. 1997.

148 *whole bussiness*: Quoted *sic* in George F. Willison, *Saints and Strangers* (New York: Reynal and Hitchcock, 1945), p. 258.

149 *not at this*: "A Sermon Preached at Plimmoth in New-England," *American Sermons: The Pilgrims to Martin Luther King, Jr.* (New York: Library of America, 1999), p. 22. Subsequent quotations are from pp. 25, 18, and 21 (spelling *sic*).

153 *hazard rating*: Sturtevant letter to Cushman, 3 Oct. 1988. Hazard rating (Class 1A, Low Hazard) confirmed in letter from Sturtevant to Cushman, 15 Apr. 1993 (DNR DSFS, Fitchburg office, file 28.10).

153 *compassionate man*: Interview with Bill Sturtevant, 10 Mar. 1999.

155 *draining the pond*: This account of the flood and its aftermath is based on documents in the DNR DSFS, Fitchburg office, file 28.10.

CHAPTER 11

157 *her poetry*: Obituary in *JCU* 5 June 1979.

158 *God's scheme*: Eva Melcher, et al., *Bark River Wanderings: Hebron and Cold Spring Townships, Jefferson County, Wisconsin* (n.p.: Bark River Woods Historical Society, [1986]).

158 *of the Bark*: Public Land Survey Interior Field Notes 1836, T6N R15E between Secs. 25 and 26 (North).

160 *Cold Spring*: Swart, *KC*, pp. 24, 77.

160 *Highway 106*: *JCU* 19 Jan. 1900.

162 *fur-trading post*: Swart, *KC*, p. 15.

162 *Claim Company*: According to Milo Jones the company subsequently took in Dwight
Foster, Enoch Darling, and David Sargent. See *Koshkonong Country Revisited: An Anthology*
(hereafter, *KCR*), ed. Hannah Swart (Fort Atkinson, WI: Fort Atkinson Historical Society,
1981), 1:18. Jones's words in the next sentence are from the same source.

162 *Oconomowoc River*: Lapham, *A Documentary History of the Milwaukee and Rock River Canal*
(Milwaukee: Milwaukee and Rock River Canal Co., 1840), pp. 8–9.

162 *at Hebron*: KCR 1:18.

163 *like timberland*: "Reminiscences," *"It Seems Like Only Yesterday . . .": Stories from Fort
Atkinson's Early Days 1836–1914* (Fort Atkinson: Fort Atkinson Historical Society, 2001),
pp. 104, 106.

163 *between them*: Caswell, "Reminiscences," p. 71.

163 *for marsh*: Public Land Survey Field Notes 1836, T6N R15E and T5N R15E.

163 *Uncle Sam's timber*: Lemuel Marvin Roberts, "Fort History," *"It Seems Like,"* p. 82.

163 *fend them off*: Richard P. Thiel, *The Timber Wolf in Wisconsin: The Death and Life of a Majestic
Predator* (Madison: U of Wisconsin P, 1993), pp. 20, 35; and Marlin Johnson, "Wolves in
Early Waukesha County," *Landmark* 18.2–3 (1975): 6–10.

163 *kettle of soap*: Typical wolf anecdotes appear in *"It Seems Like,"* pp. 26, 39–40, 183; *History of
Jefferson County*, pp. 349–50; *KCR* 1:29; and "Historical Events of Jefferson County," *Jefferson
Banner* 7 July 1927.

163 *concrete remnant*: Curtis memoir, *History of Jefferson County*, p. 547.

164 *the sawmill*: Curtis, p. 547.

165 *by the animals*: Swart, *KC*, p. 76.

165 *in the town*: *History of Jefferson County*, p. 730.

165 *the morning*: KCR 1:45.

165 *in Illinois*: Swart, *KC*, p. 76.

165 *and molasses*: Brown, *JCU* 29 Dec. 1899 (also the source for the next two sentences).

166 *as schoolmaster*: Swart, *KC*, p. 78.

166 *in 1838*: *History of Jefferson County*, p. 554.

166 *to Congress*: *History of Jefferson County*, p. 548.

166 *the 1840s*: Jerry Apps, *Mills of Wisconsin and the Midwest* (Madison: Tamarack Press,
1980), p. 37.

166 *$142,000 today*: KCR 1:87–88.

166 *and Beloit*: KCR 1:66.

166 *four winds*: KCR 1:66–67.

167 *community's postmaster*: Swart, *KC*, p. 57.

167 *Dairymen's Association*: *JCU* 23 Dec. 1870.

167 *larger one*: "Gossip from the State," *MJ* 4 Sept. 1893.

168 *single haul*: *JCU* 6 May 1898.

168 *the 1940s*: Swart, *KC*, p. 80.

168 *was situated*: DNR DSFS, Madison office, file 28.09.

168 *for a while*: According to Caswell, Darling sold the mill to a man named Wales, who sold it to
Churchill (*KCR* 1:66).

168 *Joseph Powers*: Curtis, p. 547 (also the source for the next sentence).

168 *stone operating*: History of Jefferson County, p. 555.

168 *supplied with water*: JCU 26 May 1871.

168 *grown Mississippi*: JCU 7 Apr. 1870.

169 *Powers and Doud*: JCU 1 Dec. 1870.

169 *1943 flood*: Memo of 25 Mar. 1943 (DNR DSFS, Madison office, file 28.09).

169 *for power*: Public Service Commission report, 29 July 1949 (DNR DSFS, Madison office, file 28.09).

169 *comfortable home*: "Mr. and Mrs. Robert Shipley Convert Old Mill in Hebron to a Residence Called Mill Tara," JCU 23 Dec. 1976.

169 *as the company*: Curtis, p. 547.

169 *inexpensive furniture*: Zida C. Ivey, "Story of Ancient Bedstead Spindle Spun for Daily Union by Zida Ivey," JCU 6 Apr. 1953.

169 *and modernized*: Charlene Gaynor, "Historic House Gets Couple's Loving Touch," MJ 19 Sept. 1982.

169 *families with him*: History of Jefferson County, p. 547; and Caswell, "Reminiscences," pp. 167–68.

169 *fine furniture*: Swart, KC, pp. 76–77.

170 *the proposal*: The information in this paragraph is from Swart, KC, pp. 77–79, 325.

170 *or cheese*: JCU 26 May 1871.

170 *as secretary*: JCU 23 Dec. 1870.

170 *cheese annually*: Swart, KC, p. 80.

170 *son Arthur*: KCR 2:129.

170 *until the 1940s*: A PSC report of 29 July 1949 first mentions the use of electrical power (DNR DSFS, Madison office, file 28.09).

170 *Natural Resources*: Wisconsin Department of Natural Resources, Water Regulation Handbook (Madison: WDNR, 1992), chap. 140, secs. 8–11.

170 *and 1995*: Stephen M. Born et al., The Removal of Small Dams: An Institutional Analysis of the Wisconsin Experience, Extension Report 96-1 (Madison: Department of Urban and Regional Planning, UW–Madison/Extension, 1996), pp. 1, 17.

171 *hazard rating*: DNR DSFS, Madison office, file 28.09.

171 *a member*: The DNR informed James Wagi of the results of its dam failure analysis in a letter of 17 May 1993 (DNR DSFS, Madison office, file 28.09).

171 *gates completely*: JCU 30 Aug. 1994.

171 *Dam fund*: "19th-Century Dam May Be Removed," MS 17 Oct. 1994; and Jonas Berberich, "Hebron Dam Removal Process to Begin with Lake Drawdown," JCU 1 Aug. 1996.

171 *think they do*: Jim Brown, quoted in Greg Seubert, "Dam's a Goner without Owner," JCU 12 Oct. 1994.

172 *in Slabtown*: Information in this and the next paragraph is from Born et al., pp. 23–24, 31, 36, 47.

172 *the property*: Feb. 1997 documents, DNR DSFS, Madison office, file 28.09.

CHAPTER 12

176 *of transportation*: Harry Wintermute's contributions are mentioned in a herald for the Wintermute's [*sic*] Double Show of about 1910 and an unpublished manuscript by Frank D.

Robie, "Of Millman, Melbourne and Wintermutes," p. 2, both at the Circus World Museum (hereafter, CWM); Harry's obituary in the *Whitewater Press* 1 June 1939; and *Billboard* 27 Sept. 1902: 6. Another source survives in two forms: a longer but fragmentary article entitled "Aged Showman Back on Farm," from an unidentified newspaper in the Bark River Woods Historical Society Museum (hereafter, BRWHS); and a shorter version entitled "Old Showman Back to Farm" in the *MJ* 24 Apr. 1927.

176 *show himself*: Bird Millman, quoted in Robie, p. 2.

176 *advance agent*: The piano, manufactured by the Shoenhut Company, is at the Hoard Historical Museum in Fort Atkinson. C. P. Fox mentions Thomas's other skills in "The Wintermute Bros. Circus," *Bandwagon* Nov.–Dec. 1959: 19. Harry Wintermute praises Halsey's skill as publicist in "Aged Showman" (BRWHS).

176 *smaller villages*: Charles Theodore Murray's article, which appeared in the Aug. 1894 issue of *McClure's*, is quoted in Janet M. Davis, *"Instruct the minds of all classes": The Circus and American Culture at the Turn of the Century* (Ph.D. diss., University of Wisconsin–Madison, 1998), p. 48. Fox estimates the number of lithographs posted by the Wintermutes (p. 21).

177 *wagon show*: Fred Dahlinger Jr. and Stuart Thayer, *Badger State Showmen: A History of Wisconsin's Circus Heritage* (Madison: Grote, 1998), pp. 105–106.

178 *Ziegfeld Follies*: Dixie Willson is the contemporary; see her memoir *Where the World Folds Up at Night* (New York: Appleton, 1932), p. 13. Millman's words are from an interview quoted in Robie, p. 1.

178 *local talent*: "Old Showman."

178 *after adventure*: Letter to the author, 15 Feb. 2001.

178 *four years later*: Tenth Federal Census, Population Schedule for Hebron Township, Jefferson County, Wisconsin.

178 *his show*: Ruth Ann Montgomery, *Evansville: Glimpses of the Grove* (Evansville, WI: R.A. Montgomery, 1990), p. 84.

179 *ahead again*: Quoted in "Aged Showman."

179 *canvas outfitting*: *Billboard* 27 Sept. 1902: 6. The *New York Clipper* of 26 Mar. 1892 mentions a new menagerie tent, measuring sixty by ninety feet (p. 34).

180 *next venue*: Dahlinger and Thayer describe the typical circus routine, pp. v–vi. The show times are from Wintermute handbills (CWM). The 1907 itinerary described above is also at the CWM.

180 *draft horses*: "Old Showman."

180 *dry week*: *Billboard* 27 Sept. 1902: 6.

180 *be canceled*: *Wisconsin Tobacco Reporter* 10 May 1901.

181 *aerial acts*: *MS* 21 May 1881.

181 *twenty others*: William L. Slout describes the waterproofing of canvas and the fire hazard in *Theatre in a Tent: The Development of a Provincial Entertainment* (Bowling Green, OH: Bowling Green University Popular Press, 1972), p. 100. The Great Melbourne circus advertised its use of electrical lighting at evening performances in a 1902 herald (CWM). The Edgerton and Stoughton cancellations are mentioned in the *Stoughton Courier* and the *Wisconsin Tobacco Reporter* (both 3 May 1907). Dean Jensen recounts the Ringling Bros. lightning strike in *The Biggest, the Smallest, the Longest, the Shortest: A Chronicle of the American Circus from Its Heartland* (Madison: Wisconsin House, 1975), pp. 93–94.

181 *the Second*: *Janesville Gazette* 13 May 1908.

181 *his hip*: Jensen believes that the elephant was Big Charlie (p. 82). According to Dahlinger and Thayer the attacker was an elephant named Empress (pp. 64–65).

181 *disemboweled him*: New York Clipper 11 June 1898: 243.

182 *and docility*: This description of Jargo, and that of Wallace the lion in the next paragraph, are from undated couriers and heralds at the CWM.

182 *both seriously*: Montgomery, pp. 154–55.

182 *in Hebron*: Whitewater Press 1 June 1939.

183 *for the company*: Stoughton Courier 3 May 1907.

183 *that fashion*: Davis, p. 107.

183 *as a circus*: Terry Biwer Becker, "'What's Coming? Why Fun Is Coming!': The Circus in Waukesha County, 1843–1910," Landmark 41.2–3 (Summer–Autumn 1998): 14, 17.

183 *following it*: MS 23 July 1880. In the next sentence "skin games" refers generically to cheating or swindling games. In three-card monte a player bets on the location of one of three cards that are shown face up, then turned face down and shifted around.

183 *lewd behavior*: Davis, pp. 22–23.

184 *their employees*: Dahlinger and Thayer, p. 101.

184 *Big Show*: All quotations in this paragraph are from undated Great Melbourne couriers at the CWM. The quotation in the next paragraph is from an 1892 courier for the Wintermute Bros.' Five Big United Shows, also at the CWM.

184 *to finish*: Republican Observer 3 Sept. 1908.

184 *of 1900*: New York Clipper 24 Nov. 1900: 868. Recorded in Jefferson County Deed Book v. 112, p. 153.

185 *unsuccessful operation*: JCU 7 July 1905.

185 *their shows*: The adoption of the Vanderburg name is reported in Billboard 3 Aug. 1907: 23. Jensen speculates on its origin, p. 89. The senior George Hall's Van Amburgh connection is mentioned in C. Beerntsen, "George W. 'Popcorn' Hall's Circuses," Bandwagon Jan.–Feb. 1970: 16; his son's in the Chang Reynolds Elephant Biographies, no. 733 ("Pearl") at the CWM.

185 *general farmer*: Thirteenth and Fourteenth Federal Censuses, Jefferson County, Hebron Township.

186 *debate with him*: Whitewater Register 1 June 1939. In the following paragraph, Harry's Memorial Day lecture is mentioned in "Aged Showman" and the circumstances of his death in the JCU 2 June 1939.

186 *on tour*: Jensen, p. 84. For the circumstances of Frank and Zella's meeting I am indebted to Doris Kolmos (conversation on 19 July 2001).

186 *and jokes*: "Circus Wagons Roll Down Memory Lane," MS 13 Apr. 1977.

187 *Mlle. Zella*: Herald for Wintermute Bros. and Hall, dated ca. 1915 (CWM). The postcard mentioned in the next sentence is at the BRWHS.

187 *to 1917*: Chang Reynolds Elephant Biographies, no. 733 (CWM). On the back of a photo of Pearl at the CWM, Frank Hall noted that he had leased the elephant from his father for the 1914 season. According to Fox, the lease extended for four years, perhaps 1914–1917 (p. 19).

187 *at a time*: Letter from Charles Beetow to the author, 21 July 2001.

187 *physical exertion*: Davis, pp. 111, 113, 127. The 1923 courier quoted below is reproduced in Richard E. Conover, The Circus: Wisconsin's Unique Heritage (Baraboo: Circus World Museum, 1967), p. 32.

188 *the hecklers*: Davis, p. 242.

188 *welfare caseworker*: Betty Boyd, conversation with the author on 6 May 2001.

188 *big tent*: Letter from Charles Beetow to the author, 21 July 2001.

188 *or 1931*: Letter of Frank Hall dated 13 Feb. 1931 (CWM). Other information on this period is from "Circus Wagons Roll" and an information form that Frank Hall prepared in 1928 for the Circus Fans Association (CWM).

189 *and Frank*: "Circus Wagons Roll."

189 *make it up*: From an undated courier at the CWM.

CHAPTER 13

193 *produce spindles*: Zida C. Ivey, "Story of Ancient Bedstead Spindle," *JCU* 6 Apr. 1953.

193 *make two hundred*: *JCU* 26 May 1871.

194 *to Jefferson*: Alonzo Brown, response to Eli May memoir, *JCU* 29 Dec. 1899.

194 *Virginia waterleaf*: Laurel Walker, "Spring's Beauties," *MJS* 29 May 1996.

195 *twenty-five pounds*: "About the State—Palmyra," *MS* 6 Apr. 1890, Issue 24.

195 *located here*: Eva Melcher, et al., *Bark River Wanderings: Hebron and Cold Spring Townships, Jefferson County, Wisconsin* (n.p.: Bark River Woods Historical Society, [1986]).

196 *I can*: "Beyond Ecology: Self, Place, and the Pathetic Fallacy," *The Ecocriticism Reader*, ed. Cheryll Glotfelty and Harold Fromm (Athens, GA: U of Georgia P, 1996), pp. 92–104.

198 *Impassible Marsh*: Public Land Survey Interior Field Notes 1835, T5N R15E between Secs. 11 and 14 (East).

199 *young pioneers*: Charles Rockwell, "My First Experience Rafting: Or, a Night and Day on Bark River," *Koshkonong Country Revisited: An Anthology*, ed. Hannah Swart (Fort Atkinson, WI: Fort Atkinson Historical Society, 1981), 1:36.

199 *Brink's Mill*: Melcher, et al.

200 *in London*: The information in this paragraph is from Melcher, et al.; www.wisconsinhistory.org/dictionary; "Ex-Gov. Peck Is Dead—Rose from Printery," *Milwaukee Free Press* 17 Apr. 1916; "George W. Peck Rowhouse," Historic Preservation Study Report for 1620–28 North Farwell Avenue, Milwaukee (Spring 1998), p. 4; and http://georgewpeck.com/gpbio.html.

202 *business men*: *Peck's Bad Boy and His Pa* (Chicago: Belford, Clarke, 1883).

CHAPTER 14

204 *their bait*: This account of the episode is based on John A. Wakefield, *Wakefield's History of the Black Hawk War*, ed. Frank E. Stevens (1834; Madison: Roger Hunt, 1976), p. 81; and the journals of James J. Justice (2:1323) and Nineveh Shaw (2:1334) in *The Black Hawk War, 1831–1832* (hereafter, *BHW*), ed. Ellen H. Whitney (Springfield: Illinois State Historical Library, 1973–1978).

204 *the northeast*: Joseph Street to Henry Atkinson and William Clark, 6 and 7 June 1832, *BHW* 2:536, 548.

205 *Napope &c*: *BHW* 2:745 (capitalization and punctuation *sic*).

205 *opposite side*: The number of Ho-Chunk is uncertain. Justice says two or three (*BHW* 2:1323). Wakefield says three (p. 81). White Crow identified two as the attackers, Wau-kee-aun-skaw (or Waw-kee-aun-shaw) and his son, and their surrender is called for in the treaty of 15 Sept. 1832 (*BHW* 2:1133, 1155). Old Decorah identified a different Indian as the shooter and three others, including Waw-kee-aun-shaw's son but not Waw-kee-aun-shaw himself, as "present at" the shooting (*BHW* 2:1131-32). Crawford B. Thayer assumes there were five Indians, and names them in *Hunting a Shadow: The Search for Black Hawk* (Fort Atkinson, WI: Fort Atkinson Historical Society, 1981), p. 93.

205 *Burnt Village*: According to information on www.wisconsinhistory.org, Burnt Village had
     been burned in intratribal warfare shortly before the Black Hawk War.

205 *aging warrior*: Indian casualty estimates for whole campaign range from 442 to 592 according
     to *Black Hawk: An Autobiography* (hereafter, *BHAuto*), ed. Donald Jackson (Urbana:
     U of Illinois P, 1955), p. 161n115.

205 *police action*: Cecil Eby, *"That Disgraceful Affair," the Black Hawk War* (New York: Norton,
     1973), p. 180.

206 *before 1600*: According to Birmingham and Eisenberg, the Ho-Chunk arrived in Wisconsin
     after 1200 AD (*Indian Mounds of Wisconsin* [Madison: U of Wisconsin P, 2000], p. 174). They
     were in Door County at the time of contact with the French, and claim to have come from
     there (Robert E. Bieder, *Native American Communities in Wisconsin 1600–1960: A Study of
     Tradition and Change* [Madison: U of Wisconsin P, 1995], p. 39).

206 *Apple River*: James H. Lockwood mentions Sac and Fox Indians bringing bars of lead from
     Galena to the Prairie du Chien trading post. See "Early Times and Events in Wisconsin,"
     Collections of the State Historical Society of Wisconsin (hereafter, *WHC*), ed. Lyman C. Draper
     (1856; Madison: State Historical Society, 1903), 2:131–322.

206 *southeastern Iowa*: *BHAuto*, p. 71.

206 *Revolutionary War*: Eby, pp. 69–70.

206 *and trading*: *BHAuto*, p. 47.

206 *in length*: *BHAuto*, p. 100.

206 *Osage tribes*: *BHAuto*, pp. 51–53, 104.

207 *also promised*: The treaty is reproduced in *BHAuto*, pp. 183–86. For Black Hawk's claim that
     he received no annuity, see *BHAuto*, p. 125.

207 *his woe*: *BHAuto*, p. 181.

208 *to ten thousand*: Eby, pp. 70, 72.

208 *lay uncultivated*: Eby, p. 42.

208 *the Indians*: Eby, p. 13. William T. Hagan says that about twenty families were squatting
     near Rock Island in the winter of 1828 through the spring of 1829 (*The Sac and Fox Indians*
     [Norman: U of Oklahoma P, 1958], p. 109).

208 *private ownership*: Hagen, *Sac and Fox*, pp. 111–12; and Eby, p. 13.

208 *cornfields stood*: *BHAuto*, p. 117; Eby, p. 77.

209 *of Keokuk*: Hagan, *Sac and Fox*, pp. 131, 133.

209 *the Americans*: Hagan, *Sac and Fox*, pp. 134–35.

210 *the British*: Eby, p. 84.

210 *British help*: Hagan, *Sac and Fox*, p. 138.

210 *thousand followers*: Eby, p. 257; and *BHAuto*, pp. 20–21.

210 *that purpose*: *BHAuto*, p. 137.

210 *other supplies*: *BHAuto*, p. 132.

210 *and Foxes*: Hagan, *Sac and Fox*, p. 142.

210 *have done so*: Taylor to Thomas S. Jesup, *BHW* 2:1223.

210 *six to seven hundred*: Atkinson to Roger Jones, 19 Nov. 1832, *BHW* 2:1205.

211 *Indian band*: Hagan, *Sac and Fox*, p. 153.

211 *and retreat*: *BHAuto*, pp. 141–42.

211 *thousand Indians*: Eby, pp. 133–35.

212 *in Illinois*: The number of attackers varies in different accounts; see *BHW* 2:1291–92n6.

212 *Davis settlement*: The Hall sisters and Frank E. Stevens (*The Black Hawk War, Including a Review of Black Hawk's Life* [Chicago: Stevens, 1903]) mistakenly give May 20 as the date; see *BHW* 2:1291n.

212 *into words*: Charles M. Scanlan, *Indian Creek Massacre and Captivity of Hall Girls*, 2nd ed. (Milwaukee: REIC, 1915), p. 37; and John Hall, quoted in Stevens, p. 156.

212 *bloody pulp*: Scanlan, p. 49; and Eby, p. 147.

212 *as wives*: For Sylvia's actual age, usually reported as seventeen, see *BHW* 2:1292n10.

212 *their father*: Stevens, p. 149.

213 *their hands*: Stevens, p. 151.

213 *five weeks*: Scanlan, p. 61.

213 *maple sugaring*: Scanlan, p. 63. Hagan reconstructs Black Hawk's route in "Black Hawk's Route through Wisconsin," mimeograph (Madison: State Historical Society of Wisconsin, 1949), pp. 23–25.

213 *girls' release*: Atkinson offered two thousand dollars, according to Daniel M. Parkinson ("Pioneer Life in Wisconsin," *WHC* 2:339).

213 *adoptive daughters*: Scanlan, p. 67.

213 *few days*: Stevens, p. 152.

213 *of Madison*: According to Whitney's note on the communication between John Sherman and Henry Dodge of 30 May 1832 (*BHW* II:487n1), the sisters were ransomed on May 28 (the eighth day) and delivered to Blue Mounds on June 1. According to Draper's note to Parkinson, they arrived on June 3 (*WHC* 2:339).

213 *warrior's pledge*: Scanlan, p. 71.

213 *the party*: Scanlan, pp. 82–84, 87. Cf. Parkinson, *WHC* 2:339–40.

214 *and captivity*: *BHW* 2:1287–91.

214 *in 1834*: Her account appears in Wakefield, pp. 88–92.

214 *court deposition*: Stevens, pp. 150–54. John Hall's account also appears in Stevens, pp. 154–57.

214 *unoffending infant*: Wakefield, p. 114.

214 *all over*: Quoted in Eby, p. 196. Milo Milton Quaife considers the story apocryphal; see his edition of Thomas Ford's *A History of Illinois from Its Commencement as a State in 1818 to 1847* (1854; Chicago: Lakeside, 1945), p. 184n40.

215 *the presidency*: Eby, p. 107; and Stevens, p. 278.

215 *his men*: Stevens, pp. 280–81.

215 *Early's company*: The dates are from Harry E. Pratt, *Lincoln Day by Day 1809–1839* (Springfield: Abraham Lincoln Association, 1941), pp. 16, 18.

215 *of the Bark*: *BHW* 2:511.

215 *detained there*: White Crow apparently negotiated for their release at Black Hawk's "island" camp (*BHW* 2:1341n25).

215 *the channel*: Wakefield, p. 81.

216 *mud and water*: Wakefield, p. 82.

216 *fording place*: Estimates of how many miles they traveled vary from four (Eby, p. 205) to ten (*BHW* 2:751n1) to fifteen (Wakefield, p. 83).

216 *waters beneath*: Ford, p. 199.

216 *western territories*: Wakefield, p. 83.

216 *3,500 troops*: Thayer, p. 114.

216 *very moment*: BHW 2:752.

217 *marshy redoubt*: Thayer notes that Lincoln, who wrote the order mustering out the scout battalion on July 9, may have stayed in camp to complete the paperwork (p. 132).

217 *farther north*: Eby, pp. 205–6.

217 *to Detroit*: Eby, pp. 200, 205.

217 *the Northwest*: Eby, pp. 220–21.

217 *on foot*: Pratt, p. 21; Thayer, pp. 145, 158.

217 *Rock Rapids*: Atkinson later reported the episode in such a way as to suggest that Dodge and Henry acted in accordance with his orders; see letter to Roger Jones, BHW 2:1210.

218 *edible bark*: Dodge to Atkinson, BHW 2:826.

218 *south bank*: Henry Gratiot mentions that White Crow was the guide (*BHW* 2:1304).

218 *Scuppernong Marsh*: According to Thayer they camped in a swamp now occupied by muck farms just northwest of Palmyra (p. 235).

218 *Ho-Chunk scouts*: Eby, p. 229.

218 *if possible captured*: Atkinson to Henry and Dodge, BHW 2:832.

218 *hostile behavior*: BHAuto, p. 157n110.

219 *you accept*: Black Hawk and another Sac chieftain reported five or six dead; white officers claimed to have killed as many as 68 (Eby, p. 237, 237n5).

219 *the victory*: Eby, pp. 241, 262.

219 *for supplies*: BHAuto, p. 155.

219 *in elevation*: Shaw, BHW 2:1337 (spelling *sic*).

220 *his words*: BHAuto, p. 158.

220 *the encounter*: Testimony by Kish-kas-shoi, Ana-kose-kuk, and Wee-sheet (*BHW* 2:1029, 1032, 1056).

220 *opened fire*: Joseph Throckmorton, *BHW* 2:928; Reuben Holmes, BHW 2:938; and John H. Fonda, "Early Wisconsin," WHC 5:261.

220 *the stream*: Street, quoted in *BHAuto*, p. 161n115 (spelling *sic*).

220 *Sioux warriors*: BHAuto, p. 162n118.

221 *their wounds*: Atkinson to Scott, BHW 2:935–36; and William Clark to Lewis Cass, BHW 2:994.

221 *they had to*: Parkinson, WHC 2:363.

221 *such casualties*: Shaw, BHW 2:1338.

221 *cover together*: Wakefield, p. 133; cf. p.136.

221 *arms themselves*: Robert Anderson to Larz Anderson, BHW 2:933.

221 *Black Hawk's band*: BHW 2:1168.

221 *the Ojibwe*: BHAuto, p. 160.

221 *the captives*: BHAuto, p. 162; and Street's report, BHW 2:1065–67.

221 *in the war*: Scott to Lewis Cass, BHW 2:1124.

222 *the subject*: Atkinson to Scott, BHW 2:1157.

222 *girl prisoner*: Gideon Low to Atkinson, 10 Aug. 1832, BHW 2:979.

222 *blind eye*: Among the others who blamed White Crow were Pama-ho and Ma-kauk, Ioway, and Wee-sheet (*BHW* 2:1036, 1055, 1056).

222 *Sauk war*: *Wau-Bun: The Early Day in the Northwest*, ed. Louis Phelps Kellogg (1855; Menasha, WI: National Society of Colonial Dames in Wisconsin, 1948), p. 65.

222 *turn back*: Atkinson to Black Hawk, 24 Apr. 1832, *BHW* 2:301–2.

222 *to obey*: Pama-ho, *BHW* 2:1036.

222 *to Atkinson*: Gratiot to Atkinson, 27 Apr. 1832, *BHW* 2:319, 319n1.

222 *them not to*: Ioway, *BHW* 2:1055.

223 *chief accountable*: Scott to Cass, 9 Sept. 1832, *BHW* 2:1125.

223 *prosecuting individuals*: Atkinson in Council with the Winnebago and Menominee Indians, *BHW* 2:949; Scott to the Winnebago Indians, *BHW* 2:1022.

223 *Burnt Village*: Treaty with the Winnebago of 15 Sept. 1832, *BHW* 2:1155.

223 *Fort Winnebago*: Kinzie describes the surrender and escape of the suspects (pp. 364–66, 370–72).

223 *his services*: *BHW* 2:1136, 1140–41.

223 *old lands*: Bieder, p. 132.

223 *as homesteaders*: Nancy Oestreich Lurie, *Wisconsin Indians*, rev. ed. (Madison: Wisconsin Historical Society, 2002), pp. xii, 12.

223 *gaming casinos*: The tribe's official membership rolls show 5,042 Ho-Chunk in Wisconsin in May 2011 (http://ho-chunknation.com).

223 *largest employer*: *Wisconsin's Past and Present: A Historical Atlas* (Madison: U of Wisconsin P, 1998), p. 8.

224 *in 1833*: Bieder, p. 131.

224 *pay off debts*: Eby, p. 272.

224 *the northeast*: Robert M. Sully painted portraits of Black Hawk, his son Na-she-a-kusk, and the Prophet; he sold them to the State Historical Society of Wisconsin in 1855 (*WHC* 2:12, 41–42).

225 *for donations*: Jason Berry, *The Spirit of Black Hawk: A Mystery of Africans and Indians* (Jackson, MS: UP of Mississippi, 1995), p. 50. The information in the next paragraph is from pp. 11, 129.

225 *Indian men*: Hagan, *Sac and Fox*, p. 124.

225 *free states*: *BHAuto*, p. 179.

226 *the tribe*: Nancy O. Lurie, quoted in Berry, p. 79.

226 *the wall*: Berry, p. 130.

227 *and Dodge*: *Black Hawk War*, p. 207.

227 *merciless savages*: See Reynolds's message to the Illinois legislature, *BHW* 2:1218–22; and Wakefield, p. 144.

227 *in the war*: *Lincoln in the Black Hawk War* (St. Louis: Sigma, 1910).

228 *very hungry*: Quoted in Carl Sandburg, *Abraham Lincoln: The Prairie Years* (New York: Harcourt, 1926), 1:386–87.

228 *and interpretation*: Eby's title applies to the Black Hawk War as a whole a phrase that Taylor used to describe Stillman's Run (p. 140).

228 *his death*: Thayer, p. 352.

229 *Bad Axe*: Eby, p. 19.

230 *Red man*: Third Council, *BHW* 2:1149. The other quotations in this paragraph are from *BHW* 2:1221 and *Wakefield's History*, p. 136.

230 *the Mississippi*: *BHAuto*, pp. 164–65.

230 *a swan's*: *BHAuto*, p. 100.

CHAPTER 15

234 *this episode*: *Black Hawk: An Autobiography*, ed. Donald Jackson (Urbana: U of Illinois P, 1955), p. 153. Lyman C. Draper, the editor of the *Collections of the State Historical Society of Wisconsin* (1856; Madison: State Historical Society, 1903), is one who derives the river's name from this episode (2:356).

234 *peel the bark*: Joseph Plympton to Henry Atkinson or Hugh Brady, 5 June 1832, *The Black Hawk War, 1831–1832*, ed. Ellen H. Whitney (Springfield: Illinois State Historical Library, 1973–1978), 2:529.

234 *storage boxes*: The Ho-Chunk built their lodges of grass, reed mats, and bark. See Robert E. Bieder, *Native American Communities in Wisconsin 1600–1960: A Study of Tradition and Change* (Madison: U of Wisconsin P, 1995), p. 38 and photo on p. 112. John A. Wakefield mentions the bark wigwams of the Ho-Chunk in *Wakefield's History of the Black Hawk War*, ed. Frank E. Stevens (1834; reprint Madison: Roger Hunt, 1976), p. 104.

234 *simply the Bark*: Nineveh Shaw refers to the river as the Peel Bark (*Black Hawk War* 2:1334).

234 *by mistake*: Pen and Jack-Knife [pseud.], "Up the River," *Koshkonong Country Revisited: An Anthology* (hereafter, *KCR*), ed. Hannah Swart (Fort Atkinson, WI: Fort Atkinson Historical Society, 1981), 2:127.

235 *Amia calva*: Barbara A. Nelson and Margaret S. Holzbog, *Richfield Remembers the Past* (Richfield, WI: Richfield History Committee, 1996), p. 166. Bowfin appear in Don M. Fago's inventory of the lower Bark and occasionally upstream, with concentrations in places such as Rome Pond. At least one specimen was found in Bark Lake (*The Distribution and Relative Abundance of Fishes in Wisconsin* [Madison: DNR, 1984]).

236 *from the river*: *WSJ* 2 July 1998.

236 *it happened*: Michael Lesy, *Wisconsin Death Trip* (New York: Pantheon, 1973).

236 *to death*: "A Brutal Murder," [Madison] *Daily State Journal* 22 May 1857.

236 *let go*: "A Ghastly Discovery," *MS* 16 May 1890.

237 *placid waters*: "Brother and Sister Drown," *MS* 24 May 1889.

237 *natural food*: Steve Engelbert, "Lake's Ups and Downs Help Fish," *Janesville Gazette* [1998], www.gazetteextra.com.

237 *and rafts*: Aaron Rankin, "My First Trip West—1836," *"It Seems Like Only Yesterday . . .": Stories from Fort Atkinson's Early Days 1836–1914* (Fort Atkinson: Fort Atkinson Historical Society, 2001), pp. 29, 32.

237 *the general*: Hannah Swart, *Koshkonong Country: A History of Jefferson County, Wisconsin* (Fort Atkinson, WI: W. D. Hoard, 1975), p. 229.

238 *a barrelhead*: Celeste Foster Southwell, "Fort Atkinson As It Was," *"It Seems,"* p. 263.

238 *July 7, 1832*: Cecil Eby, *"That Disgraceful Affair," the Black Hawk War* (New York: Norton, 1973), p. 204n3; and Patrick J. Jung, *The Black Hawk War of 1832* (Norman: U of Oklahoma P, 2007), p. 131. Crawford B. Thayer located the official record of the mortally wounded soldier; see *Hunting a Shadow: The Search for Black Hawk* (Fort Atkinson, WI: Fort Atkinson Historical Society, 1981), pp. 352, 410–11.

237 *the stockade*: Rankin, p. 32; and Shirley Hoard Kerschensteiner, "Early Life in Fort Atkinson," *"It Seems,"* p. 285.

238 *local clergyman*: Lemuel Marvin Roberts, "Fort History," *"It Seems,"* p. 82. Roberts's son, Dean, describes the excavation in "Preacher Kept Skull of Soldier Slain by Indians," *JCU* 6 Dec. 1945.

239 *Dairymen's Association*: KCR 1:131, 216–17; and *JCU* 23 Dec. 1870.

241 *same form*: Robert A. Birmingham and Leslie E. Eisenberg, *Indian Mounds of Wisconsin* (Madison: U of Wisconsin P, 2000), pp. 125, 127.

241 *in progress*: For Lapham's survey of the group, see *The Antiquities of Wisconsin, as Surveyed and Described* (1855; Madison: U of Wisconsin P, 2001), Plate XXVIII, no. 1.

241 *in 1919*: Birmingham and Eisenberg, p. 203.

242 *and Quarleses*: Walter A. Frautschi, "Early Wisconsin Shooting Clubs," *Wisconsin Magazine of History* 28 (June 1945): 394.

243 *Water*: Lorine Niedecker: *Collected Works*, ed. Jenny Penberthy (Berkeley: U of California P, 2002), pp. 237–38.

243 *nine years*: Penberthy, introduction to Niedecker's *Collected Works*, p. 1. This is the source of biographical information in the following paragraphs, supplemented by details from Margot Peters's *Lorine Niedecker: A Poet's Life* (Madison: U of Wisconsin P, 2011).

245 *the tuition*: Peters, p. 25.

247 *as a girl*: Collected Works, pp. 261–63.

247 *literary figure*: Quoted in Penberthy, p. 11.

247 *to Lake Koshkonong*: Niedecker and the Correspondence with Zukovsky, 1931–1970, ed. Jenny Penberthy (Cambridge: Cambridge UP, 1993), p. 108n1.

248 *water*: Collected Works, p. 268.

248 *a meadow*: Antiquities, p. 35.

249 *canoe through it*: "Reminiscences," KCR 1:66-67.

249 *to the lake*: "Reminiscences of Early Days," *"It Seems,"* p. 57.

249 *historic period*: Birmingham and Eisenberg, pp. 141, 164–71.

249 *Koshkonong alone*: Susan Lampert Smith, "On Trail of Lake Koshkonong History," *WSJ* 30 Mar. 1997.

250 *for power*: Frank Sinclair, "Lake Koshkonong," *Outdoor America* (1924): 380, 384.

250 *tear it down*: Wisconsin State Register 8 Dec. 1877, Issue 41.

250 *aquatic plants*: Sinclair, p. 380.

250 *in Paradise*: The History of Jefferson County (Chicago: Western Historical, 1879), p. 334.

250 *against waves*: The information in this paragraph is from Sinclair, p. 380; DNR, *Lower Rock River Water Quality Management Plan*, 2001, LR11 (Lower Koshkonong Creek), p. 3; and DNR, *Wisconsin Conservation Bulletin* July and August 1971.

250 *Danube River*: USGS Carp Fact Sheet at http://nas.er.usgs.gov/queries/FactSheet .asp?speciesID=4.

251 *brook trout*: "A Fish Story," MS 22 Dec. 1880.

251 *into the lake*: The Rock-Koshkonong Lake District (RKLD) webpage cites "The History of Carp in Lake Koshkonong," a paper by DNR fisheries biologist Don Bush, regarding carp introduction into the lake. See the documents at www.rkld.org/AboutUs/History.aspx.

251 *and salted*: Memoir of Jane Johnson Chadwick, www.watertownhistory.org.

251 *sucker family*: Mary Hoard describes the boats in a notebook, "Oldest Houses," under the letter F (Hoard Historical Museum).

252 *heavy fine*: "Carp Supply for New York," 19 Oct. 1903.

252 *400,000 pounds*: *JCU* 5 Feb. 1954.

252 *of the fish*: George C. Becker, *Fishes of Wisconsin* (Madison: U of Wisconsin P, 1983), p. 423; and Bush, "History," RKLD webpage.

252 *and grow*: Engelbert, "Lake's Ups and Downs."

253 *and parasites*: David Schaper, "Asian Carp: Can't Beat Them? Eat Them," *All Things Considered*, National Public Radio (hereafter, NPR), 12 July 2006; and www.greatlakesdirectory.org/il/122207_great_lakes.htm.

253 *and lakes*: Dan Egan, "Destructive Fish Continue March Northward," *MJS* 11 Aug. 2011.

253 *or grouse*: James Card, "Where These Fish Are Jumping, Arrows Are Flying," *New York Times* 16 Oct. 2009.

253 *and zooplankton*: Schaper, "An Electric Hope for the Great Lakes," *All Things Considered*, NPR, 11 July 2006.

253 *fish depend*: Bighead carp can exceed ninety pounds. One caught in Illinois weighed 85–90 pounds (Rod Kloeckner, "Commercial Fishermen Remember Monster Asian Carp," *Chicago Tribune* 30 Mar. 2009). The record weight for a silver carp is 110 pounds (Card, "Where These Fish").

253 *Koshkonong's history*: The information in this paragraph is from Schaper, "Asian Carp" and "An Electric Hope"; and two articles by Dan Egan in the *MJS*: "Explanation for Carp May Be a Fish Story," 15 Aug. 2010; and "More Evidence of Asian Carp Found Above Electric Fish Barrier," 20 July 2011.

254 *into the river*: *MJS* 28 Sept. 2003.

254 *ocean freighters*: Lee Bergquist, "Zebra Mussels found in 10 More Wisconsin Lakes," *MJS* 20 May 2003.

254 *Lake Michigan*: See two 2011 articles by Dan Egan in the *MJS*: "'The lake left me. It's gone,'" 13 Aug.; and "In Lake Michigan, Resilient Whitefish, Fishermen Fight for a Comeback," 16 Aug.

254 *fifty thousand species*: Andrew C. Revkin and Carol Kaesuk Yoon, "As Alien Invaders Proliferate, Conservationists Change Their Focus," *New York Times* 20 Aug. 2002.

254 *garlic mustard*: Gov. Jim Doyle and the Wisconsin Council on Invasive Species, "Opening Up a Can of (Exotic) Worms: Non-Native Earthworms Changing Northern Hardwood Forests," news release of 3 May 2005; Sophia Estante, "Worming into New Territory," *Wisconsin Natural Resources* Aug. 2005; and Anne Minard, "Researchers Build a Case for Earthworm's Slimy Reputation," *New York Times* 28 Oct. 2003.

254 *loosestrife alone*: Tom Christopher, "Can Weeds Help Solve the Climate Crisis?" *New York Times* 29 June 2008.

254 *human immigrants*: Banu Subramaniam, "The Aliens Have Landed!: Reflections on the Rhetoric of Biological Invasions," *Making Threats: Biofears and Environmental Anxieties*, ed. Betsy Hartmann, Banu Subramaniam, and Charles Zerner (Lanham, MD: Rowman and Littlefield, 2005), pp. 135–48.

254 *settlers arrived*: William Cronon, *Changes in the Land: Indians, Colonists, and the Ecology of New England* (New York: Hill and Wang, 1983); and Mann, *1491: New Revelations of the Americas Before Columbus* (New York: Random-Vintage, 2006).

254 *climate change*: Christopher, "Can Weeds."

255 *tends otherwise*: *A Sand County Almanac* (1949; New York: Ballantine, 1970), p. 262.

255 *of origin*: Revkin and Yoon, "As Alien Invaders Proliferate."

Index

About the Author

Photo by Elizabeth J. Bates

Milton J. Bates has lived most of his life in Wisconsin. After completing a doctorate in English at the University of California–Berkeley, he taught at Williams College and Marquette University, retiring in 2010. He has held a Guggenheim Foundation Fellowship and Fulbright lectureships in China and Spain. His previous books include studies of the poet Wallace Stevens and of the Vietnam War. He lives with his wife in the Upper Peninsula of Michigan.